Class and Stratification

An Introduction to Current Debates

Rosemary Crompton

Polity Press

Copyright © Rosemary Crompton 1993

The right of Rosemary Crompton to be identified as author of this work has been asserted in accordance with the Copyright, Designs and Patents Act 1988.

First published in 1993 by Polity Press in association with Blackwell Publishers

Editorial office:
Polity Press
65 Bridge Street
Cambridge CB2 1UR, UK

Marketing and production:
Blackwell Publishers
108 Cowley Road
Oxford OX4 1JF, UK

238 Main Street
Suite 501
Cambridge, MA 02142, USA

ISBN 0 7456 0946-5
ISBN 0 7456 0947-3 (pbk)

British Library Cataloguing-in-Publication Data
A CIP catalogue record for this book is available from the British Library.

Library of Congress Cataloging in Publication Data
A CIP catalog record for this book is available from the Library of Congress.

Typeset in 10 on 11½pt Times
by Best-set Typesetter Ltd., Hong Kong
Printed in Great Britain by T.J. Press (Padstow) Ltd, Padstow, Cornwall.

This book is printed on acid-free paper.

Contents

4   Problems of Class Analysis

5   Rethinking 'Class Analysis'

6   Citizenship and Entitlements

**7   Lifestyle, Consumption Categories and Consciousness
    Communities**

Introduction and Acknowledgements

Introductions to books are usually the last thing to be written, and this one is no exception. I would like to take this opportunity, however, to describe some of the factors which led me to write this textbook, not least because many of the themes developed within it are rather different from positions taken up in my previous work – particularly *Economy and Class Structure* (Crompton and Gubbay 1977).

During the 1960s and 1970s, sociology underwent a period of rapid expansion as an academic subject. Within the social sciences, sociology had always been a critical discipline. During this period, therefore, one major focus of sociological criticisms was the ideas and hypotheses relating to the 'end of ideology' thesis. This thesis included arguments to the effect that industrial societies were characterized by a broad consensus on values and attitudes, and that conflicts relating to 'class' were rapidly becoming outdated in such societies. In contrast, sociological sceptics argued that, even in welfare capitalism, class conflicts persisted, and that class inequality and conflicts could not be eradicated or even 'managed' in capitalism. During the 1960s and 1970s, therefore, 'class theory' came to assume an increasingly important place within sociology. This was accompanied by a revival of interest in the classical theorists, particularly the work of Marx. In particular, Braverman's *Labor and Monopoly Capital* (1974) provided a number of insights as to how the divisions revealed by the Marxist analysis of the labour process might be mapped on to the structure of jobs and occupations. *Economy and Class Structure*, written during the 1970s, reflected these developments. It sought to provide a Marxist alternative to the predominantly Weberian mapping of social classes within sociology which had prevailed hitherto.

Theoretical ideas relating to social class in sociology had been grafted on to an existing approach to social stratification in which 'classes' were taken to be occupational aggregates. Other existing conventions were also carried forward into these new developments in 'class analysis' – most notably, the assumption that as the class of the household corresponded to that of the main breadwinner, and that as the 'head of household' would usually be a man, then the 'class structure' could be reliably assumed to correspond to the structure of male employment. Without exception, therefore, in Britain all of the major surveys in the area of class and stratification had, until the 1970s, drawn upon men-only samples.

This practice came under increasing attack from the feminist critique within sociology which developed from the early 1970s. These criticisms, however, were not only directed at the exclusion of women from empirical investigations, but also at the underlying assumptions upon which the identification of a class structure within the structure of employment was predicated. That is, it was argued that the class (employment) structure was itself 'gendered'. Logically, therefore, the effects of 'class' and 'gender' could not be disentangled within the structure of employment. These feminist arguments were paralleled by developments in social theory, which, particularly in Giddens's account of 'structuration', argued that action could not be separated from structure in sociological investigations – including investigations into 'social classes'.

As a consequence of these and other developments, 'class analysis' in sociology moved in a number of different directions. However, during the 1980s, debates within sociology itself were somewhat over-shadowed by the crisis which sociology faced as an academic discipline in Britain, as departments were 'rationalized' and subject to increasing economic pressures, and sociologists themselves underwent the (often painful) process of adapting to 'new times'. Perhaps because of these developments, a number of key sociological concepts – in particular, class – came under increasing, and critical, scrutiny. The end – or at least, the irrelevance – of class analysis in sociology was ever more frequently argued.

By the end of the 1980s, therefore, the empirical work of those pursuing a theoretical interest in class within sociology had fragmented into (at least) three areas: first, the macro-level analysis of large data sets, gathered by those who had developed theoretical, relational, approaches to 'social class' (Goldthorpe and Wright); second, socio-historical accounts of class formation (Lash and Urry 1987; McNall et al. 1991); and third, a growing interest in the *cultural* construction and reproduction of class associated with a developing 'sociology of consumption' and fuelled by the emphasis on consumerism which seemed, increasingly, to characterize contemporary societies (Bourdieu

1986). Those sociologists not directly concerned with these debates carried on doing what they had always done – that is, using the convenient sociological shorthand whereby 'occupation' was taken to be a measure of 'class' without worrying too much about the finer details – even though, as we shall see, this assumption is highly problematic. It is one of the major arguments of this book that the largely unacknowledged fragmentation of approach within 'class analysis' in sociology is one of the reasons why its practitioners were not well placed to respond to the growing tide of criticisms of both the class concept and class analysis in general, which had emerged by the end of the 1980s.

This book, therefore, was written with the aim of providing an overview of the field which would facilitate the moving forward of debate in an area which had, in my view, got somewhat bogged down in arguments between and within different schools of 'class analysis'. The unfortunate result was that many outsiders – even within the sociological community – had lost any real sense of what was going on. Despite claims to have provided an 'overview', however, there are a number of gaps in this text which I would freely acknowledge. As reflects my own interests, the question of gender is discussed reasonably thoroughly, but the important topic of race and ethnicity is discussed only in relation to the question of citizenship. Other crucial stratification issues – such as, for example, age – are not discussed at all. Nationalism, which following the break-up of the Eastern bloc is emerging as a central topic for the 1990s, is not considered. I can only apologize in advance for these and other deficiencies.

It would have been pleasant to record the fellowships, scholarships, and sabbatical leaves which had contributed to the writing of this book, but unfortunately there were none. Roger Burrows organized a debate on class at the 1990 British Sociological Association Conference, to which I contributed along with Ray Pahl and Gordon Marshall, and which was important in getting me started. Gordon Marshall was the first to suggest that I was writing a book, not an article, and has read the first draft of chapter 5. Communications with Mike Savage over the last few years have done much to clarify my thinking, as did conversations with Bob Holton in 1990. I would also like to thank David Held and Tony Giddens at Polity Press for their advice and comments, as well as an anonymous Polity reader for detailed comments on the first draft. Gerald Crompton has had to listen to far more monologues on class and stratification than an economic historian has any reasonable right to expect. Justine Clements has made the final alterations to my word-processed text, for which many thanks. Many others have contributed, directly and indirectly, to the writing of this book and I hope that a general acknowledgement will suffice – the good bits (if any) are theirs, and the faults are all mine.

Rosemary Crompton
University of Kent

1
Explaining Inequality

Introduction

All complex societies are characterized, to varying extents, by the unequal distribution of material and symbolic rewards. It is also the case that no persisting structure of economic and social inequality has existed in the absence of some kind of meaning system(s) which seek both to explain and to justify the unequal distribution of societal resources.

'Social stratification' is a general term which describes these systematic structures of inequality. In pre-industrial or traditional societies, inequalities and thus social stratification were widely held to be natural, and/or to reflect an aspect of a cosmology which provided an account of the society itself. Thus, for example, in ancient Greece Aristotle asserted that: 'It is thus clear that there are *by nature* free men and slaves, and that servitude is just and agreeable for the latter . . . Equally, the relation of the male to the female is *by nature* such that one is superior and the other inferior, one dominates and the other is dominated' (cited in Dahrendorf 1969: 18). A pre-established harmony is being asserted between things natural and things social. This is a view which effectively rules out any sociological treatment of the issue – if inequalities are 'natural', then there is no need to investigate them further.

Besides this assumption of 'naturalness', inequalities have been viewed as deriving from the divinely ordained structuring of society, as in the Hindu caste system in classical India. In this system, social rank corresponded to religious (ritual) purity. Lower castes polluted the higher and, as a consequence, a series of restrictions were imposed on low-caste individuals and their families. Thus the caste system corresponded (although not precisely) to the overall structure of social inequality.[1] Two religious concepts sustained the system, *karma* and *dharma*. Karma teaches a Hindu that he or she is born into a particular caste or sub-caste because he or she deserves to be there as a consequence of actions in a previous life. Dharma, which means 'existing according to that which is moral', teaches that living one's present life according to the rules (dharma) will result in rebirth into a higher caste and thus ultimate progression through the caste system. Both existing inequalities of caste, therefore, as well as any possibility of change in the future, are related to universal religious truths and are thus beyond the reaches of systematic sociological examination.

The justification of material inequality as stemming from some 'natural' or divine ordinance, therefore, is a common feature of traditional or pre-industrial societies. Such accounts not only explain inequality, they also assert that it is part of the natural order of things that the 'best' should get the majority share of the rewards that society has to offer. In feudal Europe as in classical India, stratification was accompanied by religious and moral justifications. From the ninth century onwards, Western Europe was an essentially rural society, in which an individual's condition was determined by access to the land. This was largely controlled by a minority of lay and ecclesiastical proprietors. It was a hierarchical society, in which the enserfed peasantry were subject to the domination of secular and ecclesiastical lords. The Church possessed both economic and moral ascendancy. As Pirenne (1936) has argued, the Church's conception of the feudal world 'was admirably adapted to the economic conditions of an age in which land was the sole foundation of the social order'. Land had been given by God to men in order to enable them to live on earth with a view to their eternal salvation. The object of labour was not to grow wealthy, and the monk's renunciation was the ideal 'on which the whole of society should fix its gaze'. To seek riches was to fall into the sin of avarice, and poverty was of divine origin (Pirenne 1936: 423).

In traditional societies, therefore, relative economic stagnation was also associated with social rigidity in respect of stratification systems. These societies, however, did not endure, and throughout the seventeenth, eighteenth and nineteenth centuries Western Europe, and much of the rest of the world, was transformed by the development of capitalist industrialism – the most significant element of the process which has been described as the coming of 'modernity'. The profound economic and social changes which took place throughout these centuries were accompanied by a developing critique of the traditional systems of belief which for over two millennia had served to explain material inequalities and render them legitimate.

In direct opposition to the idea that human beings are naturally or divinely unequal at birth, therefore, there developed from the seventeenth century onwards the argument that, by virtue of their humanity, all human beings were born *equal*, rather than unequal.[2] From this assumption derives the beginnings of a sociological approach to the explanation of inequality. If equality, rather than inequality, is assumed to be the 'natural' condition of human beings, then how are persisting inequalities to be explained and justified? If each individual is endowed with natural rights, why do some individuals dominate others? These questions remain as the central problems of social and political theory. In the sphere of political thought, some of the first answers to these questions were supplied by the social contract theorists. Hobbes (1588–1679) argued that in a state of nature life was 'nasty, brutish and short', characterized by the war of 'every man against every man'. The solution to this 'problem of order' was submission to the state, in the absence of which there would be chaos. Locke (1632–1704) also argued that the 'natural rights' to life, liberty and property are best protected by the authority of the state. In a famous statement which has resounded through history. Rousseau (1712–78), asserted that 'man was born free, and he is everywhere in chains'. He did not consider that complete equality could ever be achieved but argued that direct democracy, expressed through the 'general will' would afford the greatest protection for the individual. Thus the foundations of the argument that all 'citizens' were entitled to political rights, as expressed in universal suffrage and democratic institutions, were laid in the eighteenth century.

The passing of traditional society and the growth of capitalist industrialism was accompanied by an emphasis on the rationality of the modern social order. Not customary rules, but rational calculation, were held to be the principles which should govern economic conduct in the developing capitalist societies. The expansion of markets and transformation of the processes of production which accompanied the Industrial Revolution would have been difficult to achieve without the erosion of customary rights in trade and manufacture – which affected all its aspects and included cartels, wage and price fixing, restrictions on the mobility of labour, and so on. Thus the political changes which created the formally free individual also created the landless labourer – who was, however, entitled to sell what only she or he possessed – labour, or the capacity to work. Labour itself had become a commodity.

The English and French revolutions were first amongst the political changes which accompanied the transition to capitalist industrialism. However, the 'bourgeois freedoms' which they achieved came under critical scrutiny from that foremost social theorist of the nineteenth century, Karl Marx. As expressed in the *Communist Manifesto*, Marx saw the unfolding of human history as an outcome of economic, rather than merely political, conflicts: 'The history of all hitherto existing society is the history of class struggles' (Marx and Engels 1962: 34). Inequality was, and always had been, a reflection of differential access to the means of production and what was produced. For Marx, state power was inseparable from economic power, and the 'sovereign individual' of capitalism was but a necessary condition of the development of the capitalist mode of production. Political equality could coexist with material inequalities and indeed, by defining the inequalities associated with the dominant system of production, distribution and exchange as 'non-political', bourgeois ideology served to make them legitimate. The landless labourers created as a consequence of political and economic change constituted a new class which was emerging as a consequence of the development of industrial capitalism – a class which would eventually transform capitalist society – the proletariat.

The development of capitalist industrialism has been identified as a major element in the transition to 'modernity'. The idea of modernity describes not just the development of industrialism *per se*, but also of the corresponding modes of surveillance and regulation of the population of nation states – nation states have been identified as one of the characteristic social forms accompanying the transition to modernity. Modernity is accompanied by the extensive development of *organizations*, that is, reflexively monitored systems which have the capacity to act upon the social world. The transition to modernity has ushered in a world which is peculiarly dynamic, a world which is in the process of constant change and transformation.

In this book, 'class' will be discussed as a peculiarly modern phenomenon. As we shall see, the concept of class has a number of different meanings. To describe class as 'modern', however, is to suggest that it is primarily a characteristic of modern stratification systems, of 'industrial' societies, in contrast to the 'traditional' structures of inequality associated with ascribed or supposedly natural characteristics such as those of feudal estates or religiously defined hierarchies, as well as gender and race. In the modern world, class-based organizations – that is, organizations claiming to represent classes and class interests – have been the dynamic source of many of the changes and transformations which have characterized the modern era. This does not mean that 'classes' did not exist prior to modernity, but rather that the discourse of 'class' has become one of the key concepts through which we can begin to understand it.[3]

'Class', therefore, is a major organizing concept in the exploration of contemporary stratification systems. However, although inequalities associated with the structures of production, distribution and exchange assume greater significance with the transition to industrialism, this does not mean that established forms of social distinction and dif- ferentiation simply disappear overnight. Customary inequalities, particularly those associated with ascribed statuses associated with age, gender and race, have persisted into the modern era.

Not only customary inequalities, but many of the ideas which underpinned them, persisted into the modern age. Hirsch (1977) has argued that the 'moral legacy' of pre-capitalist institutions supplied the social foundations for the developing capitalist order. The ideologies associated with religion and custom in traditional societies, besides identifying the levels of material reward which were properly associated with the different ranks in society, and giving hope for the future beyond this life, supplied a powerful moral justification for the unequal distribution of resources. They also included rules relating to individual behaviour such as truth, trust, customary social obligations and the restraint of appetites. Hirsch argued (1977: 117) that by the late twentieth century capitalism was facing a 'depleting moral legacy': 'The social morality that has served as an understructure for economic individualism has been a legacy of the precapitalist and preindustrial past. This legacy has diminished with time and the corrosive contact of the active capitalist values.' In a related argument, Goldthorpe (1978) extended the logic of Hirsch's analysis to argue that the period of rapid inflation in Britain during the 1970s was in part a consequence of the decay of the *status order*, that is, it reflected an erosion of customary assumptions which had provided a normative underpinning for the differential distribution of rewards in a market society. If customary assumptions relating to inequality have and are being eroded then how do unequal societies cohere, particularly given the presumption of a fundamental equality amongst human beings?

Social order and theories of social differentiation

Inequality is a feature of all complex societies. One response, therefore, to the question posed above might be to argue that material inequalities are not, in themselves, necessarily a bad thing. Indeed, this has been a consistent theme in neo-liberal arguments concerning inequality. Such arguments distinguish between legal or formal equalities – for example, equality before the law; equality of opportunity – and equality of outcome. However, the pursuit of equality of outcome – for example, through programmes of affirmative action – contradicts, the neo-liberals argue, the principle of legal or formal equality. This is because positive or affirmative treatment for supposedly disadvantaged groups would treat the supposedly advantaged as less than equal. Thus in recent years we have witnessed, for example, the phenomenon of white male applicants to college courses in the United States utilizing equal-opportunity legislation in order to challenge the allocation of a quota of places on prestige courses to ethnic-minority applicants. Another important strand in neo-liberal arguments has been that, in any case, material inequalities are positively beneficial in modern societies. Economists such as Hayek have argued that in a capitalist society, the pursuit of self-interest encourages innovation and technological advance. Inventors and entrepreneurs may succeed or fail, but society as a whole will nevertheless benefit from the advances which these dynamic individuals have achieved – mass transport and communication, consumer goods such as cars, washing machines, and so on.[4] Capitalism is dynamic *because* it is unequal, and attempts at equalization will ultimately result in the stifling of initiative. Thus neo-liberals such as Berger have argued that: 'If one wants to intervene politically to bring about greater material equality, one may eventually disrupt the economic engine of plenty and endanger the material living standards of the society' (1987: 48).

These neo-liberal arguments have their parallel in the functionalist theory of stratification in sociology (Davis and Moore 1945; reprinted 1964). 'Social inequality', they argued, 'is thus an unconsciously evolved device by which societies insure that the most important positions are conscientiously filled by the most qualified persons' (1964: 415). In the particular case of advanced industrial societies, individuals must be induced to train for positions requiring a high level of skills, and compensated for having to take risks. In brief, their theory suggested that in industrial societies, characterized by a complex division of labour, a new consensus concerning inequality was emerging as a replacement for the old. Whereas the old consensus was grounded in customary, religious (and therefore non-rational) perceptions of worth, the new consensus reflected the rationality of modern industrial societies. Differentiated groupings are not percieved as necessarily antagonistic; they are, therefore, often described from within the functionalist perspective as socio-economic 'strata', rather than 'classes'.

The immediate origins of functionalist theories of stratification may be found in the Parsonian structural-functionalism which dominated sociological theory in the United States after the Second World War. These ideas will be discussed at greater length in chapters 2 and 3. Functionalist theories of stratification also reflected elements of Durkheim's analysis of the ultimate social consequences of the division of labour in industrial society. Durkheim (1968) was acutely aware of the negative consequences of the division of labour (poverty, social unrest etc.) consequent upon the development of industrial capitalism, but he argued that, nevertheless, 'normal' forms of the division of labour would lead to the development of 'organic solidarity' – that is, solidarity through interdependence – in complex industrial societies.

Functional theories of stratification, therefore, suggested that inequality in complex societies was rendered legitimate via an emerging consensus of values relating to the societal importance of particular functions. It is important to recognize that such theories incorporate a moral justification of economic inequality which has been commonplace since the advent of economic liberalism – that is, in a competitive market society, it is the most talented and ambitious – in short, the *best* – that get to the top, and therefore take the greater part of societies' rewards. However, for many commentators, such arguments rest upon the presumption of equality of opportunity (as Durkheim expressed it, the 'equality of the partners to the contract' in the division of labour). Thus the conditions and possibility of equality of opportunities have loomed large in debates on stratification.

Equality of opportunity is a powerful justification for inequality. If all have an equal opportunity to be unequal, then the unequal outcome must be regarded as justified and fair, as a reflection of 'natural' inequalities of personal endowments, rather than of structured social processes. Although a true equality of opportunity has never, in fact, been achieved, the assumption that it was nevertheless a Good Thing dominated the liberal consensus which prevailed in most Western societies after the Second World War, and which saw the extension of state expenditure on education, health and welfare. However, neo-liberals have always argued against such assumptions, and in recent decades the political and policy influence of such views has been increasing. Within the sociological field, Saunders (1990a) has argued for a return to the functionalist perspective in stratification theory and research.

Two closely associated arguments, therefore, have been used by functionalists to explain and justify material inequalities in a society of political and legal equals. These are, first, that unequal rewards provide a structure of incentives which ensure that talented individuals will work hard and innovate, thus contributing to the improvement of material standards for the society as a whole; and, second, that a broad consensus exists as to the legitimacy of their superior rewards, as such innovators are functionally more important to society.

Others, however, have stressed the continuing tensions, instability and tendencies to crisis which are associated with persisting structures of inequality. Marx predicted that the underlying structure of class inequality, associated with differential access to the ownership and control of productive resources, would lead, via the class struggle between labour and capital, to the revolutionary overthrow and eventual transformation of capitalist industrialism. Many theorists of stratification who are not Marxists, however, have also stressed the inherent instability of capitalist market societies, rather than any tendency toward an emergent consensus and stability. In contrast to the functionalists, 'conflict theorists' of stratification such as Dahrendorf (1959), Rex (1961) and Collins (1971) have emphasized the significance of power and coercion in any explanation of inequality. However, although such writers stress the persistence of conflict and are sceptical of the emergence of any genuine agreement concerning the existing structure of inequalities, they do not, unlike Marx, envisage the imminent break-up of the social and stratification order.

This is in part because persisting conflict exists in an uneasy tension with tendencies to regulation in capitalist market societies. The 'depleting moral legacy' which Hirsch identified may be argued to have been supplemented to some extent by institutions developed within the framework of capitalism. Dahrendorf (1988), Lockwood (1974) and Rex (1986), for example, have all drawn upon T. H. Marshall's account of 'citizenship' (1963), arguing that the development of social citizenship (for example, universal provisions such as education and welfare state benefits) in particular has contributed to the mitigation of class inequalities (chapter 6 below). During the twentieth century, there have been long historical periods (extending over many decades in countries such as Sweden) in which such a corporatist bargain has been struck between capital and labour (Therborn 1983).

A feature common to all authors who may be characterized as working within the 'conflict' approach to social stratification is that they all identify social *classes* as the primary 'actors' within stratification systems in industrial societies. However, there is a marked lack of precision or agreement as to the definition and meaning of 'class'.

Stratification and the debate on social class

In recent years, a common theme within sociology (and, indeed, in commentaries on society and politics more generally) has been that 'class' is becoming increasingly irrelevant in the late twentieth century. Thus Pahl (1989: 710) has argued that 'class as a concept is ceasing to do any useful work for sociology', and Holton and Turner have asserted that 'class' is 'an increasingly redundant issue' (1989: 194). The retreat from class, it may be suggested, is becoming the sociological equivalent of the new individualism. In this book it will be argued that although it is certainly the case that much confusion surrounds the use of the term, there are insufficient grounds for the wholesale rejection of class as an 'outmoded nineteenth-century concept'.

It is paradoxical that these recurring statements as to the redundancy of 'class' within sociological analysis should be emerging at a time when the level of non-sociological interest in the topic shows little sign of diminishing. For example, in the contest for the Conservative Party leadership (and Prime Ministership) in Britain during 1990, much was made of the 'classlessness' – or rather, upward mobility – of the eventual winner, John Major.[5] This was a powerful argument, and supporters of his opponents were driven to attempt to demonstrate their *lack* of 'class advantages' despite their patrician backgrounds and antecedents. This led Douglas Hurd (another contestant for the leadership) to describe his father as a farmer (classless?), who had managed to 'scrape together' the funds to send his son *on a scholarship* to Eton, and a supporter of Heseltine (a third competitor) to recount that his candidate had personally applied the wallpaper in the boarding-house which was the foundation of his (Heseltine's) property empire. In the same week as the leadership contest Lord Justice Harman ruled that the Conservative Westminster City Council could not sell property whose leasehold specified that the properties should be used as 'dwellings for the working class . . . and for no other purpose'. Westminster had argued that the term 'working class' no longer had any meaning. However, the judge ruled that although parliament no longer used the term in housing legislation this did not mean that it no longer had any meaning in ordinary English speech (the protagonists were well aware that, once on the open market, the properties would rise in value to a level outside the reach of the 'working class'). 'Class' is still, apparently, a topic worthy of a full-page article in a quality Sunday newspaper (*Observer*, 6 October 1991), and a BBC Television series extending over several weeks.

Sociologists might argue that the use of the term 'class' in academic discourse is in fact quite different from its use in ordinary speech, the everyday use of the word being much closer to the notion of social distinction or prestige. This would seem to be confirmed by the journalistic view: 'observation of class difference has, over the years, been reduced to a question of style . . . The new anthropologists of class are no longer sociologists' (*Observer*, 6 October 1991). However, why should style be considered off limits for sociology? In any case, the same journalists who defined class as 'style' continued: 'Anyone who ever really believes that we are heading towards a classless society only has to look at the class backgounds of those entering higher education to find otherwise. Tory policies on education have, if anything, made education more class-based than ever.' These arguments have little, if anything, to do with 'style'.

'Class', therefore, is a word with many meanings. Although these meanings will be extensively rehearsed throughout this book, it is nevertheless useful to attempt a summary at this early stage.

First, 'class' may be used to describe groups ranked in a hierarchical order – for example, the class of plebeians in ancient Rome (Calvert 1982). The system of feudal estates – lords, villeins, freemen, serfs etc. – was also a structure in which different legal rights, and formal inequalities, were associated with particular 'classes' in society. As we shall see, Weber described such legal and quasi-legal orders as being composed of 'status groups'; nevertheless, the term 'class' is still frequently employed to describe the hierarchical ranking of groups in society.

This association of class with hierarchy has led to a second common use of the term – to indicate social standing or *prestige*. Thus the term 'upper class' or 'lower class' is frequently used as a shorthand to describe an individual's social attributes. In contemporary usage, however, the use of the term 'class' in this sense would not carry with it any indication of legal status or formal entitlements. When occupations are ranked according to their perceived levels of prestige or social standing, these are described as status scales.

A third common use of 'class' is as a general description of structures of material inequality. Thus ·in modern societies, unequally rewarded groups are often described as 'classes'. These groupings, however, are not characterized by any formal, legal distinctions; rather, they summarize the outcome, in material terms, of the competition for resources in capitalist market societies. 'Classes' may correspond to income groups, but a very common basis for classification in modern societies is occupation – for example, the Registrar-General's 'social-class' groupings. These occupational groupings are amongst the most useful indicators of patterns of material advantage and disadvantage in modern societies, and are widely used in social-policy, market and advertising research, and so on.

The term 'class', however, has not just been used to *describe* levels of material inequalities, social prestige, or legal or traditional rankings. 'Classes' have also been identified as actual or potential social forces, or social actors, which have the capacity to transform society. Marx considered the struggle between classes to be the major motive force in human history. His views were certainly not shared by conservative commentators; nevertheless, from the French Revolution and before, 'classes' – particularly the lower classes – have been regarded as a possible threat to the established order. Thus 'class' is also a term with significant *political* overtones. The use of the single word 'class', therefore, may describe legal or traditional rankings, social prestige or material inequalities, as well as revolutionary or conservative social forces. It is a concept which is not the particular preserve of any individual branch of social science – unlike, for example, the concept of marginal utility in economics. Neither is it possible to identify a 'correct' sociological perspective, or an agreed use of the term. The variety of meanings which have been attached to the concept of class, it will be argued, has contributed to the lack of clarity which characterizes many contemporary debates in stratification. However, two further sets of factors have also added to the general muddying of waters which were never particularly clear: first, debates in social theory, and second, the very rapidity of the social and economic changes which these theories sought to explain.

Debates in social theory have had a profound impact on the manner in which sociologists and others have approached the empirical study of the social world. What Giddens (1982a) and others have described as the 'orthodox consensus' that emerged in the social sciences during the 1950s and 1960s had decisively shaped class analysis in sociology in the immediate postwar period. The 'orthodox consensus' was influenced by the logical framework of positivism; thus social science investigations were closely modelled on those of the natural sciences, and social facts treated as 'things'. The predominance of a broadly functionalist approach has already been briefly described, and the third element of this consensus, according to Giddens, was the influence of a conception of 'industrial society', whereby the technology of industrialism and its attendant social characteristics (rationality of technique, extensive division of labour, and so on) was seen to be the main motive force transforming the contemporary world. Although the orthodox consensus had its critics – for example, the 'conflict theorists' identified above – these critiques were developed and shaped within its framework. In particular, as we shall see in chapters 2 and 3, this approach structured research and theorizing in the area of class and stratification in a number of significant respects. First, classes were concieved as objective entities which could be empirically investigated – and to this end, the occupational structure was conventionally regarded as providing a framework within which the 'class structure' could be located. Second, much of the debate between 'functional' or 'consensus' approaches, on the one hand, and 'conflict' theories, on the other, took place on the terrain of stratification theory. Developments in occupational stratification systems were a key feature of the industrial-society thesis. It was argued that the stratification systems of advanced industrial societies would have a tendency to converge, and moreover that this would be in the direction of more open structures in which 'middle-class' occupations predominated (Mayer 1963).

In the area of empirical research in particular, it may be suggested that the 'orthodox consensus' in sociology has not in fact been eclipsed to the extent which Giddens suggests. Nevertheless, in the field of class analysis, one aspect on which the developing critique did have a considerable impact concerned the question of class action, which was inseparable from the conceptualization of 'class' itself. Mainstream class and stratification theory – as represented, for example, by writers such as Bendix and Lipset (1967b), had appropriated the Marxist distinction between a class 'in itself' and a class 'for itself' – that is, between a class which existed as a historical reality, on the one hand, and a class which had acquired a consciousness of its identity and a capacity to act, on the other. Bendix and Lipset, however, viewed the question of class action as contingent – a class might, or might not, manifest a particular consciousness (this approach, it should be noted, fits unproblematically with broadly 'positivist' modes of social investigation). However, the developing critique of positivism – as expressed, for example, in Giddens's theory of 'structuration' – argued that neither subject nor object, 'structure' nor 'action', should be regarded as having primacy. These arguments meshed with those already developed by some Marxist theoreticians – particularly historians such as E. P. Thompson – regarding the indivisibility of class from the notion of consciousness.

Thus there developed within 'class analysis' in sociology an important – but not widely acknowledged – divergence between, on the one hand, those pursuing the empirical investigation of the 'class structure' and, on the other, those class analysts treating consciousness and structure as facets of the *same* phenomenon. This divergence was reflected in different methods of empirical investigation. Those primarily concerned with the investigation of the class structure – and they included both Marxists and non-Marxists – tended to work with large data sets, to which increasingly sophisticated statistical techniques can be applied, whereas those conceiving of structure and action as a unity have relied more on historical and case-study techniques of empirical investigation. Chapter 2 will explore the way in which the insights of the two major nineteenth-century theorists of social class – Marx and Weber – have been developed in theoretical and empirical sociology.

As we have seen, however, the notion of 'class' has also been widely used to describe the broad contours of inequality in contemporary societies, rather than being primarily concerned – or even concerned at all – with the issues of class consciousness and action. In nineteenth-century investigations of the poor, for example, the unfortunates had to be identified – indeed the empirical definition of 'poverty' absorbed much of the energies of early investigators. As, increasingly, extensive national statistics were gathered, so classification schemes were devised to bring order to the data. In a society where increasing numbers were dependent on paid employment, one obvious indicator of social advantage or disadvantage was occupation. Thus from the beginning of the twentieth century it has become commonplace for statisticians to divide the population into occupational aggregates or classes, depending (more or less) on the material rewards accruing to particular occupational groupings. The term 'class' is universally employed to describe these occupational aggregates, although they are clearly not of the same order as the 'classes' discussed in the theoretical work of Marx and Weber. However, occupational indices developed in the context of applied or policy research have constantly overlapped with theoretical discussions and empirical research relating to social class, and class consciousness and action, and therein lies the source of much confusion.

Chapter 3, therefore, has a major focus on different strategies which have been developed to investigate the class *structure*. All of these accounts focus mainly upon employment and the associated structure of occupations. However, although the structure of employment in industrial societies is the major empirical source of the generation of these 'classes', there is no agreed index of classification. It will be suggested that class indexes can be usefully divided into three broad categories.

These are, first, the 'commonsense' indexes which lack theoretical pretensions, and which arrange occupations into an approximate hierarchical order to which a number of (hopefully not too arbitrary) cut-off points are applied. In an industrial society, occupation is an excellent indicator of both levels of material reward and social standing, and over the years, such indexes have been found to correlate with a range of factors, such as rates of infant mortality, access to education, voting behaviour, and so on. Second, there are indexes of occupational prestige or status, which attempt to measure the societal ranking or worth of particular types of occupations within the population at large. Occupational prestige scales were intially constructed with a view to the investigation of social mobility. The similarity of occupational prestige scales as between different nation states, and the relative 'openness' (or otherwise) of occupational structures, have been essential data in the development and investigation of the 'industrial-society' thesis, which, as we have seen, Giddens has described as a key element of the 'orthodox consensus' developed within postwar sociology. Both commonsense occupational indexes and occupational prestige scales are descriptive indexes. They are also hierarchical, and thus 'gradational' measures of a more or less particular quantity (income, prestige, social standing, and so on). However, the third category of class index identified in chapter 3, that is, 'relational' or theoretical class schemes, have been constructed with explicit reference to class theories – particularly those of Marx and Weber. Thus they claim to be a measure of the dynamics and actualities of class *relations*, rather than simply to describe structures of inequality or prestige. The two major examples of theoretically grounded, relational class schemes which will be investigated are the Marxist class scheme of Erik Wright, and the neo-Weberian class scheme of John Goldthorpe. Both of these authors claim that their class schemes are not hierarchical or 'gradational', but 'relational'.

However, although these three different types of class scheme have been constructed for very different purposes, there are in practice considerable similarities between the location of occupations and employment statuses as between the different schemes. Thus the three types of scheme are often treated as equivalent. However, the fundamental differences in the bases and assumptions on which they have been constructed suggest that considerable care should attend upon their application, particularly in respect of theoretical arguments relating to social class. However, the very different nature and claims of the different 'class' indexes available have not been widely acknowleged within the sociological community, and this has been a further source of confusion in the area of 'class analysis'.

It is against this diversity of approaches to social class, therefore, that the growing body of criticism of class analysis has to be evaluated. Since the nineteenth century, there is no time when class has not been a contentious issue, but the recent pace of social and economic change has served to increase the range and intensity of the debate.

The growing critique of 'class analysis'

As we shall see in chapter 2, a major point of contrast between the theoretical approaches of Marx and Weber concerns the question of class action. Although Marx's writings are famously ambiguous on the point, there can nevertheless be little doubt that he viewed class conflict as the major motor of historical change, and thus some kind of class action to be inevitable. Weber, on the other hand, regarded class conflict as contingent – that is, as highly likely to occur, but by no means inevitable. He certainly did not regard such conflict as the only or even the major, force of societal transformation. In a similar vein, much recent debate has focused on 'the declining significance of class'.

Changes in the structure of work as employment, as well as in the kinds of persons engaged in it, have supplied much of the empirical basis for arguments concerning the declining significance of class in late twentieth-century industrial societies. In Britain, America, and much of Western Europe, there has been a massive decline in the numbers employed in heavy manufacturing and traditional extractive industries such as mining, steelmaking, shipbuilding and heavy engineering. The reasons for this decline are complex. Technological innovation has played a major part, as has technical obsolescence – newly automated processes simply require fewer people, new forms of energy replace old – but there have also been shifts in the global division of labour – South East Asia, for example, is now the centre of the shipbuilding industry. The collapse of heavy industry in the West was enormously accelerated by the impact of the world recession which followed upon the oil crisis of the 1970s (cause and effect are virtually impossible to disentangle here). The economic restructuring which followed decline and massive unemployment did increase the number of jobs available, but mainly in the service economy of finance and retail services. These changes have all led to a decline in the numbers of what had long been considered to be the traditional 'working-class', that is, geographically concentrated, manual employees in heavy industry. There has been a corresponding growth in non-manual. 'white-collar' employees, who had conventionally been regarded as located in the 'middle' classes or strata.

Together with these changes in the occupational structure, it has also been argued that 'work' as employment has become of considerably less significance in the shaping of social attitudes. People in employment spend less of their time in paid work, and increasing numbers of people are less dependent on paid work for their livelihood than in a previous era. This is partly because technical change and continuing economic uncertainty mean that there is simply less work (as employment) available, but also because the expansion of state provisions (in education, health and welfare) has made people less dependent on the sale of their labour in order to obtain the services they need. Thus work as employment is of declining importance as a source of social identity in the second half of the twentieth century, and to borrow Gorz's title (1982), it is argued that we should bid a 'Farewell to the Working Class'.

The real implications of these changes in work and employment have, however, been hotly contested. In particular, in 1974 Braverman's influential book, *Labor and Monopoly Capital*, argued that the capitalist mode of production embodied an inherent tendency towards the routinization and 'deskilling' of labour. These tendencies affected all workers, and thus the apparent 'upgrading' of the labour force consequent upon the growth of non-manual employment was more apparent than real. White-collar workers, and even management, would in their turn become deskilled employees. Braverman's intervention stimulated considerable controversy as the real nature of the changes, in class terms, which were occurring in respect of the occupational structure; but a (perhaps unintended) consequence of the revitalized debate on the class structure was that the question of class action was increasingly treated as a separate issue – or even not considered at all.

The question of class action, however, still remained problematic. The definition and relative size of the 'working class' might be contested, and the evidence of occupational class schemes might continue to demonstrate that occupational class and voting behaviour were still closely related; nevertheless, it would be difficult to make a strong case to the effect that the working class (or any other class) in the West has been engaged in sustained revolutionary activity since the end of the Second World War. The collapse of 'state socialism' in the Eastern bloc seems to have been accompanied by a turning away from socialist ideals, rather than their revitalization. During the 1970s and 1980s, therefore, there have developed a number of important political debates which have challenged the significance of 'class' for contemporary politics.

These debates are also linked to the wider social and economic changes which took place during the 1970s, which have already been briefly discussed in respect of their effects on employment. It is increasingly being suggested, amongst theoreticians of the political left, that these changes are in fact epochal and signify a significant shift in the development of capitalist industrialism. Many different labels have been used to describe this transition – from modernity to postmodernity, from organized to disorganized capitalism, from Fordism to post-Fordism. They describe the continuing break-up of older, mass production industries and the growth of new, computer-based production and 'flexible specialization'. Individuals are being forced to adapt rapidly to these 'new times', long-term employment in mass industries and mass bureaucracies, which provided a solid foundation for the articulation of industrial-class action, is rapidly becoming a thing of the past. 'Old politics' stands accused of 'productivism'; the 'new socialism', it is argued, must recognize that there are no objective class interests as such, but that there are many different points of antagonism, and thus potential for oppositional organization between capitalism and the population of late twentieth-century industrial societies. These kinds of arguments, therefore, not only attempt to take on board the apparent decline in political significance of the old-style working class, but also to identify new focuses of political concern.

In contrast to the distributional issues which were the focus of the 'old politics', it is argued that the growth of 'new social movements' has transformed the political scene. Such movements are concerned with the environment, the possibility of world peace, and the rights of various groups which have been historically excluded from full economic and political participation – women and subordinate ethnic groups in particular (Offe 1985a). The notion of rights is being extended, beyond those of adults, to include those of animals and children. It is a feature of new social movements that their support cuts across class boundaries, thus further weakening the basis of the old class politics, and class-based political action.

These political arguments, therefore, have been widely employed in debates relating to the declining significance of 'class'. The growth of 'second-wave' feminism, which accompanied the increasing participation of women in paid employment, has also been of considerable importance. Class politics, it might be argued (as well as the institution of citzenship itself) were decisively shaped by the interests of male employees, as well as male owners and controllers of the means of material production. Men might have subordinated other men, and struggled for power and control, within the 'public' sphere of employment, politics and warfare, but, as the feminist critique demonstrated, women were subordinate not only in the public sphere but also within the 'private' sphere of domestic and family life. The orthodox terrain of class theory and analysis seemed to have little to contribute as far as an analysis of the position of women was concerned. The increase in women's employment also served to highlight major weaknesses as far as occupational class schemes were concerned. Such schemes had been devised in relation to a model of predominantly male employment. The persistence of occupational segregation by sex, despite the increase in the employment of women, meant that such schemes could no longer be implicitly treated as gender-neutral. The persistence of the gendered division of labour, however, continues to create apparently insuperable obstacles to the development of a single classification which would encompass both men and women.

More generally, if work as employment is declining in its significance towards the close of the twentieth century, then it has been argued that other factors, notably consumption, are becoming more relevant for the analysis of stratification systems. Consumption is providing the basis for new social cleavages; Saunders (1987), for example, has argued that the major social cleavage in contemporary societies is that between those whose consumption needs are largely met through the market, on the one hand, and those largely dependent on state benefits on the other. Similar arguments are developing in the debate concerning the emergence of a putative underclass in the United States. It is also as consumers that many individuals express their environmental concerns; another example of this reasoning would be the supposed increase in significance of the 'gay' pound and dollar. In short, people's identities are being increasingly expressed and manifest through consumption, rather than production. As a consequence, outdated nineteenth-century class theories, obsessed with productivism, should, it is argued, be finally abandoned.

The kinds of criticism reviewed above have focused upon the question of whether 'classes' should still be regarded as actual or potential significant social forces in the late twentieth century. They do not suggest, however, that capitalist societies are not still highly unequal. Following from this point, although 'work' *may* possibly have declined as a significant source of social identity, work is still the most significant determinant of the material well-being of the majority of the population. Thus descriptive class indexes continue to demonstrate the persisting structure of inequality in contemporary societies. It still makes sense to describe late capitalist society as being dominated by a 'ruling class' which is economically dominant, and has the capacity to influence crucially political and social life (Scott 1991).

In chapter 4, criticisms of class analysis will be examined in some detail. Chapter 5 will evaluate the response to these criticisms from the varying perpectives which class analysis encompasses. It will also develop an argument to the effect that despite the economic and political changes and developments which have indeed taken place during the turbulent 1970s and 1980s, class and stratification theory does *not* have to be fundamentally recast in order to accommodate them. One general criticism will, however, be accepted. Recent debates *have* been hampered by an excessive focus on 'class' to the exclusion of other sources of structured social inequality. Much of the fire and brimstone, however, has been occasioned by people talking past, rather than to, each other. In a classic commentary on postwar sociology, Merton had observed that: 'In sociology as in other disciplines, pseudofacts have a way of inducing pseudoproblems, which cannot be solved because matters are not as they purport to be' (1959: xv). The lack of agreement relating to a number of basic concepts – particularly 'class' – within stratification theory and research, it may be suggested, has tended to generate a number of 'pseudo-debates'. Nevertheless, the rich tradition of stratification theory and research can still supply essential concepts through which to analyse our rapidly changing times – most particularly, through an analysis of the interrelationship between class and status.

In chapter 6, the development of citizenship will be explored as an example of a particular application of the status concept. In all advanced industrial nation states, citizens have become entitled to a guaranteed – if modest – level of material support whether or not they are engaged in market activities. As Esping-Andersen (1990) has put it, certain services – for example in the areas of health and education – have to varying extents been 'de-commodified'. Marshall has described these as the rights of social citizenship, which he views as extensions of the rights of civil and political citizenship acquired from the eighteenth century onwards. Civil and political citizenship rights were intitially granted to white adult males only, but the universalistic ideologies of liberal democracy have made it difficult to resist the sustained claims of excluded groups. Thus women and ethnic groups have made successful claims to citizenship status. Class struggles, it may be argued, were significant in the extension of citizenship rights, but the struggles of feminists, and ethnic minorities, to achieve these rights should be distinguished from those of class. Indeed, white male 'class' interests have often been seen as being at variance with those of other, non-class, groups within the stratification order. A further twist to the development of social citizenship in the twentieth century is that some commentators of the right have asserted that the state provision of non-market supports has contributed to the development of a permanent underclass in advanced industrial societies.

One feature of the underclass debate is that it has been argued that within this grouping there has developed a particular culture, or set of moral perspectives, which serves to perpetuate its disadvantaged situation. This somewhat dubious argument is examined in chapter 6. Although it will be argued that it should not be accepted, it does serve to highlight the significance of the non-economic determinants of the stratification order. It has been stressed that, even in capitalist market societies, status claims have been of continuing significance in determining the distribution of material rewards and resources. The renewed emphasis on the significance of consumption, however, has brought to prominence the role of status, as expressed in 'lifestyles' and consumption practices, in the structuring of inequalities. For example Bourdieu (1973, 1986) has argued that cultural capital should be considered as playing a similar role to that of economic capital in the production and reproduction of inequalities.

Culture has been argued to play an increasingly significant role in the changing circumstances of 'consumer capitalism'. In particular, it has been suggested that cultural producers are a significant element within the 'new middle class', a grouping which, along with the 'underclass', has been identified by numerous commentators as a significant new stratification development associated with late twentieth-century industrialism. The 'new middle class' incorporates not just the symbol producers, but also the 'need merchants' who exist to prepare the labour inputs for the new service economy. This economy increasingly demands social, rather than technical or practical skills, and with these demands there develops the providers – therapists, fitness experts, counsellors, and so on. These new debates on the new middle class are examined in chapter 7.

Concluding summary

From the first, 'class' has always been a term with a variety of meanings. It has served to describe, in a relatively straightforward fashion, structures of material and symbolic inequality, as well as to describe social forces which have a capacity to act upon the world. Over the last two decades, however, research and theorizing in the area of class and stratification has undergone further fragmentation in response to economic and political changes, as well as changes in the perceptions of social scientists as to how the social world may best be investigated. This fragmentation has given rise to a proliferation of approaches to class and stratification analysis.

This book, therefore, has a relatively modest purpose. It does not seek to draw a new 'class map', or to develop a further original (and final?) approach to the analysis of social stratification. Rather, it attempts to provide a map of class and stratification analysis for the undergraduate student. This will involve the identification of weaknesses, as well as strengths, but it will nevertheless be argued consistently that the investigation and exploration of structured social inequality should remain as one of the central problem areas of sociology.

Notes

1   The 'ideological' origins and nature of the caste system have been challenged, particularly by Marxist anthropologists (Meillassoux 1973). It is argued that in reality caste differentiation reflected degrees of material power and domination, rather than ritual purity.

2   As we shall see in ch. 6, some categories of human beings, notably women, were initially excluded from this 'fraternal social contract'. See Pateman (1988, 1989).

3   As we shall see in ch. 2, Marx argued that feudal societies, like capitalist societies, were class-stratified. However, it may be suggested that the discourse of 'class' is peculiarly modern, and this is the major reason why the term will be restricted to modern industrial societies in the subsequent discussion.

4   An obvious counter-argument to this view is that many of the goods and services created by innovators have not benefited either the environment or society in general. Tobacco and Thalidomide might be cited as examples.

5   In this argument, there was an echo of the election campaign of 1963. The then Conservative Cabinet was largely composed of Old Etonians, and the Labour leader (Harold Wilson) made much in his challenge of his own humble origins, stressing the contrast with the social backgrounds of the Conservative leadership. The Labour Party won the election.

2
Class Analysis:
The Classic Inheritance and
its Development

Introduction

As described in chapter 1, the term 'class' is widely used as a general label to describe structures of inequality in modern societies. Such descriptive accounts of inequality, however, will incorporate implicit or explicit assumptions as to *why* a particular individual, occupation, or social category should be located in a particular class. 'Class' has also been used in more abstract terms to describe a social force – most particularly by Marx, who described all history as 'the history of class struggles'. The notion that 'classes' can have transformative capacities is not limited to Marxism. The social forces (or 'actors') identified by class theorists such as Marx and Weber, however, do not correspond neatly to the class categories identified in descriptive accounts of the 'class structure'. Nevertheless, as we shall see in this chapter, both Marx's and Weber's theoretical accounts of social class have generated insights which have guided the particular allocation of individuals, occupations or social categories within specific class schemes. As a consequence of this practice, the 'classes' produced by the application of class schemes to the structure of employment have often been treated, implicitly, as if they also constituted actual or potential class actors. It will be argued that there are many difficulties with this assumption.

Social class and inequality have been amongst the central topic areas within sociology. It is not surprising, therefore, that the investigation of these topics over the last half-century should have been significantly shaped by debates taking place within sociology itself. Thus debates in social theory, as well as the specific theoretical contributions of Marx and Weber, have also had an important impact on class analysis. Our primary objective in this chapter, besides giving an account of Marx's and Weber's classic contributions, will also be to explore the impact of these varying theoretical inputs on the developing project of class and stratification analysis.

The ideas of both Marx (1818–83) and Weber (1864–1920) continue to shape debates in class theory in the late twentieth century. However, their contributions have been extensively reinterpreted and reformulated by succesive generations. Of these two 'founding fathers', Marx was primarily a political activist, rather than an academic social theorist. From the 1960s however, there was a revival of academic interest in Marx's work which ran in parallel with the theoretical debates in sociology which were then current – in particular, the developing critique of normative functionalism or the 'consensus' perspective (Lockwood 1964). As noted in chapter 1, the dominant paradigm in Anglo-American sociology in the 1950s and early 1960s was essentially positivist – that is, it held to the view that sociology was the study of observable and objective *facts* about the social world (rather than being concerned with, for example, theological or metaphysical speculation). It had a primary emphasis on the study of social structures or systems, rather than individuals. As the conflict theorists claimed, it was also concerned mainly with the functional coherence and normative integration of these systems, rather than on any conflicts or underlying tensions (Smelser 1988: 10). These kinds of sociological assumptions had also shaped the 'industrial society' thesis – that is, the idea that all Industrial Societies have a tendency to converge in a similar, non conflictual, direction (Kerr et al. 1973).

However, critics of positivism argued that social facts cannot be objectively located but are theory-dependent – that is, they are not simply 'out there' but are socially *constructed*. Thus even apparently objective facts such as census data are gathered with regard to theoretical assumptions which may not always be explicit (Hindess, 1973). The emphasis on social structures or systems was criticized (Wrong 1966) for its 'oversocialized' conception of human nature. The recasting of social theory was associated with an increasing emphasis on the significance of human *action*; it was emphasized that human beings are neither (to paraphrase Garfinkel) structural nor cultural 'dopes' but act reflexively with the social world. The emphasis on stability and integration characteristic of normative functionalism was increasingly rejected in favour of perspectives that emphasized conflict rather than consensus, domination rather than integration (Rex 1961).

As a consequence of these theoretical debates, sociology has fragmented into a number of separate paradigms, and it would be difficult, if not impossible, to describe a 'dominant paradigm' in contemporary sociology. These divisions have also been reflected in its sub-fields.

Despite a common origin in Marx's and Weber's work, therefore, class theory in sociology has developed in a number of different directions. However, these differences have not always been recognized explicitly by the many contributors to debates on 'class'.

Marx

Marx's aim was to provide a comprehensive analysis of capitalist society with a view to effecting its transformation; he was a committed revolutionary as well as a social theorist. In the *Communist Manifesto*, Marx and Engels (1962: 34) describe the course of human history in terms of the struggle between classes:

> Free man and slave, patrician and plebeian, lord and serf, guild-master and journeyman, in a word, oppressor and oppressed, stood in constant opposition to each other, carried on an uninterrupted, now hidden, now open fight, a fight that each time ended, either in a revolutionary re-constitution of society at large, or in the common ruin of the contending classes.

There can be little doubt, therefore, as to the centrality of class in Marx's work, but, although the theme is constant, he nowhere gives a precise definition of the class concept. Indeed, it is somewhat poignant that his last manuscript breaks off just at the moment at which he appeared to be on the point of giving such a definition, in a passage beginning: 'The first question to be answered is this: What constitutes a class? – and the reply to this follows naturally from the reply to another question, namely: What makes wage-labourers, capitalists and landlords constitute the three great social classes?' (Marx 1974: 886).

For Marx, class relationships are embedded in production relation-ships; more specifically, in the patterns of ownership and control which characterize these relationships. Thus the 'two great classes' of capitalist society are bourgeoisie and proletariat, the former being the owners and controllers of the material means of production, the latter owning only their labour power, which they are forced to sell to the bourgeoisie in order to survive. However, Marx did not have, as has sometimes been suggested, a 'two-class' model of society. It is true that he saw the bourgeoisie and proletariat as the major historic role-players in the capitalist epoch, but his analyses of contemporary events made it clear that he saw actual societies as composed of a multiplicity of classes. That is, Marx used the term 'class' both as an analytical concept in the development of his theory of society, and as a descrip-tive, historical concept. For example, in his account of the (1852)

Bonapartist coup d'etat in France, 'The Eighteenth Brumaire of Louis Bonaparte' (1962a), a variety of social groupings are identified including the landed aristocracy, financiers, the industrial bourgeoisie, the middle class, the petty bourgeoisie, the industrial proletariat, the lumpenproletariat and the peasantry.

• Marx's account of antagonistic class relationships did not rest upon ownership and non-ownership alone. Rather, ownership of the material forces of production is the means to the exploitation of the proletariat by the bourgeoisie within the very process of production itself. The key to Marx's understanding of this process lies in the labour theory of value, a concept which Engels described as one of Marx's major theoretical achievements. In a capitalist society, argues Marx, labour has become a commodity like any other, but it is unique in that human labour alone has the capacity to create *new* values. Raw materials (commodities) such as wood, iron or cotton cannot by themselves create value; rather, value is added when they are worked on by human labour to create new commodities which are then realized in the market. The labour which is purchased (and therefore owned) by the capitalist will spend only a part of the working day in the creation of values equivalent to its price (that is, wages); the rest of the working day is spent in the creation of surplus value, which is retained by the capitalist. (Surplus value does not simply describe profit, but is distributed to a number of sources including taxes, payments to 'unproductive' labourers and new capital investment, as well as profits or dividends.) Thus even though the labourer may be paid a wage that is entirely 'fair', that is, it represents the value of this labour in the market, and the worker has not been cheated or swindled in any legal sense (cheating and swindling *may* occur, of course) – he or she has nevertheless been exploited.

It has been emphasized that Marx was not just concerned to provide a description of the nature of exploitation in class societies, but also to give an account of the role of social classes in the transformation of societies themselves. Thus for Marx, classes are social forces, historical actors. For Marx, men (and, it should be said, women) *make* their own history, although not necessarily in the *circumstances* of their own choosing. Some commentators have suggested that for Marx a class only existed when it was conscious of itself as such. However, in *The Poverty of Philosophy*, he appears to make an unambiguous distinction between a 'class in itself' and a (conscious) 'class for itself', when he writes of the proletariat that 'this mass is already a class in opposition to capital, but not yet a class for itself' (1955: 195). This ambiguity in Marx's work has been of considerable significance in the development of sociological analyses of class.

Marx's account of the generation of human consciousness is central to his theory of historical materialism, the social-scientific core of Marxist theory. This is summarized in the Preface to *A Contribution to the Critique of Political Economy*:

> In the social production of their life, men enter into definite relations that are indispensable and independent of their will, relations of production which correspond to a definite stage of development of their material productive forces. The sum total of these relations of production constitutes the economic structure of society, the real foundation, on which rises a legal and political superstructure and to which correspond definite forms of social consciousness. The mode of production of material life conditions the social, political, and intellectual life process in general. It is not the consciousness of men that determines their being, but, on the contrary, their social being that determines their consciousness. (*Marx 1962b: 362–3*)

Two related – and contentious – insights may be drawn from this account. First, that it is the economic 'base' that determines the political and ideological 'superstructure' of human societies; and second, that it is material being that determines human consciousness, rather than vice versa. These arguments may be illustrated via a summary of the account of the transition from feudalism to capitalist industrialism, as outlined by Marx and Engels in the *Communist Manifesto*. The relations of production in feudal society – the system of manorial estates held by right rather than purchase, with an unfree peasantry bound to labour on the land through feudal obligations, were the material basis of an ideological superstructure in which the existing social order was given divine justification through the Catholic Church. Feudal society was static and technologically underdeveloped, and the network of customary rights and obligations which underpinned it acted as a hindrance to the development of the dynamic capitalist order. The feudal aristocracy was, however, ultimately unable to resist the power of the rising bourgeoisie, the 'revolutionary class' in the feudal context. Thus after centuries of feudal stagnation, the transition to capitalism was nevertheless achieved – often accompanied by more or less violent events (such as, for example, the French Revolution). The triumphant bourgeoisie may have broken with feudal restrictions and consolidated their rights in the ownership of the means of production (that is, capital), but in creating the class that had only its labour to sell as its means of subsistence – that is, the proletariat – the bourgeoisie had created their own 'grave diggers': 'Society as a whole is more and more splitting up into two great hostile camps, into two great classes directly facing each other: Bourgeoisie and Proletariat' (Marx and Engels 1962: 35). The proletariat would constitute the revolutionary class within capitalist society, and through its struggles would usher in first socialism and eventually, true communism.

Marx's distinction between base and superstructure has been the subject of extensive debate. He has been widely accused of economic reductionism – the assertion that the economic base *determines* social, political and intellectual development. Such a mechanistic model would, indeed, constitute a gross oversimplification of the complexities of human behaviour, and in a letter written after Marx's death, his collaborator Engels emphasized that the theory of historical materialism should not be interpreted as claiming that the economic situation was the *sole* cause of human behaviour. Rather, he argued that although it might be 'ultimately' determinant, at any particular moment, other social relations – political, ideological – would also be affecting human actions. The base/superstructure debate, however, was not closed as a consequence of Engels's intervention

Marxist theory has developed in a number of different directions. By the 1970s two broad strands within Marxism relating to the base/superstructure debate had emerged: 'humanist' and 'scientific'. As Urry (1981: 8) has noted, these perspectives incorporated 'the reproduction of certain of the problems which have already been encountered within orthodox sociology'. This was the structure/action debate; the contrast between, on the one hand, sociological perspectives which emphasize above all the significance of human action in explanations of social institutions and behaviour, and, on the other, the functionalist or structurally deterministic accounts of society which such 'action' approaches criticized. Thus, humanist Marxism – as in, for example, the work of Gramsci – tends to treat the base/superstructure distinction as a metaphor which can all too easily be interpreted in a deterministic fashion. Gramsci emphasizes the value of Marx's analysis as a means of developing a critique of the dehumanizing aspects of modern capitalism, a critique which will ultimately enable the actor to transcend his or her 'alienation'. As with the action approach within sociology, therefore, a central role is given to the human actor.

'Scientific' Marxism was the self-assigned label of French structural Marxists such as Althusser (1969) and Poulantzas (1975). Althusser argued that ideology and politics were not determined by the economy in a mechanistic fashion, as some simplistic interpretations of Marx had assumed. Rather, they should be seen as conditions of its existence and are therefore 'relatively autonomous' – although, echoing Engels, Althusser held that the economic was determinant in 'the last instance'. The work of Althusser and Poulantzas was also characterized by a distinctive epistomology, or view of how knowledge about the world is acquired. Knowledge about the social world, they argued, does not proceed by observation but through theoretical practice or 'science' – of which Marxism was an example. Thus we do not 'know' classes by observing them but rather through the theoretical identification and exploration of the class structure, and individuals are the 'bearers' or 'agents' of these structures of social relations. This approach, therefore, emphasizes above all the primacy of class *structures*. The manner in which individuals are distributed within these structures is, from their perspective, of comparatively minor importance; the important task for the 'scientist' is to identify the structure itself, and thus the 'real interests' of the individuals located within it. It is not difficult to see the parallels here with functionalism and structural over-determinism in sociology (Connell 1982). Different classes are being identified according to their 'functional' relationship to the capitalist mode of production as a whole, which is described in Marx's account of the exploitation of workers within the labour process and the way in which different groups in society are related to this process.

As we have seen, Marx had drawn a distinction between a 'class in itself' and a 'class for itself'; this has been described as a distinction between a set of 'objective' conditions which define the class, and the 'subjective' consciousness which this class possesses (Braverman 1974). However, what is the nature of this subjective consciousness? It has been argued (Abercrombie and Turner 1978) that Marx's work provides two, conflicting, accounts of the generation of class consciousness. On the one hand, the passage cited above from the *Critique of Political Economy* could be used to argue that each class develops its 'own' consciousness: that factory workers, for example, will develop a common understanding of their exploited position. On the other hand, the same passage could be used to argue that the dominant class has the capacity to generate a dominant ideology – that the employers, for example, will have the capacity to generate amongst factory workers a belief that the prevailing arrangements are beneficial for all concerned. Thus in *The German Ideology*, Marx and Engels state: 'The ruling class are in every epoch the ruling ideas, i.e. the class which is the ruling *material* force of society, is at the same time its ruling *intellectual* force' (1970: 64). Thus a subordinate class may, as a consequence, hold to views which are at variance with its own 'objective' interests – a phenomenon which has been described by later Marxists as a 'false consciousness' of their true class situation.

Throughout the 1980s, the debate on class continued amongst Marxist theorists. Structural Marxism no longer has the influence it once had – at least in part, it may be suggested, because of the electoral failure of the left (see Preface in Benton 1984). The revival of Marxist scholarship in the 1960s was accompanied by an optimism of the left which persisted throughout much of the 1970s; the 1980s, however, witnessed the electoral rise of the 'New Right' – Thatcherism in Britain, Reaganomics in the United States. Political theorists including Przeworski (1985), Laclau and Mouffe (1985), and Wood (1986) have examined the possibilities of the development of socialism in these changing circumstances. Much of this discussion has involved a fundamental revision of some basic Marxist political ideas. In particular, the central place which the proletariat or working class occupied within Marx's original writings has increasingly been called into question. Wood (1986: 3–4) has summarized these revisions (which she describes, somewhat scathingly, as the 'New True Socialism') as follows: first, the absence of revolutionary politics amongst the working class reflects the fact that there is no necessary correspondence between economics and politics (that is, the link between base and superstructure is regarded as tenuous, even non-existent). Second, there is no necessary or privileged relation between the working class and socialism, and so a socialist movement can be constituted independently of class (thus dissolving the link between 'class' and 'consciousness'). Third, socialism is in any case concerned with universal human goals which transcend the narrowness of material class interests and may therefore address a broader public, irrespective of class. Thus the struggle for socialism can be conceived as a plurality of democratic struggles, bringing together a variety of resistances to many forms of inequality and oppression (for example, those associated with gender and race).

These arguments amongst Marxist theoreticians have not been directly concerned with class and stratification research in sociology, but they have nevertheless had a considerable impact. The American sociologist Erik Wright (1989) has systematically developed both his 'class map' as well as his strategy of analysis in response to inputs from these sources. More generally, however, it may be suggested that contemporary debates within theoretical Marxism have contributed to more general arguments to the effect that 'class' is no longer a relevant analytical concept as far as late twentieth-century societies are concerned.

Marx, therefore, saw classes as real social forces with the capacity to transform society. His class analysis did not simply describe the patterning of structured social inequality – although an explanation of this structuring can be found in the relationships to the means of production through which classes are to be identified. His theories have been enormously influential and are open to a number of different interpretations. Two major problems have been identified which are still the focus of considerable debate within sociology: first, the relative significance of the 'economy' (or class forces) as compared to other sources of social differentiation in the shaping of human activities; and second, whether or not consciousness is integral to the identification of a class. As we shall see, the position of Max Weber, the other major theorist whose ideas have been central to the development of sociological perspectives on class, was rather different on both of these issues.

Weber

The contrast between Marx's and Weber's analysis of class may at times have been overdrawn, but it cannot be doubted that their approaches to social science were very different. Marx was a committed revolutionary, Weber a promoter of 'value-free' social science; and although Weber could not be described as an idealist, he was highly critical of Marx's historical materialism. Marx claimed to have identified abstract social forces (classes) which shaped human history – although, as we have seen, the extent to which Marx considered such structures *can* be identified independently of human action is itself a topic of much debate. Weber, in contrast, was an explicit methodological individualist. That is, he argued that all social collectivities and human phenomena have to be reducible to their individual constituents, and explained in these terms.

As far as class is concerned, for Weber:

> We may speak of a 'class' when (1) a number of people have in common a specific causal component of their life chances, in so far as (2) this component is represented exclusively by economic interests in the possession of goods and opportunities for income, and (3) is represented under the conditions of the commodity or labour markets. (*Gerth and Mills 1948: 181*)

Thus 'class situation' reflects market-determined 'life chances'. The causal components contributing to such life chances include property, giving rise to both positively and negatively privileged property classes (that is, owners and non-owners), and skills and education, giving rise to positively and negatively privileged 'acquisition' or 'commercial' classes. Weber was aware of the (almost) infinite variability of 'market situations' and thus of the difficulty of identifying a 'class', and his discussion in *Economy and Society* incorporates the listing of over twenty positively and negatively privileged, property and acquisition, classes. This empirical plurality is resolved by Weber's description of a '*social* class', which 'makes up the totality of those class situations within which individual and generational mobility is easy and typical' (Giddens and Held 1982: 69). He identified as 'social classes' (a) the working class as a whole; (b) the petty bourgeoisie; (c) technicians, specialists and lower-level management, and (d) 'the classes privileged through property and education' – that is, those at the top of the hierarchy of occupation and ownership. In short, at the descriptive level, Weber's account of the 'class structure' of capitalist society is not too different from that of Marx, despite the fact that their identification of the *sources* of class structuring (production relationships on the one hand, market relationships on the other) *are* very different.

Marx and Weber, however, differed profoundly as far as the question of class action was concerned. For Weber: ' "classes" are not communities; they merely represent possible, and frequent, bases for communal action' (Gerth and Mills 1948: 181). 'Associations of class members – class organizations – may arise on the basis of all . . . classes. However, this does not necessarily happen . . . The mere differentiation of property classes is not "dynamic", that is, it need not result in class struggles and revolutions' (Giddens and Held 1982: 69–70). Indeed, in a passage which clearly refers to the Marxist notion of 'false consciousness' he writes that:

> every class may be the carrier of any one of the innumerable possible forms of class action, but this is not necessarily so. . . . That men in the same class situation regularly react in mass actions to such tangible situations as economic ones in the direction of those interests that are most adequate to their average number is an important . . . fact for the understanding of historical events. However, this fact must not lead to that kind of pseudo-scientific operation which has found its most classic expression in the statement of a talented author, that the individual may be in error concerning his interests but that the class is infallible about its interests. (*Gerth and Mills 1948: 184–5*)

Weber's historical sociology, therefore, was developed in conscious opposition to Marxist theories of historical development – at least in its more economistic versions – as in Weber's analysis of the genesis of modern capitalism in *The Protestant Ethic and the Spirit of Capitalism*. In this book, he explored the unintended consequences of Calvinist ideology, and its impact on historical development, through an examination of the 'elective affinity' between Protestantism and the 'spirit of capitalism', which affected the development of capitalism itself. Weber argued that rational, ascetic Protestantism, as developed within a number of Calvinist churches and Pietistic sects in Europe and America during the seventeenth century, provided, through its rules for daily living (diligence in work, asceticism, and systematic time use) a particularly fruitful seedbed for the development of capitalism. It would be misleading to argue that Weber had developed his argument in order to advance an alternative, 'idealist', interpretation of history, he did not seek 'to substitute for a one-sided materialistic an equally one-sided spiritualistic causal interpretation of culture and of history' (Weber 1976: 183). However, as Marshall (1982: 150) has argued, the question as to whether Marx's materialist or Weber's pluralistic account of the rise and development of capitalism is to be preferred is not, ultimately, an empirical one but, rather, a question of the 'validity of competing frameworks for the interpretation of social reality'. Although Weber's account of the rise of capitalism cannot be described as 'idealist', therefore, it does lead, inevitably, to an account of the relationship between the 'ideological' and 'material' realms of human activity which would be in conflict with Marx's analysis.

Weber's analysis is also to be distinguished from Marx's in that he not only denies the inevitability of class action and conflict, but also the identification of class as a primary source of differentiation in complex societies. For Weber, ' "classes", and "status groups" are phenomena of the distribution of power within a community' (Gerth and Mills 1948: 181), and in certain circumstances, status may be the predominant source which regulates entitlements to material rewards. Status is associated with honour and prestige and, indeed, may often come into conflict with the demands of the market, where, to use an old phrase suitably adapted: 'every man (and woman) has his (or her) price'. In contrast: 'in most instances', wrote Weber, 'the notion of honour peculiar to status absolutely abhors that which is essential to the market: higgling' (Gerth and Mills 1948: 193). Thus in Weber's analysis the feudal lord or abbot, for example, would belong not to a dominant class but to a status group. 'Status', in Weber's writings, is a complex concept. First, there is the meaning which has already been described: that which reflects the etymological link with 'estate' or 'stande' and describes positions which represent particular life chances or fates for the status group in question. Second, status groups have been identified as 'consciousness communities', as when, for example, Collins (1971: 1009) describes status groups as 'associational groups sharing common cultures . . . Participation in such groups gives individuals their fundamental sense of identity.' Third, status has been used to describe consumption categories or 'lifestyle', as 'the totality of cultural practices such as dress, speech outlook and bodily dispositions (Turner 1988: 66).

The crucial differences between Marx's and Weber's accounts of class may be summarized as follows: first, for Marx, class relationships are grounded in exploitation and domination within *production* relations, whereas for Weber, class situations reflect differing 'life chances' in the *market*; second, Marx's historical materialism gives a primacy to 'class' in historical evolution which is at odds with Weber's perspective on historical explanation; and finally (and following from this point), whereas for Marx, class action is seen as inevitable, for Weber, classes 'merely represent possible, and frequent, bases for communal action' (Gerth and Mills 1948: 181).

Class and sociology after the Second World War

Sociology had been well established in the United States before the Second World War, and 'At the beginning of the 1950's . . . one could find large numbers of studies dealing with almost every aspect of behaviour in the United States. No other society had ever been subjected to such detailed examination' (Bendix and Lipset 1967a: 6). A strong tradition of empirical investigation, therefore, was well established. This included research into social stratification, which, as in studies such as Warner's (1963) anthropologically inspired *Yankee City* series, first published in the 1940s, had a focus on occupational inequality and social mobility, often in small communities. As has frequently been noted, in such studies 'class' was in practice operationalized as a particular dimension of the Weberian concept of *status* in that it was mainly concerned with social prestige rankings within the community. The pre-eminent sociological theorist in the United States was Talcott Parsons; as we have seen, the structural functionalism which characterized his approach had a tendency to emphasize order rather than conflict, and thus to direct attention away from the conflict and tensions in society which are the focus of *class* (rather than status) analyses.

Sociology in Britain was relatively underdeveloped in the 1950s, and had been much influenced by the Fabian tradition of social improvement and reform. Thus a preoccupation with structured social inequality had always been present. An example of this tradition of British 'political arithmetic' would be Glass's *Social Mobility in Britain* (1954), which had used an occupational (class) scale in its statistical analyses of social mobility. In Continental Europe, sociology was more deeply rooted in established traditions of philosophy and social theory. The intellectual diaspora which was a consequence of the rise of fascism brought many European scholars to the United States and Britain, and with it an increasing emphasis on the significance of 'theory' in sociology.

The first major reader in the field of class and stratification to be published in English after the Second World War – *Class, Status, and Power* (1953; 2nd edn 1967), edited by Reinhard Bendix and S. M. Lipset – reflected this mingling of influences. The title was itself a deliberate play on a section of Weber's *Economy and Society*, 'Class,

Status, and Party', which had been of considerable significance in shaping sociological thinking about 'social class'. The importance of the distinction between economic 'classes' and 'status rankings' (the latter describes the conceptualization of class in Warner's research) was increasingly emphasized. However, the use of the 'class' concept by the different contributors to the volume reflected the variety of definitions of the term which has been noted in chapter 1. Thus there were a number of papers on class theory, in which class was discussed as an abstract force, whereas other contributions used the same word – class – to describe the occupational aggregates used in, for example, empirical analyses of residential segregation. Bendix and Lipset's article – 'Karl Marx's theory of social classes' (1967b) – provided a guide to 'Marx on Class' for a whole generation of sociology students in Britain and America.

They identified a 'basic ambiguity', which has already been noted, in Marx's theory concerning class action:

> on the one hand, he felt quite certain that the contradictions engendered by capitalism would inevitably lead to a class-conscious proletariat and hence to a proletarian revolution. But on the other hand, he assigned to class-consciousness, to political action, and to his scientific theory of history a major role in bringing about this result. (*1967b: 11*)

In other words, is class consciouness and therefore conflict inevitable, or not? As Bendix and Lipset demonstrated, Marx's own work provided an extensive discussion of the circumstances in which class consciousness *might* develop (conflicts over the distribution of material resources, alienation and deskilling within the labour process, concentration of workers within factories, combinations to raise wages, increasing polarization within society, and so on), but, they argued, ambiguity still remained as to whether it *would* develop. However, if the question of class consciousness is viewed as contingent rather than inevitable (and this, it will be remembered, was Weber's position), then the question becomes an empirical one – in what circumstances does class consciouness develop? As Lockwood has noted: 'once shorn of its deterministic assumptions, the Marxian problem of the relationship between class position and class consciousness could become a subject of far-reaching and systematic sociological inquiry' (1958; 1989: 217).

The development of theoretical accounts of the 'class structure'

The way was laid open, therefore, for the analytical and empirical separation of class structure from consciousness, between the 'objective' and 'subjective' dimensions of class. Within this emerging sociological perspective, a central problem is that of the identification of the class structure itself – that is, a structure of positions which may or may not give rise to consciousness. The structure of employment became the major focus of such attempts. Dahrendorf's work was extremely influential in this regard. In *Class and Class Conflict in an Industrial Society* (1959: 151), he drew upon the work of both Marx and Weber in deriving the class structure from 'positions in associations (i.e., occupations) co-ordinated by authority and defin[ing] them by the "characteristic" of participation in or exclusion from the exercise of authority'. In a similar vein to Bendix and Lipset, he argued that: 'The general theory of class consists of two analytically seperable elements: the theory of class formation and the theory of class action, or class conflict' (1959: 153). This analytical separation of 'structure' and 'action', as we have seen, assumed considerable significance in sociology and has had an important effect on the development of 'class analysis'.

Like Dahrendorf, Lockwood in *The Blackcoated Worker* drew upon the theoretical analyses of both Marx and Weber in his now-classic 1958 account of a 'socio-economic group that had long been a discomfort to Marxist theory: the growing mass of lower non-manual or white-collar employees' (1958; 1989: 218). (In fact, Lockwood's research focused entirely on clerical occupations.) He described 'class position' as including three factors: 'market situation', that is 'the economic position narrowly conceived, consisting of source and size of income, degree of job-security, and opportunity for upward occupational mobility'; secondly, 'work situation', or 'the set of social relationships in which the individual is involved at work by virtue of his position in the division of labour'; and finally, 'status situation', or the position of the individual in the hierarchy of prestige in the society at large. Experiences originating in these three spheres were seen as the principal determinants of class consciousness. (1989: 15–16). It must be emphasized that Lockwood was not merely concerned descriptively to locate clerks in the class structure. A central issue in his work is the question of class consciousness and action, and he explored the differentiation of 'class situation' within the clerical category which gave rise to variations in the level and type of trade union activity amongst clerical workers – trade unionism is here being viewed as an expression of class consciousness. Nevertheless, in maintaining, like Dahrendorf, an analytical separation between structure (formation) and action, Lockwood's work left open the possibility that 'class analysis' might come to have a primary focus on one or the other. Although, therefore, his original work was concerned as much with the question of class consciousness and action as it was with class structure, it might be suggested that one of its enduring legacies has been that it provided, within a neo-Weberian framework, the means to locate empirically particular groups of occupations within the 'class structure'. In particular, Lockwood's concepts of 'work' and 'market' situation have been the key elements in Goldthorpe's (1987) development of a theoretical class scheme, based on the occupational structure, which has been widely employed in empirical research.

Another sociologist who has devoted considerable effort to the theoretical identification of a 'class structure' within the structure of employment relationships is the American Marxist E. O. Wright. Wright's initial development of his Marxist 'class map', which was to become the basis of his own theoretical class scheme, was carried out in a conscious dialogue with structural Marxism (Wright 1976). Thus although Wright's theoretical perspectives are clearly very different from those of Lockwood, Dahrendorf, Goldthorpe and other 'left Weberians', his work is, like theirs, an attempt to identify sets of 'class positions' within the structure of employment. Wright's earlier work was much infuenced by Braverman, whose *Labor and Monopoly Capital* (1974) was modelled on Marx's analysis of the labour process in *Capital*, vol. 1. Braverman argued that with the development of mass production, work had become increasingly routinized and, as a consequence, there had been a continuing 'proletarianization' of the labour force – despite the apparent increase in 'white-collar' or 'middle-class' employment. Braverman's account of the 'deskilling' of craft work and the rationalization of the labour process had a considerable impact on industrial sociology. In respect of class analysis, however, his work had the effect of driving a further wedge between structure and action: 'No attempt will be made to deal with the modern working class on the level of its consciousness, organization, or activities. This is a book about the working class as a class *in itself*, not as a class *for itself*' (1974: 26–7; emphasis in original).[1] His account, therefore, focused entirely on developments within the labour process and did not discuss the possibility of class resistance or action. Thus although it is highly unlikely that Braverman would have had any sympathy with structural Marxism, his work had a similar impact. The 'analytical separation between class formation and class action' (Dahrendorf) was increasingly coming to represent distinct areas of theoretical and empirical activity (Crompton and Gubbay 1977).

Since the Second World War, therefore, we can trace the emergence of a distinctive sociological strand of 'class analysis'. Marxist and Weberian theories of social class are employed, as in the work of authors such as Lockwood, Dahrendorf and Braverman, to generate theoretical accounts of how particular jobs and occupations might be located within a structure of class positions. Increasingly, these accounts are used to elaborate and refine a predominant empirical approach within social stratification as a whole, in which employment aggregates are described as 'classes'. That is, 'classes' are identified theoretically within the structure of employment. Following from Bendix and Lipset's appropriation of Marx's distinction between a class 'in itself' and 'for itself', class structure and class action are regarded as analytically seperable. Thus these theoretically identified employment aggregates may be regarded as 'classes' – although the question of class action is contingent, rather than inevitable. This strategy, therefore, brings together within a single framework theoretical analyses of social class with empirical analyses of inequality. It is an approach with tremendous explanatory and analytical promise but, as we shall see, it also embodies a number of serious, and probably irresolvable, difficulties.

Culture, class and history

We have summarized above a number of sustained attempts, deriving from different theoretical perspectives, to indentify *a priori* a 'class structure' located within the structure of work and employment. A number of different factors served to push class analysis in this direction, including the established convention in American and British sociology of identifying 'classes' as occupational aggregates, the influence of both structural-functionalism and structural Marxism, and the revival of sociological interest in the labour process. However, these developments ran in parallel with other approaches to the study of social class, which tended to be associated with a humanistic, rather than a structuralist, Marxist perspective, and a methodological approach which drew primarily upon history and anthropology.

A broadly historical approach to the topic of social class, similar to that found in the work of Weber and Marx, has been a constant theme in the work of sociologists. In Britain, the work of Bottomore (1991) and Bauman (1982) might be cited as examples. From the 1960s there has been a continuing dialogue between sociology and history, much of which has been concerned with the concept of 'class' (Stedman Jones 1976; Neale 1983, Abrams 1980). A major example is E. P. Thompson's *Making of the English Working Class*, first published in 1963. In this book, and in his other work, Thompson argues explicitly against the more determinist versions of the model of economic 'base' and ideological 'superstructure' which had been developed from Marx's work. As Kaye (1984: 172) has argued; 'In his historical studies . . . Thompson has persistently pursued an intellectual struggle against those varieties of Marxism and social science which are characterized by economic determinism and the denial of human agency'. A rejection of determinism and emphasis on human agency might suggest the possibility of close parallels with Weber, but Thompson has from the first been associated with a tradition of Marxist history which, in Britain, has a lengthy pedigree. This tradition includes authors such as Maurice Dobb, Christopher Hill, and Eric Hobsbawm, who have written extensively on the development of capitalism and the transition from feudalism, the English Revolution, rural protest, and the development of Empire. The concept of 'class', and class struggle, has a central place in all of their writings, but Thompson's account of the 'making' of the English working class in the eighteenth and nineteenth centuries develops a distinctive perspective on 'class' which has had a major impact. Although his work is focused on the British case, it has been extremely influential in other countries.[2]

Thompson defines 'class' in the manner of an abstract force which nevertheless has real consequences: 'By class I understand a historical phenomenon, unifying a number of disparate and seemingly unconnected events ... I emphasise that it is a *historical* phenomenon. I do not see class as a 'structure', nor even as a 'category', but as something which in fact happens' (Thompson 1968: 9). Like Marx, Thompson sees class as embedded in relations of production, but he is emphatic that classes cannot be discussed or identified independently of class *consciousness*: 'class experience is largely determined by the productive relations into which men are born – or enter involuntarily. Class-consciousness is the way in which these experiences are handled in cultural terms: embodied in traditions, value-systems, ideas, and institutional forms' (1968: 10). Thompson's emphasis on the significance of experience and conciousness has led to criticisms from other historians that his work is excessively culturalist – that is, it represents a shift away from the investigation of *economic* structures and relations which, it may be argued, should occupy a central place in any Marxist historical investigation (Johnson 1979). This specific point relating to Thompson's work will not be pursued here – although the interrelationship between the 'economic' and the 'cultural' will be explored in some depth in chapter 7. For the moment, however, we will explore a topic of some relevance to class analysis in sociology, and which assumes a central place in Thompson's work – that is, the possibility (or otherwise) of identifying a class 'structure' independent of class consciousness.

Kaye has argued, following Wood, that Thompson has 'reformulat[ed] class analysis as class-struggle analysis' (1984: 201), but nevertheless Thompson does not claim that there are no 'objective' class relations. As we have seen, Thompson is explicit that the productive relations which determine class experience have an existence apart from the individual, but he *does* insist that 'class is a relationship, and not a thing . . . "It" does not exist, either to have an ideal interest or consciousness, or to lie as a patient on the Adjustor's table' (1968: 11). In taking up this position, Thompson was arguing against what he perceived to be the dominant sociological approach to 'class analysis', which was briefly described in the previous section of this chapter. He was equally critical of the structural-functional approach of Parsons and Smelser as well as the 'conflict' approach of Dahrendorf (1959). Smelser (1959) had carried out a detailed historical study of the Lancashire cotton industry which had used Parsons's 'general theory of action' in order to construct a set of empty theoretical 'boxes' to be filled by empirical research. This was informed by the principle that structural differentiation created new roles which then functioned more effectively in the new circumstances. On an extreme reading of this approach, human actors are thereby reduced to puppets. Dahrendorf had developed a model of the 'class structure' in which 'classes are . . . based on a structural arrangement of social roles' (1959: 148). Thus Dahrendorf's analysis focuses on the structuring of these roles, rather than on their incumbents: 'Classes are based on the differences in legitimate power associated with certain *positions*, i.e., on the structure of social roles with respect to their authority expectations. It follows from this that an individual becomes a member of a class by playing a social role' (Dahrendorf 1959: 149; my emphasis). It is not difficult to see how this approach would be at variance with that of Thompson, who describes Dahrendorf's work as 'obsessively concerned with methodology', and as excluding 'the examination of a single real class situation in a real historical context' (Thompson 1968: 11).

Besides its impact on the development of social history, Thompson's work has also been influential in the area of cultural studies, within which there has developed an approach to 'class analysis' very different from that of those who have concentrated upon the identification and investigation of the macro-level class structure. Much of this work has been influenced by Gramsci's humanist Marxism. As we have indicated above, Gramsci rejected the base/superstructure dichotomy of economistic Marxism, and emphasized the pervasive importance of culture and ideology to the persistence of structures of class domination. Culture, he argued, is neither apolitical, nor a mere reflection of the ideology of the dominant class. Central to Gramsci's thought is the concept of *hegemony*, that is, the manner in which the active *consent* of the subordinate classes to their domination is achieved. Thus 'every struggle between classes is always also a struggle between cultural modalities' (Hall 1981); winning the struggle of ideas is as important to the 'class struggle' as are economic and political struggles.

Thus within cultural studies there have been developed ethnographic accounts of the manner in which individuals in different classes both resist and reproduce their class situations. An influential example of this genre is Willis's *Learning to Labour* (1977), a study of working-class male adolescents. Willis illustrated how, in his terms, the explicitly oppositional working-class culture (that is, opposed to 'middle-class' values, including conformity, an emphasis on the importance of formal education, and so on) which was developed within the school context nevertheless reflected that within the working-class world of work which these youths were about to enter, and thus, paradoxically, reinforced their subordination. It is a feature of this cultural approach to class analysis, therefore, that no distinction is made between 'structure' and 'action', and that 'culture' is defined as encompassing both the meanings and the values which arise amongst distinctive social groups and classes, as well as the lived traditions and practices through which these meanings are expressed and in which they are embodied (Hall 1981: 26).

Much of the work stimulated by Thompson has focused on the working class, but in recent years, the lifestyles of the 'new middle classes' have become objects of intense scrutiny, following the work of Bourdieu (1986). This dimension of the ongoing analysis of the relationship between class structures and cultural developments will be reviewed in chapter 7 of this book.

Once again, the indivisibility of structure and action

Methodologically speaking, the development of 'theoretical' or 'relational' employment-based class schemes, on the one hand, and historico-cultural ethnographies, on the other, represent opposite poles in the development of 'class analysis'. However, these are by no means the only direction that class analysis has taken in sociology. The development of theoretical class schemes, focused on the structure of employment, depends on the analytical separation of the study of class structure from that of class action, of 'subjective' and 'objective' dimensions, but the validity of this separation has always been contested – and not only by those committed to an ethnographic approach. For example, Stark (1980) has been highly critical of Braverman's separation of the investigation of a class 'in itself' from a class 'for itself'. He argues against the type of class analysis which 'proceeds by identifying the members who 'make up' the class; this aggregate is then given the properties of a purposive actor' (1980: 96–7). As a consequence of this separation, he argues, Braverman's history was empirically inadequate in that it did not examine either worker resistance or the purposive strategies of the emergent managerial class. Rather than simply identifying classes as aggregates of 'places', Stark argues, in a manner reminiscent of Thompson, for a 'relational' approach:

> a class is not 'composed of' individuals; it is not a collection or aggregation of individuals. *Classes*, like the social relations from which they arise, exist in an antagonistic and dependent relation to each other. Classes are constituted by these mutually antagonistic relations. In this sense . . . the object of study is not the elements themselves but the relations between them. (*1980: 97*)

Thus the transformation of method, he argues, must also be accompanied by a shift in the level of abstraction of class analysis, away from an obsessive over-concern with the 'mode of production' to the study of the *interaction* of organizations and groups.

Stark's arguments, therefore, may be seen as an example of the ongoing parallel between debates in Marxist theory and those in mainstream sociology during the 1960s and 1970s. Giddens, whose work was influential in developing the critique of positivism, first developed his ideas on 'structuration', which has become the core of his social theory, in his book *The Class Structure of the Advanced Societies* (1973; 1981). He introduced the concept of 'structuration' as a means of focusing upon '*the modes in which* "economic" relationships become translated into "non-economic" social structures' (1981: 105) – that is, *social* classes.[3] Two types of structuration were identified. First, mediate structuration, which describes the links between particular market capacities – the ownership of productive property; the possesion of educational and technical qualifications; and manual labour power – and identifiable groups in society. Mediate structuration is governed by the extent of social mobility. Second, proximate structuration points to the factors which shape local class formation, including relationships of allocation and authority within the enterprise (here his discussion has close parallels with Dahrendorf's), and the impact of 'distributive groupings' in the community and neighbourhood. Thus Giddens's initial identification of a 'social class' incorporates both structure and agency. On the question of class consciousness, Giddens extends the original Marxist concept to a number of levels. He argues that 'structuration' will result in a common class *awareness*, but not necessarily class *consciousness* – that is, any sense of opposition to other social classes. He argued that, in contrast to Marx's analysis, a *revolutionary* consciousness which might lead to the transformation of society is most likely to develop at the historical moment of the emergence of the capitalist order, when material disparities are at their greatest and the imposition of authoritative control most rigorous.

In mature capitalism, in contrast, the working class is characterized merely by *conflict* consciousness, and social democracy is the characteristic form of developed capitalist society.

Giddens's account of the 'class structure', therefore, reflected the developing critique of positivism and structural over-determination within sociology itself, in that class relationships were presented as being *actively* structured, rather than simply being taken as given. The introduction of the notion of 'structuration' has led his subsequent work in a more methodological direction, and he has not returned to a further substantial treatment of class analysis. He notes that the book has today a 'somewhat "archaic" feel', and 'if I were to go over the same ground again today, the book would need thoroughgoing revision, and I would modify parts of it substantially' (Giddens 1990: 298). Some indication of the direction such revisions might take are given in later essays which explore the interrelationship of class and 'citizenship' (see chapter 6 below), and the significance of the labour process to the nature of exploitation within capitalism (Giddens and Mackenzie 1982). It may be noted that the question of action arises at two points in his analysis; first, that which relates to the 'structuration' of the different classes, and second, the nature and possibilities of class action once 'structuration' has occurred.

Given this emphasis on the active structuring of class relationships, it is not surprising that Giddens's approach to class analysis struck a resonant chord with historians influenced by Thompson's work.[4] The possibilities of the development of class consciousness and action consequent upon class formation has also been a continuing focus of empirical research in British sociology. Much of this work was stimulated by Lockwood's influential article, 'Sources of variation in working class images of society' (1966). For the most part, Lockwood argued, individuals 'visualise the . . . structure of their society from the vantage points of their own particular *milieux*, and their perceptions of the larger society will vary according to their experiences . . . in the smaller societies in which they live out their daily lives' (1966: 249). He thus developed a typology of working-class images of society ('traditional proletarian', 'traditional deferential', and 'privatised'), which corresponded to variations in the characteristic 'work' and 'community' situations experienced within the working class. Thus particular structural locations are seen as corresponding to particular societal images.

Lockwood's work stimulated a number of empirical studies which explored the link between particular occupational groups, structural locations, and social imagery – for example, Newby's (1977) study of agricultural workers, Brown and Brannen's study of shipbuilders (1970), as well as wide-ranging review and debate (Bulmer 1975). This work makes no empirical separation between the investigation of structure and action, and was often consciously related to the 'action' perspective which developed within sociology from the 1960s (Willener 1970). Thus within sociology there has been a continuing exploration of the origins and significance of class action. This kind of research, however, has more usually taken the form of the case study, rather than relying primarily on the large-scale sample survey (Marshall 1988).

A major response, therefore, to the break-up of the 'orthodox consensus' in sociology from the 1960s onwards was a renewed emphasis on the significance of human *action* for sociological investigations and explanations. Empirical studies of social class influenced by this perspective have often taken the form of micro-level studies of particular groups and occupations, within their specific social context. Much of this work has overlapped with the sociology of work and occupations, in particular that stimulated by the 'labour process' debate (Crompton and Jones 1984; Smith 1987). Another perspective which developed during the 1970s, and which has been particularly infuential within human geography and urban sociology, was a return to *political economy*. As the label implies, this strand of analysis tends to be interdisciplinary, and has often been informed by Marx's work. In the next section, therefore, we will discuss the applications of the class concept within urban sociology, where it has has been employed in a somewhat eclectic manner, and has incorporated both objective and subjective, aggregational and relational, dimensions of class analysis.

Social class, urban sociology and the turn to 'realism'

The concept of social class has occupied a central position in both urban sociology and radical geography. These sub-disciplines have been highly responsive to current developments in social thought, and have been much influenced, in succession, by structuralist Marxism (Castells 1977), political economy, the rediscovery of the labour process and the 'deskilling' debate (Massey 1984), philosophical realism (Sayer 1984) and, most recently, debates about 'postmodernism' (Harvey 1990). There has also been a continuing focus on the interpretation of contemporary social developments; in particular the debates relating to the restructuring of Western economies following the recession of the late 1970s and early 1980s have loomed large in empirical and theoretical discussions in Britain. This flexibility and openness of approach has been a source of both strength and weakness. On the one hand, it has encouraged a theoretical pluralism which appropriately reflects the complexity of the issues under investigation. On the other, them somewhat eclectic approach to be found within the New Human Geography has resulted in a tendency to borrow and mix concepts developed within rather different theoretical traditions, and a failure to appreciate that the confusions thus imported have resulted in a number of pseudo-debates which have not proved particularly fruitful (for example, some of the arguments surrounding the relative significance of class and consumption sector which are examined in chapter 7 of this book).

The influence of Marxism within urban sociology has meant that there has been a continuing emphasis within it on the significance of class *structure*. This has often been taken, in an unproblematic fashion, to be represented by the occupational structure. As a consequence, radical urban sociology has made extensive use of occupational class schemes – in all their variety (Sarre 1989). Thrift and Williams (1987: 5) distinguish five major concepts which are 'fairly consistently used in a class analysis, namely class structure, the formation of classes, class conflict, class capacity and class consciousness'. These concepts are more or less appropriate at different levels of analysis, which they describe as both spatial – cross-national, regional, individual communities – as well as temporal. Class structure, which is defined as 'a system of places generated by the prevailing social relations of production' (p. 6) is 'the most abstract' of the five concepts, and Thrift and Williams emphasize that class structure 'is only one element of class and it is unfortunate that in the literature it has all too often become an end in itself' (p. 7) – a comment which may be taken as a criticism of structural Marxism. Thus they do not claim that the class structure alone determines action, and stress that other social forces such as 'race, religion, ethnicity and gender, family and various state apparatuses' will 'not only blur the basic class divides but also generate their own divisions' (1987: 7).

The formation of classes, class conflict, class capacity and consciousness, they argue, demands a relational approach, as these processes can only be studied in the context of action, that is, actions (struggles) which shape the very emergence of 'classes' themselves. Here we have in their discussion of 'class' aspects which have close parallels with E. P. Thompson's Marxist humanism, but these are used in combination with a 'class structural' approach.

Urban sociology has also been much influenced by the 'realist' theoretical approach. Philosophical realism became influential as a possible solution to the theoretical problems raised by the critique of positivism (Keat and Urry 1975; 1981). 'Realism' directs attention not just at events, but at the underlying processes or mechanisms which produce them. These relatively enduring social entities are held to have causal properties which give rise to events – but the mere existence of a causal property does not mean that an event *will* occur. The realization of particular causal properties often depends on the blocking, or realization, of others, and empirical investigations guided by 'realist' principles have reflected this complexity (Bagguley et al. 1989). 'Realist' accounts have tended to focus on class *formation*, which has many parallels with Giddens's account of 'structuration'. In the 'realist' approach, therefore, the separation of the investigation of class structure from that of class action would be rejected.

Thus for example Keat and Urry claim that:

> The term 'class' is used by Marx in a realist manner. It refers to social entities which are not directly observable, yet which are historically present, and the members of which are potentially aware of their common interests and consciousness. The existence of classes is not to be identified with the existence of inequalities of income, wealth, status or educational opportunity. For Marx, and generally for realists, class structures are taken to cause such social inequalities. The meaning of the term, 'class', is not given by these inequalities. Rather it is the structure of class relationships which determines the patterns of inequality. (*1975: 94–5*)[5]

It may be noted, however, that Keat and Urry's description of Marx as a 'realist' incorporates an 'objectivist' characterization of the class structure, despite their stress on class *relationships*. Nevertheless, Keat and Urry are particularly critical of what they describe as the 'positivisation' of class in American stratification studies that is the identification of 'classes' as aggregates of individuals without reference to 'causal properties' but 'in terms of various kinds of demographic, social, and psychological criteria' (1975: 95). Thus in his subsequent work (Abercrombie and Urry 1983; Lash and Urry 1987), Urry has taken a socio-historical approach in his empirical investigations of the class structure. In particular, he has devoted considerable attention to exploring the emergence of the 'service class', and its 'causal powers' in contemporary capitalism.[6]

Theoretical 'realism' within urban sociology, therefore, sees classes as having 'causal powers' which are 'realized' in the struggle with other classes. Thus empirical analysis informed by this approach is socio-historical. Savage et al.'s recent (1992) work on the middle classes in Britain provides a clear statement of this approach to 'class analysis'. As indicated above, the major focus of the 'realist' approach is upon class *formation*, and this is reflected in their work. They argue that the 'middle classes' have access, to varying degrees, to three assets – or potential 'causal powers'. These are, first, property; second, organizational assets (that is, access to positions in organizational hierarchies, and the power that goes with them); and third, cultural assets, that is, the 'styles of life', or 'habitus', which serve to buttress and perpetuate structures of power and advantage (there are obvious parallels between cultural assets and the Weberian concept of status). Savage et al. draw upon a wide range of empirical material to suggest how relatively stable social collectivities have emerged on the basis of these 'causal powers'.

The 'realist' approach, therefore, may be characterized as having its major empirical focus upon processes of class formation, rather than upon descriptions of the class structure. The emphasis upon the contingency of the realization of particular 'causal powers' means that, in practice, empirical accounts of the processes of class structuring carried out within this framework are multidimensional. The stress upon contingency and multidimensionality within the realist approach has sometimes resulted in a certain vagueness which 'takes everything into account'. This is a source of both strength and weakness. In particular, it is difficult to provide empirical tests of association and causal relationships – as, for example, those who have developed theoretical class schemes (Goldthorpe, Wright) have attempted to do. However, this weakness may also be seen as a strength, in that the 'realist' approach is a flexible one and has provided a number of important insights into contemporary social developments.[7]

Conclusions

Marx and Weber, despite their very real theoretical differences, both conceptualized social classes as groups structured out of *economic* relationships, and both saw classes as significant social 'actors' in the context of capitalist industrialism. For Marx, class struggle would have a central role in the ultimate transformation of capitalism. Weber did not hold to this view, but there can be little doubt that he saw class conflict as a major phenomenon in capitalist society. In the late twentieth century, a criticism that is increasingly made of both authors (particularly Marx), and indeed, of 'class analysis' in general is that such arguments place too much emphasis on the significance of economically determined classes at the expense of other, competing sources of social identity such as nationality, gender, locality, or ethnic group. In short, it is argued, nineteenth-century sociology cannot adequately grasp the complexities of late twentieth-century society.

This chapter has not discussed these arguments in any detail (they will be examined in chapter 4), but as we have seen there has developed within Marxism theoretical approaches to class which have modified considerably – indeed, abandoned – the economism of earlier theoretical conceptualizations. The discussion above has been mainly concerned with the fate of the class concept itself, particularly in relation to the ongoing debates relating to structure and action in sociology. Weber's rejection of the inevitability of the development of class consciousness and thus action was an element in his overall rejection of Marxist economism and determinism. In sociology (and history), however, the question of class consciousness has been incorporated into a more general debate concerning the nature of social reality, which has crucially shaped the perspectives of a number of different authors who would all claim to be doing 'class analysis' – although the diversity of their work belies the common label.

In the course of this chapter, there have emerged a series of dichotomies relating to both sociology and class analysis, some of which may be summarized as follows:

	Sociology
structure	action
	Class analysis
class in itself	class for itself (Marx)
objective	subjective (Braverman)
class formation	class action (Dahrendorf)
aggregational	relational (Stark)

The persistence of such dichotomies in the social sciences has often been criticized, as when, for example, Bourdieu writes that:

> One can and must transcend the opposition between the vision which we can indifferently label realist, objectivist or structuralist on the one hand, and the constructivist, subjectivist, spontaneist vision on the other. Any theory of the social universe must include the representation that agents have of the social world and, more precisely, the contribution they make to the construction of the vision of that world, and consequently, to the very construction of that world. (*1987: 10*)[8]

It might be argued, however, that although Bourdieu has described the essence of sociological 'good practice', the overarching theory that would succesfully achieve this integration has not yet been developed – or rather, there is certainly no consensus that it has been. Giddens's theory of 'structuration', as well as the development of philosophical 'realism', have both been offered as theoretical solutions,[9] but neither has gained universal acceptance; there is no dominant theoretical paradigm in sociology. In the light of these constraints two, rather different, emphases on the question of 'action' have been identified within discussions relating to class. These are, first, an insistence upon the active construction of classes themselves (class formation or 'structuration'), as when, for example, Therborn writes that: 'Classes must be seen, not as veritable geological formations once they have acquired their original shape, but as phenomena in a constant process of formation, reproduction, re-formation and de-formation' (1983: 39) – that is, the role of action in the constitution of 'classes' *in* themselves. Theories of class formation can be distinguished from theories of class action – the question of whether a 'class' acts *for* itself. Weber, as we have seen, would regard such a possibility as contingent, and this would also be Bendix and Lipset's position. To adopt the first position, some may suggest, renders the second redundant – a class 'in itself' is simultaneously a class 'for itself'. In contrast, the second position assumes that the examination of class structure may be undertaken independently of the examination of class action.

These debates are not mere abstractions. They have not only crucially affected perceptions of class, but also the way in which research into social class has been carried out. In the next chapter, therefore, we will focus on the work of class analysts whose starting-point is the class *structure* – that is, attempts to measure 'social class'.

Notes

1 It has to be said that, whatever Braverman's other strengths, his understanding of class analysis in sociology was rudimentary. His description of 'class analysis' in sociology was confined to a discussion of self-rated class which he took to represent the investigation of class consciousness, and his discussion of Lockwood's work treats it as a historical, rather than a sociological, account of clerical work.

2 See, for example, Dawley (1979).

3 It is of interest that Giddens uses Willis (1977), a 'cultural' investigation of the 'class structure', as an example of the empirical application of 'structuration' (Giddens 1984: 289ff).

4 See Kaye (1984: 234–5); also Gregory (1982).

5 Note that Pawson (1989) has argued convincingly that although their critique may be valid, Keat and Urry's methodological prescriptions are essentially structuralist.

6 This aspect of Urry's work will be discussed at some length in chs 3 and 4.

7 Urry's work, and the work of those influenced by him, has been taken as a representative example of the way in which 'realism' has been employed in British sociology. However, it should be recognized that there are many 'realisms' (Wacquant 1989), and indeed, that Wright, whose methodology is clearly very different from Urry's, would also claim to be a 'realist'.

However, as Burawoy (1989) has remarked: 'the realist view of science is strong in stating its ontological premises but weak in dealing with the epistemological problems it raises'; thus a plurality of method might be anticipated.

8   To avoid confusion, it should be pointed out that Bourdieu is here using the term 'realist' to describe those who, having determined empirically the properties and boundaries of the class structure, argue that these are 'real' classes. These approaches will be discussed at length in ch. 3.

9   These are not the only offerings; see Archer (1982) on 'morphogenesis'. The diversity of theoretical approaches serves to emphasize the point that there exists no dominant theoretical paradigm.

3
Measuring the 'Class Structure'

Introduction

In the previous chapter, the postwar development of the theoretical concept of class from its origins in the work of Marx and Weber has been analysed in parallel with theoretical debates in sociology. It has been suggested that empirical research on class within the social sciences has moved in a number of different directions. First, there are those variants of class analysis in which the starting-point, and sometimes the primary emphasis, has been on the analysis of the class *structure* as a whole. Alternatively, some authors have laid more emphasis on the active *processes* of class structuring, and on class relationships. Similarly, some authors have stressed above all the primacy of economic factors in the structuring of classes; others have also emphasized the significance of cultural and ideological processes.

In this chapter, the discussion will focus primarily on empirical accounts of class *structures*. In chapter 1, it was noted that the division of the population into unequally rewarded groups is commonly described as a 'class structure', and in modern industrial societies this usually means a focus on the structure of employment. The division of the occupational order into economic 'classes' is probably the most frequent 'taken-for-granted' use of the class concept in contemporary sociology (Westergaard and Resler 1975). However, it is important to distinguish between, on the one hand, class schemes which simply *describe* the broad contours of occupational inequality and, on the other, theoretically derived class schemes which purport to incorporate, at the empirical level, the actualities of class *relations*. Thus there are a wide variety of employment-based class schemes, constructed for a variety of different purposes. A simple but important point – which is all too often overlooked – is that all class schemes are social constructs, or rather, the constructs of sociologists. Therefore different class schemes, when applied to the same occupational structure, can produce quite different 'class maps'. For example, it is a feature of Wright's scheme, which will be discussed later in this chapter, that it produces more 'proletarians' than other classifications.

In this chapter, different class schemes will be discussed in relation to three broad analytical categories. These are (a) occupational class schemes which have been devised primarily for use as commonsense descriptive measures in empirical research – often research with a social policy objective; (b) subjective scales of occupational prestige or social ranking; and (c) 'theoretical' occupational class schemes, constructed with explicit reference to the theoretical approaches of Marx and Weber. It may be objected that no system of classification can be said to be independent of 'theoretical' assumptions, even if they are not overt (Hindess 1973). Nevertheless, the differentiation between class schemes on the basis of their theoretical claims is commonplace (Nichols 1979, Marshall et al. 1988), and, as we shall see, the development of particular theoretical schemes has been associated with the development of distinctive sub-areas of 'class analysis' using the scheme in question.

Occupations

The economic, technical and social changes brought about by the development of capitalist industrialism have been accompanied by a continuing division of labour and differentiation of occupations. The point need not be laboured that 'occupation' has become, for the majority of the population, probably the most powerful single indicator of levels of material reward, social standing, and 'life chances' in general in modern societies (Blau and Duncan 1967: 6–7). Thus throughout this century it has become commonplace for social researchers of all kinds (in academia, government and commercial agencies, and so on) to divide up the occupational structure into aggregates corresponding to different levels of social and material inequalities, which are commonly known as 'social classes'. Reid (1981: 6), for example, defines a 'social class [as] a grouping of people into categories on the basis of occupation', and Parkin has asserted that: 'The backbone of the class structure, and indeed of the entire reward system of modern Western society, is the occupational order' (1972: 18).

However, despite its acknowledged usefulness as a social indicator, there are a number of difficulties in using occupation as a measure of 'class'. Two major areas of difficulty may be identified. First, despite its utility as a summary measure, employment and occupational titles do not, in fact, adequately incorporate the many different dimensions of inequality in modern societies. Secondly, it has been argued that 'occupation' by itself cannot adequately capture the actualities of class *relations* in either a Marxist or a Weberian sense. To begin with the first set of difficulties: occupational title does not give any indication of capital or wealth holdings and thus, as Nichols has argued 'in the . . . "social classes" of the census the owners of capital are lost to sight' (1979: 159).[1] Furthermore there is the fact that only a minority of members of an industrial society will be 'economically active', and therefore have or be seeking an occupation, at any time. A variety of strategies are available for allocating the 'economically inactive' to an occupational class, including giving all household members the same 'class' as that of the 'head of household' or 'main breadwinner'; locating the retired in the 'class' indicated by their last occupation, and so on. Finally – and more fundamentally – although 'class processes' – that is, the structures of production and market relationships – will obviously have a massive impact on the occupational structure, there are also other factors, in particular the ascriptive differences associated with gender and race, which are of considerable significance in structuring the division of labour. It is important also to recognize that many of the claims made by occupational groups in the constant jockeying for material advantage which is a feature of the activities of trade unions and professional groupings are in fact *status* claims, for example, those related to established relativities which have been fiercely protected by skilled-craft groupings. The occupational structure, therefore, will also bear the imprint of these other factors.

The second area of difficulty relates to the capacity of occupational class schemes to describe class relations in a theoretical sense. The Marxist distinction between the 'technical' and the 'social' division of labour has been used to argue that 'occupation' does not grasp the essential components of the Marxist class concept: 'Occupation typically refers primarily to sets of job tasks, that is, it refers to positions within the technical division of labour . . . the concept of class refers primarily to the social relations at work, or positions within the social division of labour' (Abercrombie and Urry 1983: 109). An entire strategy of class analysis – Wright's Marxist model – has been based on this conceptual division. Although Weber's approach to social class was very different from that of Marx, he too regarded social classes as something more than occupational aggregates. For Weber, a social class is made up of the 'totality of those class situations within which individual and generational mobility is easy and typical'. Thus Goldthorpe, a leading neo-Weberian class analyst, has identified mobility boundaries as crucial to the identification of 'social classes'.

'Commonsense' occupational class schemes (category (a) above) invariably reflect some kind of hierarchical ordering of occupations, although the assumptions underlying the hierarchy are not always made explicit. These can include income or other material benefits, social status, 'cultural level', and so on. Subjective scales of occupational rankings are similarly hierarchical, 'gradational' classifications. In contrast what are here described as theoretical schemes or approaches attempt to encompass in their construction the actualities of class *relationships*.

The investigation and analysis of occupational *hierarchies* – particularly subjective rankings – has been closely associated with models of society which have stressed the importance of the social solidarity and functional interdependence associated with the division of labour in complex societies, whereas the development of theoretical class analysis and 'relational' class schemes has had more of an emphasis on cleavage and conflict.

Thus the dominant paradigm in sociology (normative functionalism) established in the United States after the Second World War was associated with a view of the occupational structure as a hierarchy of rewards and prestige into which the population was sorted according to its capabilities. In Davis and Moore's (1945) functional theory of stratification, the structure of social inequality was seen as a mechanism through which the most appropriate and best-qualified persons were allocated to the functionally most important positions in society, and as a consequence, the question of individual 'status attainment' has been a key topic in stratification research in the United States (Blau and Duncan 1967).

In contrast, 'conflict' theories of stratification considered the division of labour and the development of 'classes' to be likely to be a non-resolvable source of conflict and tension in society. This difference is reflected in the class schemes of those authors, such as Goldthorpe and Wright, whose analysis has been grounded in Marx's and Weber's theoretical arguments. Davis and Moore's theory has also been criticized from within a modified functionalist perpective which incorporates aspects of a 'conflict' view. How can some occupations, it was argued, be regarded as functionally 'more important' when, in a highly complex society, *all* occupations are necessary in respect of the whole? (Consider the chaos when public service workers go on strike.) The 'sacrifices' made by those undergoing training (in terms of earnings forgone) are usually made by others (parents) and, in any case, are massively over-compensated by the subsequent level of reward. Systems of stratification can also bring with them rigidities, and levels of social conflict, which are positively *dysfunctional* as far as the social order is concerned (Tumin 1964).

'Commonsense' occupational hierarchies and the analysis of social 'classes'

In Britain, the most frequently used class scheme has been that of the Registrar-General – for example, most of the empirical material in Reid's (1981) comprehensive summary of occupational class differences in employment, mortality, family arrangements, education, politics and so on is organized using the Registrar-General's classification. It was first developed in 1913 by a medical statistician, (Stevenson), who was engaged in a wider debate concerning levels of infant mortality. As Szreter (1984) has demonstrated, Stevenson, although no eugenist himself, initially developed the scale in the context of a debate with eugenists such as Francis Galton, who believed that the social and occupational structure more or less reflected a natural hierarchy of ability and morality in society. From the first, therefore, the Registrar-General's scheme has been hierarchical.

The Registrar-General's social-class classification has been devised with the aim of including within each category unit groups

> so as to secure that, as far as is possible, each category is homogeneous in relation to the general standing within the community of the occupations concerned. This criterion is naturally correlated with . . . other factors such as education and economic environment, but it has no direct relationship to the average level of remuneration of particular occupations. (*HMSO 1966: xiii*)

It has been through a number of revisions since its inception (Hakim 1980), but the most commonly used version, devised for the 1971 census, is:

I	Professional etc. occupations
II	Intermediate occupations
III (N)	Skilled non-manual occupations
III (M)	Skilled manual occupations
IV	Partly skilled occupations
V	Unskilled occupations

As Reid's (1981) compendium *Social Class Differences in Britain* demonstrates, these occupational groupings correlate with a wide range of inequalities in income, health and education. Indeed, given the origins of the index, a somewhat salutary indication of its staying power can be drawn from the fact that although rates of infant mortality have of course declined considerably since the early years of this century, considerable social-class differences in infant mortality rates still persist. In 1981, for example, the infant mortality rate per 1,000 live births in England and Wales was 7.7 for Social Class I, but 18.8 for Social Class V (McPherson and Coleman 1988: 427). Nevertheless, the Registrar-General's scale contains a number of anomalies and difficulties in the classification of particular occupations (Nichols 1979). In older versions of the scale, the category of 'manager' presented particular problems, and drawing the boundary between manual and non-manual employment has been a constant source of contention. These and other classification difficulties resulted, from the 1951 census onwards, in the creation of a more detailed classification of socio-economic groups (SEGs). The seventeen-point SEG scale includes details such as size of establishment in relation to 'managerial' occupations, and collapsed versions have been widely used in government surveys such as the General Household Survey.

The Registrar-General's class index was devised and has been developed by the Office of Population and Census Statistics (OPCS), but this is not the only governmant department in Britain collecting details of occupations. In particular, the Department of Employment (DE) developed in the 1960s and 1970s a detailed classification of occupations (Classification of Occupations and Directory of Occupational Titles: CODOT), which was integrated into the 1980 census Occupational Classifications. It was felt that the combination of OPCS and DE categorizations had not been particularly successful and, from the 1991 census, these should be replaced by a new classification, the Standard Occupational Classification (SOC). This hierarchical classification assumes that occupations involve a set of typical work activities, which are then classified into major, minor and unit groups according to, first, the level of skill and qualifications involved, and second, the nature of the work activities (Thomas and Elias 1989). These unit groups will then be the basis of a new 'social class' classification.

Despite the fact that they have been subject to a process of almost constant revision, occupational class scales used by government departments have nevertheless remained remarkably similar in their broad outlines – managerial and professional occupations at the top, unskilled workers at the bottom. Other industrial countries have also developed very similar hierarchical scales – for example, Blau and Duncan (1967), as well as devising their own socio-economic index, utilized a scale of socio-economic status devised by the United States Bureau of the Census which closely resembles the Registrar-General's SEG scale. Another scale in wide commercial use is that developed first for the

National Readership Survey and is commonly used by market research agencies. This divides the population into A, B, C1, C2, D and E – corresponding to upper middle, middle, lower middle, skilled, semi-skilled and unskilled working classes. Again, the occupations comprising the different 'classes' closely resemble those of the other hierarchical scales in general use.

Scales of occupational prestige or 'status'

Marsh (1986) has described the Registrar-General's and other, similar scales as describing 'groups differentiated by lifestyle'; this label would be particularly appropriate to market research, where occupational coding is often carried out on the doorstep (an excellent source of information concerning 'lifestyle'!) by the interviewer concerned. The Registrar-General's and market researcher's 'class' categories have also often been described as status or prestige scales (Weber described status groups as being differentiated 'above all, by different styles of life'). However, the 'prestige' label is probably more appropriate for occupational scales which have been deliberately constructed according to the reputed prestige or desirability of occupations.

Occupational prestige scales have often been described as 'subjectivist'; that is, as reflecting the subjective assesment of the relative prestige of occupations within a population. One of the earliest and best-known of such scales is that of North and Hatt, constructed in 1947 in the United States for the National Opinion Research Center (NORC) in Chicago, where a cross-section of ninety occupations were ranked by a national sample of the population on a scale ranging from 'excellent' to 'poor' standing (see Reiss et al. 1961). The resulting scale of occupational prestige closely resembles that of the socio-economic classifications reviewed earlier: higher professional and powerful occupations such as physician or Supreme Court justice being ranked at the top, and low-skilled occupations such as street sweeper and garbage collector at the bottom. There proved to be a very high statistical correlation between the results of the earlier and later scaling exercises, and a comparison of similar 'subjectivist' rankings carried out in a number of other countries suggested that there was also a high level of cross-national consensus on occupational prestige rankings (Hodge et al. 1967).

These empirical findings supplied a justification for two, closely related, functionalist arguments concerning social stratification. First, the wide measure of recorded agreement concerning the relative prestige of different occupations corresponded to the distribution of material rewards and power attached to the occupations in question. It was therefore argued that the results of this 'moral referendum'

(Parkin 1972) concerning occupational prestige suggested that the distribution of occupational inequality was, indeed, regarded as legitimate by the population at large, and that, as Davis and Moore had argued, the actual pattern of material rewards and status rankings reflected the functional importance of different occupations for the society, as well as being a measure of the training and talent required to fill these positions (Davis and Moore 1945). Second, the cross-national similarity of the prestige rankings of particular occupations was argued by Hodge et al. to reflect an underlying 'logic of industrialism', a theoretical argument which Giddens (1982a) has identified as a central component of the 1960s 'orthodox consensus'. All industrial societies, it was argued, required a similar division of labour and associated structure of occupational prestige (or 'classes'). These two conclusions are brought together in the following extract:

> Development hinges in part upon the recruitment and training of persons for the skilled, clerical, managerial, and professional positions necessary to support an industrial economy. Thus, aquisition of a 'modern' system of occupational evaluation would seem to be a necessary precondition to rapid industrialisation, insofar as such an evaluation of occupations insures that resources and personnel in sufficient numbers and of sufficient quality are allocated to those occupational positions most crucial to the industrial development of a nation. (*Hodge et al. 1967: 320*)

Similar scales of occupational ranking have also been constructed in Britain – for example, the Hall–Jones scale which was developed as part of a major investigation of social mobility in Britain immediately after the Second World War (Glass 1954). More recently, Goldthorpe and Hope (1974) constructed a new scale for the Oxford Mobility Study where respondents were asked to rank a set of twenty occupations in terms of their 'perceived social desirability' (rather than scoring individual occupations, as in the construction of the NORC scale). Respondents then nominated twenty of their 'own' occupations for inclusion in the ranking.

However, Goldthorpe has been highly critical of both functionalist theories of stratification and inequality, as well as the associated 'logic of industrialism' arguments, which have developed out of work relating to the NORC scale. His approach shares much in common with those authors, such as Lockwood, Dahrendorf, Rex and Collins, who emphasized not interdependence and integration, but the significance of persisting economic and political inequalities, and the social conflicts and competition associated with them, in the shaping of the stratification order. The conflict perspective was highly critical of the capacity of hierarchical scales of prestige or lifestyle to render any account of *class* conflicts. Such scales, it was asserted, measured social status, rather than class, and the apparent agreement on matters such as prestige rankings was an indication not of any moral consensus, but rather, simply represented a general awareness of the empirical distribution of material and symbolic rewards to particular occupations (Parkin 1972: 40–1). The relative distribution of rewards described in hierarchical schemes reflected, it was argued, the *outcome* of class processes, rather than giving any account of the underlying structure of class *relations* which had brought them about. For example Rex, in a commentary on data presented according to the Registrar-General's 'social class' categories, wrote:

> It is figures like this which drive the theoretically oriented sociologist to something like despair . . . The . . . table . . . is said to be a classification according to 'social class'. But the implications of this term are left open to be filled by the reader according to his own ideological preconceptions. Surely it would be more valuable if statisticians, who continually claim to be using sociological concepts, were to find out what groupings were of real sociological importance and then seek to describe these, rather than the groupings which are of little importance, but which happen to be easily measurable. (*Rex 1970, cited in Halsey 1988: 3–4*)

Rex is arguing here that descriptive occupational indexes such as those of the Registrar-General are theoretically inadequate. What is required for a truly sociological exploration of the issue, therefore, are measures which identify these 'groupings of real sociological importance' – that is, social classes. A parallel argument was developed by Wright (1979), who built upon Ossowski's distinction between *gradational* and *relational* class theories in his critique of existing empirical approaches to 'class analysis'. Gradational class schemes – such as prestige or income hierarchies – describe but do not explain. Gradational differences, he emphasized, are the *outcome* of class relations. Wright divided relational conceptions of class into two categories: (a) those deriving primarily from Weber's work, where 'class' is seen as deriving from social relations of exchange; and (b) those deriving primarily from Marx's theories, where 'class' is seen as grounded in production relationships.

Thus these kinds of criticism of empirical 'class analyses' using commonsense and hierarchical scales have led to the development of 'theoretical' class schemes (Crompton 1991); that is, class schemes which attempt to divide the population into 'social classes' which correspond to the kinds of groupings described by Marx and Weber. As has been noted in chapter 1, this strategy attempts to bring within a single framework of analysis theoretical approaches to social class and the detailed empirical investigation of the 'classes' themselves. Two such programmes of class analysis, associated with particular 'relational' class schemes, have achieved particular prominence since the 1970s: that devised by John Goldthorpe, which as often been described as 'Weberian', and Erik Wright's explicitly Marxist class scheme.

Theoretical ('relational') class schemes: I   Goldthorpe

Goldthorpe's class scheme is constructed via the aggregation of occupational categories within the Hope–Goldthorpe scale of 'general desirability' into a sevenfold set of 'class' categories.[2] The key concepts guiding the allocation of occupations to classes are 'market' and 'work' situation; two of Lockwood's three factors comprising 'class situation' (see chapter 2 above):

> we . . . bring together, within the classes we distinguish, occupations whose incumbents share in broadly similar *market* and *work* situations . . . That is to say, we combine occupational categories whose members would appear, in the light of the available evidence, to be typically comparable, on the one hand, in terms of their sources and levels of income and other conditions of employment, in their degree of economic security and in their chances of economic advancement; and, on the other hand, in their location within the systems of authority and control governing the processes of production in which they are engaged. (*Goldthorpe 1987: 40*)

The Hope–Goldthorpe categories which from the basis of the scheme also incorporate employment status: 'Thus, for example, "self-employed plumber" is a different occupation from "foreman plumber" as from "rank-and-file employee" plumber' (1987: 40). The seven categories of the Goldthorpe class scheme, aggregated into the threefold service/ intermediate/working categories widely employed in the presentation of his empirical results, are as follows:

Service	I	Higher-grade professionals, administrators and officials; managers in large industrial establishments; large proprietors.
	II	Lower-grade professionals, administrators and officials; higher-grade technicians; managers in small business and industrial establishments; supervisors of non-manual employees.
Intermediate	III	Routine nonmanual – largely clerical – employees in administration and commerce; rank-and-file employees in services.

IV   Small proprietors and self-employed artisans.
V   Lower-grade technicians, supervisors of manual workers.
Working   VI   Skilled manual workers.
VII   Semi-skilled and unskilled manual workers.

This arrangement of occupations into 'classes' closely resembles that of conventional hierarchical schemes reflecting prestige and/or lifestyle, such as the ABC scheme used by market researchers, or that of the Registrar-General. However, Goldthorpe is adamant that his class scheme does *not* have a hierarchical form but, rather, reflects the structure of class *relations*: 'Our class schema should not then be regarded as having – nor should it be expected to have – a consistently hierarchical form' (1987: 43). Goldthorpe's scheme has been subject to a wide range of criticisms. Its 'relational' (and therefore non-hierarchical) nature has been questioned (Marsh 1986; Prandy 1991). The allocation of occupations to particular class categories has been disputed; in particular, its seeming endorsement of the manual/non-manual distinction as a *class* boundary, even in the case of routine white-collar workers. This point is closely related to a further issue which has caused considerable controversy: the class situation of women. Goldthorpe's scheme is not particularly suitable as far as women's employment is concerned. However, he has always maintained that this is not a problem as the basic 'unit' of class analysis is the family and, therefore, the class situation of the female members can be inferred from that of the 'male breadwinner'. These criticisms are significant, and will be reviewed in the next chapter. For the moment, however, it is important to be aware that Goldthorpe's approach to 'class analysis' incorporates considerably more than the development and application of his class scheme.

For Goldthorpe, the construction of a class scheme is only the starting-point of his overall strategy of 'class analysis'. It divides the occupied population according to 'market' and 'work' situations, but it must then be established to what extent actual 'classes' have been formed within this structure; or, to use Goldthorpe's phrase, the extent to which a class can be said to have a 'demographic identity'; that is, whether classes have emerged as 'specific social collectivities . . . collectivities that are identifiable through the degree of continuity with which, in consequence of patterns of class mobility and immobility, their members are associated with particular sets of positions over time' (1983: 467). Thus patterns of social mobility are crucial to the identification of a 'class'. Once the extent of demographic identity has been established, the further question may be pursued as to the extent to which 'socio-political class formation' has also taken place; that is, 'the degree of distinctiveness of members of identifiable classes in terms of their life-chances, their life-styles and patterns of association, and their socio-political orientations and modes of action' (1983: 467). For example, Goldthorpe suggests that, in Britain, the extent of mobility associated with classes III and V of his scheme implies that these 'classes' are inchoate and unformed and thus highly unlikely to generate class-based socio-political action (1987: 335). In contrast, he argues, Britain posseses a 'demographically mature' working class which might be expected to generate systematic socio-political action, as well as an emerging 'service class' which, although not as stable as the working class, is nevertheless in the process of development as a significant social force.

Goldthorpe's approach to class analysis, therefore, follows a systematic structure → consciousness → action model which, as we shall see in the next chapter, has occasioned much criticism. Goldthorpe does not ignore the question of class action but he draws an analytical separation between class formation and class action and treats them empirically as quite separate phenomena. In recent years, the major empirical application of Goldthorpe's class scheme has been the cross-national investigation of patterns of social mobility – indeed, social mobility is one of the cornerstones of his approach to 'class analysis'. This topic will therefore be discussed before we examine our second major example of a 'relational' class scheme – Erik Wright's Marxist model.

Social mobility

Social mobility research measures the mobility of individuals between occupations and/or occupational origins, both between generations and over the lifecycle. It may be considered as one of the 'bedrock' topics of stratification theory but, especially since the 1970s, the increasing sophistication of the statistical techniques employed in its investigation has moved it beyond the reach of any concise (or simple) summary. An interest in social mobility extends across the political spectrum. Evidence of high rates of social mobility may be used to argue that the society in question is characterized by achievement rather than ascription, that individuals reap their rewards according to their personal qualities, rather than on the basis of 'unfair' advantages such as inherited wealth, or personal connections – in short that a true meritocracy is in operation. Besides the powerful legitimation of structures of occupational inequality which such arguments bestow, social mobility also acts as an important 'safety valve' in advanced industrial societies:

Mobility provides an escape route for large numbers of the most able and ambitious members of the underclass, thereby easing some of the tensions generated by inequality. Elevation into the middle classes represents a *personal* solution to the problems of low status, and as such tends to weaken collectivist efforts to improve the lot of the underclass as a whole. It has often been suggested that upward mobility undermines the political base of the underclass most seriously by siphoning off the men best fitted for leadership. (*Parkin 1972: 50*)

This argument has been pithily – if unsociologically – expressed in the well-known ditty, sung to the tune of the socialist anthem 'The Red Flag': 'The working class can kiss my arse; I've got the foreman's job at last.' In a rather more serious vein, Marx wrote that: 'The more a ruling class is able to assimilate the foremost minds of a ruled class, the more stable and dangerous becomes its rule' (1974: 601).

In the United States, the study of social mobility has assumed particular significance because of its apparent association with what have been regarded as significant 'core values' of American society – that is, the belief that individual hard work, application and effort will eventually bring their rewards; that, regardless of social background or family connections, inherited wealth or aristocratic title, it is, indeed, possible for the suitably talented individual to rise from a log cabin to the White House. The widespread popularity of such classic liberal ideas relating to individual opportunity was not, of course, confined to the United States, as nineteenth-century books such as Samuel Smiles's *Self-Help* (1859) indicate.

The extent of social mobility, therefore, has been widely used as a measure of the 'openness' of industrial societies, and high mobility rates seen as an indication that the liberal promise of equality of opportunity has indeed been achieved. Blau and Duncan's (1967) statistical investigation of a sample of nearly 21,000 men aged 20 to 64 (drawn in 1962) in the United States appeared to confirm that, even if this happy state had not yet arrived, the United States was well on the way to it. Blau and Duncan used techniques of path analysis in order to explore (amongst a variety of other empirical associations) the relationship between social origins, education and career beginnings on subsequent career success. They concluded that although social origins did indeed have an influence, educational background and training, and early work experience, had a more pronounced effect on chances of success (1967: 402).[3] They also demonstrated that rates of social mobility in the United States were high, and argued that this was a consequence of the 'advanced level of industrialization and education'; other industrial countries would, in due course, catch up (p. 433).

Thus, for Blau and Duncan, there can be little doubt that increasing social mobility is inevitable, as well as a Good Thing. The underlying optimism of their perspective is very evident:

a fundamental trend towards expanding universalism characterizes industrial society. Objective criteria of evaluation that are universally accepted increasingly pervade all spheres of life and displace particularistic standards of diverse ingroups [and] intuitive judgments . . . The growing emphasis on rationality and efficiency inherent in this spread of universalism finds expression in rapid technological progress and increasing division of labor and differentiation generally . . . The strong interdependence among men and groups engendered by the extensive division of labor becomes the source of their organic solidarity, to use Durkheim's term, inasmuch as social differentiation weakens the particularistic ingroup values that unite men. (*1967: 429*)

Blau and Duncan's work has been subject to extensive criticism, both methodological and theoretical. It might be suggested (in an argument parallel to that of Tumin's criticism of Davis and Moore) that, far from being a source of integration, extensive social mobility might actually be a destabilizing element in industrial societies. Through the process of mobility, people lose their previous attachments to social collectivities which had contributed to their sense of self-worth and psychological stability, and the resulting 'status inconsistency' might be a source of social disruption (Lipset and Bendix 1959). More extensive criticisms, however, were developed by class and associated 'conflict' theorists.

Blau and Duncan's model of mobility takes the occupational structure to be a finely graded hierarchy, into which individuals are sorted according to their (individual) attributes. However, as critics such as Crowder (1974) have pointed out, a substantial degree of the variance in status attainment is not explained by the Blau–Duncan model, and indeed, the wide distribution of income *within* educational attainment categories suggests that the relationship between income and education is not linear. Crowder argued that the large residual paths of the model are not to be explained, as Duncan had suggested, by 'pure luck', but rather, are the outcome of systematic *structural* constraints which shape not only the occupational system but also processes of allocation within it. Amongst these structural constraints are the institutions of political power and private property, and material and ideological constraints which specify the extent of control and the 'appropriate' behaviour associated with particular positions. In short, Crowder argues, Duncan's models are in essence 'sub-models which direct attention to the issues of ascription and achievement, but which may not be used to characterize the entire reward distribution system since most of the control of the distribution of rewards is completely outside these sub-models and therefore not explainable in terms of achievement and ascriptive characteristics of income recipients' (1974: 38).

Goldthorpe would be in broad agreement with these kinds of criticism of Blau and Duncan. He *does* have a positive interest in social mobility inasmuch as it is associated with greater equality of opportunity, but not with its association with the stability or legitimacy of liberal democracy – which, he suggests, 'falls some way short of being "the good society itself in operation"'.[4] Goldthorpe therefore favours not a graded hierarchy of occupations but his theoretical *class* scheme. The use of such a scheme attempts to incorporate explicitly the kinds of structural constraints absent from the Blau–Duncan model. Goldthorpe claims that his scheme encompasses the dynamics of class relations; it is *relational*, rather than gradational. Recent advances in statistical techniques, in particular, log-linear modelling, have made it possible to employ non-linear class schemes such as Goldthorpe's in social-mobility research. In contrast, Blau and Duncan's statistical techniques (path analysis) presupposed a hierarchical (that is, gradational) ordering of the underlying categories (income, education, occupational status).

Log-linear models also offer a solution to other technical problems which have historically beset research in social mobility – in particular, the 'problem of the marginals'. Social mobility investigations record movement within an occupational structure at two (or more) points in time – but the structure itself is not stable. As industrial societies have developed, so there have occurred massive changes in the structure of occupations, first from agricultural to industrial occupations, then, during the course of this century, from predominantly 'manual' to 'non-manual' occupations. For example, in Great Britain, non-manual workers increased from 18.7 per cent of the occupied population in 1911 to 52.3 per cent in 1981, with a corresponding decline in the proportion of manual workers (Price and Bain 1988: 164). Thus in any standard mobility tabulation comparing fathers' occupations with sons' occupations, the marginal distributions will vary, reflecting the difference in the occupational structure at different times. In a simple 2 × 2 table comparing manual with non-manual, for example, there will be more manual fathers and, conversely, more non-manual sons. To put the point another way, given long-term changes in the occupational structure, a certain amount of 'upward' mobility is 'built-in' or 'forced', given the under-supply of non-manual sons.

In earlier studies of social mobility such as that of Glass (1954) this problem had been resolved by drawing a distinction between 'structural' and 'exchange' mobility. The discrepancies between the marginal distributions in the mobility table are used to provide a measure of 'structural' mobility brought about through occupational changes. The further extent of mobility revealed in the table was described as 'exchange' mobility – that is, mobility net of structural effects. Equality of opportunity or 'openness' has been assessed in studies such as those of Glass by comparing the actual distribution of destinations, once structural mobility has been allowed for, with a baseline model of 'perfect mobility'. The notion of 'perfect mobility' describes the distribution within the different 'classes', by social origin, which might be expected if social origin had no measurable effect on final destination.

There are a number of statistical problems associated with the approach sketched out above – in particular, it assumes an artificial distinction between different 'types' of mobility (Goldthorpe 1987: 74–5; Heath 1981). In consequence, approaches to the study of inequalities of opportunity have been developed which distinguish between 'absolute' and 'relative' mobility rates. 'Absolute' mobility describes the total mobility revealed in a mobility table, which would include the structural mobility brought about by changes in the occupational structure (or occupational 'upgrading' over time). 'Relative' mobility chances are calculated by comparing, for people from different backgrounds, their chances of entering different 'classes' (that is, computing the 'odds ratios'). This has been described as a measure of 'social fluidity'; as a measure of 'whether or not changes in the structure of objective mobility opportunities over time are being equally reflected in the mobility experience of individuals of all origins alike' (Goldthorpe 1987: 75). Odds ratios have the added advantage that they may also be represented in *log-linear* models of mobility; these are statistical models which do the same job for binary variables as multiple regression does for continuous variables (Heath 1981). The complexities of log-linear modelling cannot possibly be dealt with here but, in brief, the 'expected' cell frequencies of the model are compared with those actually observed (that is, the model is tested for 'goodness of fit'); the results of such testing enable the investigator to suggest likely *causal* relationships between the factors encompassed within the model.

Goldthorpe has employed these improved statistical techniques in the Oxford Mobility Study, the first major study of social mobility in England and Wales to be carried out after Glass's postwar research. As is well known, Glass's research appeared to demonstrate that Britain was not a particularly 'open' society, in that long-range mobility (that is, from bottom to top, or from top to bottom) was relatively rare, and there was a high degree of self-recruitment to the 'elite' positions in British society. What mobility there was tended to be only short-range;

that is, to positions more or less adjacent in the occupational hierarchy, from manual worker to supervisor, or clerk to lower-level manager. In particular, if mobility did occur across the boundary between manual and non-manual occupations (see by many as representing the fundamental line of cleavage within the class structure), then this was highly likely to be only between adjacent classes – for example, from skilled manual to lower-level non-manual – within what has been described as the 'buffer-zone' of the class structure overall (Glass 1954; see also Westergaard and Resler 1975; Goldthorpe 1987).

Goldthorpe's 1972–4 enquiry into social mobility revealed a rather different picture.[5] It suggested that a considerable amount of *long-range* mobility had in fact occurred – for example, 28.5 per cent of those in class I in the 1972 survey were from class VI and VII backgrounds (1987: 45). The sheer extent of mobility which had occurred also served to undermine the 'buffer-zone' hypothesis. The extent of mobility revealed by the Oxford survey might, of course, have been anticipated given the long-term changes in the occupational structure which have led to an inexorable expansion of the middle and upper 'classes'. As a consequence, the extent of upward mobility in the population is far in excess of downward mobility.

However, Goldthorpe argues that these results did *not* demonstrate that Britain had become a more 'open' society. This (apparently) contradictory assertion can be demonstrated by evidence using the distinction between absolute and relative rates of social mobility, employing the techniques of odds ratios. These demonstrate the chance ('odds') of a service class son being recruited to the service class, rather than to the working class, with the odds on the same pair of destinations for those who start in the working class. The analysis of relative mobility chances, or patterns of social fluidity, within the Oxford sample demonstrated that, despite high rates of absolute social mobility, there were marked, and persistent, differences in the *relative* chances of men of different social backgrounds moving into higher-level occupations. Put simply, the data revealed a 'disparity ratio' of 1 : 2 : 4 for the chances of access to classes I and II for men from 'Service', 'Intermediate', and 'Working' classes (1987: 50). Thus Goldthorpe concludes:

> the pattern of relative mobility chances . . . associated with the British class structure . . . embodies inequalities that are of a quite striking kind: in particular, those that emerge if one compares the chances of men whose fathers held higher-level service-class positions being themselves found in such positions rather than in working-class ones with the corresponding chances of men of working-class origins. Where inequalities in class chances of this magnitude are displayed – of the order . . . of over

30:1 – then, we believe, the presumption must be that to a substantial extent they do reflect inequalities of opportunity that are rooted in the class structure. (*1987: 328*)

This kind of reasoning has been criticized by those who have accused Goldthorpe of 'political bias' in the presentation of his data in respect of the British case. Saunders (1990a) has argued that Goldthorpe, as well as other 'left-wing' sociologists who have followed a broadly similar strategy in their analysis of contemporary British mobility patterns (in particular, Marshall and his colleagues at the University of Essex (1988)) have been excessively concerned with relativities, rather than absolutes in respect of social mobility. In contrast, Saunders emphasizes the significance of the *absolute* increases in mobility rates which have been brought about by economic expansion since the Second World War. He also argues that presumptions as to the lack of 'openness' in British society are founded upon the unwarranted assumption that the different talents, aptitudes and abilities which shape 'life chances' *are* randomly distributed within society:

Goldthorpe and many other contemporary sociologists effectively end up denying that . . . natural inequalities can have any importance in influencing people's destinies. If, for example, the working class accounts for half of the population, then for Goldthorpe and for the Essex researchers we should expect half of all doctors, managers and top civil servants to have originated in the working class. If we find, as Goldthorpe did, that only one quarter of such groups are from working-class origins, then according to this reasoning we are justified in assuming that the 'shortfall' is entirely due to social barriers and that British society is therefore just as class-ridden and unjust as its critics have always maintained. In the idealised world of John Goldthorpe and other 'left' sociologists, people's destinies should be randomly determined because talents are randomly distributed. British society is thus found wanting because people of working-class origins are not in the majority in all the top jobs. This argument is ludicrous, yet in modern sociology it is all too rarely questioned. (*1990a: 83*)

Saunders's accusations of left-wing 'bias' within British sociology are mirrored by his own right-wing 'bias'. He states a clear political preference for the neo-liberal argument, developed by economists such as Hayek, that a relative lack of regulation, together with its associated inequalities, within the capitalist marketplace is more dynamic than its 'regulated' alternatives and thus of more material benefit to the population as a whole. Goldthorpe has stated an equally clear preference for a degree of market regulation or 'corporatism' (Goldthorpe 1984). There are theoretical arguments, and empirical evidence, which would be supportive of either perspective, but ultimately, judgements as to the superiority – or otherwise – of the alternatives on offer are unavoidably political. Saunders's arguments also incorporate the neo-liberal assumption that an absence of regulation will allow the 'best' to achieve the most. That the greatest share of the available rewards do go to the 'best' or 'functionally most important' is, as we have seen, a central argument of 'functionalist' theories of stratification.

For the moment, however, we will examine the way in which Goldthorpe's class scheme, as well as the associated emphasis on *relative* mobility rates associated with techniques of log-linear modelling, have been developed in the context of international comparisons of social mobility. In a recent review, Kurz and Müller (1987) have argued that three main developments have characterized social-mobility research during the last ten years; these are: (a) the revitalization of the class perspective, (b) intensive comparative research efforts, and (c) the large-scale application of the log-linear modelling approach. As we have seen, the 'revitalization of the class perspective' was associated with 'conflict' critiques of 'status attainment' perspectives, critiques which emphasized the *structural* constraints on individual status attainment deriving from institutionalized differences in the societal distribution of power and resources (Collins 1971; Crowder 1974). The status attainment perspective was also associated, particularly in Blau and Duncan's work, with the thesis of universalism – that is, the argument that an increasing objectivity and rationality of social evaluation, which would come to characterize all 'industrial societies', would lead to similar (and increasing) rates of social mobility. Comparative studies of social mobility, therefore, can test the validity of such assumptions.

However, different countries industrialize at different rates, and the process of industrialization does not always result in a uniform occupational outcome.[6] Such differences between the units of comparison have rendered cross-national comparisons highly problematic. Thus Featherman, Jones and Hauser (FJH) (1975) have advanced a modified version of the thesis of universalism. Absolute mobility rates may vary between different societies because of factors such as differences in the occupational structure, the size of the agricultural sector, and so on, but nevertheless, the underlying 'mobility regime' – that is, *relative* mobility rates – would show a basic similarity in all societies with market economies and nuclear family systems. Using a version of Goldthorpe's class scheme, the international group of researchers associated with the CASMIN project (Comparative Analysis of Social Mobility in Industrial Societies) has carried out a series of comparisons of relative social mobility. Their results have largely confirmed the FJH hypothesis in that basic patterns of relative mobility chances proved to be similar between different countries:

Immobility is greatest among farmers, followed by the petty bourgeoisie and the service class. The immobility at the peak of the socioeconomic hierarchy . . . is greater than that at the bottom, in the working class. Mobility is more likely in the 'middle' of the socioeconomic hierarchy (or the class structure) than at the peak. Short-range mobility occurs more often than long-range mobility. (*Kurz and Müller 1987: 425*)

Deviations from this basic pattern were 'largely attributable to nation-specific, historically formed features' (p. 426) – that is, they did not correspond to any particular societal 'type' – a finding which would have invalidated the FJH thesis. Although it is argued that the FJH thesis underestimates the role of political interventions, these do not correspond to any consistent mobility pattern; in short, it seems there is a 'family resemblance' (Erikson et al. 1982) between the mobility regimes of industrialized nations. Thus the source of variation in mobility rates between different countries has to be sought outside of the mobility table itself – Kurz and Müller, for example, suggest, following Maurice et al. (1986), that national differences in educational systems may be highly significant in explaining national variations in the extent of work-life mobility.

Goldthorpe's class scheme, as well as the associated reliance on log-linear modelling, has by no means gained universal acceptance in mobility research (Payne 1987, Kelley 1990). These technical questions cannot be pursued here. What are the *consequences* of social mobility for stratification systems? One important feature of advanced industrial societies which the finding of constant social fluidity does demonstrate is that, despite legislative efforts (such as educational reform etc.) to achieve greater 'openness' and equality of opportunity, this has not, as yet, been completely achieved. Although overall rates of upward mobility have risen, differential *relative* rates of class mobility prospects have proved remarkably resistant to change. In respect of the British case, Goldthorpe has argued that Britain is characterized by both a 'mature' working class (that is, a working class which has been self-recruiting over several generations), as well as a 'service class' whose 'demographic consolidation is likely to be matched by a steady strengthening of its socio-cultural identity' (1987: 341). As a demographically and socio-culturally 'mature' social formation, Goldthorpe argues that the working classes' interests lie in a social-democratic strategy of 'politics against markets'; that is, some form of corporatist strategy. However, the British Labour Party has singularly faied to provide leadership in this respect, and 'opportunities have been repeatedly missed to define and politicize issues in class terms' (1987: 350). Meanwhile, the 'service class' must be viewed as having a major interest and commitment to preserving its situation of relative advantage and thus the status quo of structured social inequality. Although Goldthorpe has been a trenchant critic of Marx's work, therefore, it is paradoxical that he would seem to hold to the view that the main hopes of a more equal (and therefore, by implication, 'better') society lie in the organization of the working class.

These conclusions have been widely criticized. Goldthorpe's emphasis on the stability of relative mobility rates and thus the 'maturity' of the working class, it is argued, simply flies in the face of the extensive fragmentation of the 'class structure' which has in fact occurred, as well as the fact that in any case, Goldthorpe's 'classes' show little indication of an awareness of their interests as such, but tend, rather, to be preoccupied with their homes, families and other aspects of consumption (Pahl 1989, Saunders 1990b). Many of those who have been critical of Goldthorpe have not been fully aware of the complexities of his approach, and these issues will be dealt with in the next chapter. For the moment, we will leave the topic of social mobility and move on to our next example of a 'theoretical' class scheme – Erik Wright's Marxist 'class map'.

Theoretical ('relational') class schemes: II Wright

Goldthorpe has been described as a 'neo-Weberian' or 'left Weberian' sociologist. In contrast, Wright has, since the middle of the 1970s, been following a self-consciously *Marxist* project, a central feature of which has been his efforts to develop a Marxist class scheme; as he has put it, one of the central objectives of his work has been 'to generate a concept capable of mapping in a nuanced way concrete variations in class structures across capitalist societies' (1989: 274). His project has been developed in constant dialogue with other Marxist theoreticians, and in the light of empirical research findings generated by the Comparative Project of Class Structure and Class Consciousness, an international research project which is co-ordinated by Wright. Wright is quite frank that his goal of generating an adequate Marxist 'class map' has not, as yet, been achieved. However, in his efforts to move towards an adequate measure, his class scheme has been through a series of transformations.[7]

Like Goldthorpe, Wright is critical of orthodox sociological strategies for measuring the 'class structure'. He dismisses hierarchical or grada-tional schemes as 'static taxonomies': 'While it might be the case that most of the participants in the storming of the Bastille had status scores of under 40, and most of the French aristocracy had scores above 70, such labels do not capture the underlying dynamics at work in the revolutionary process' (1979: 8). Thus we have, yet again, the

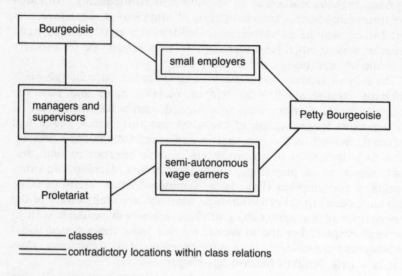

FIGURE 1   *Wright's first Marxist class map*

criticism that such schemes do not tap the dynamics of class *relationships*. Wright also draws a sharp distinction between 'class' and 'occupation' (1980). Occupations, he argues, are understood as positions defined within the *technical* relations of production; classes, on the other hand, are defined by the *social* relations of production.

> a carpenter transforms lumber into buildings; a doctor transforms sick people into healthy people; a typist transforms blank paper into paper with words on it, etc. Classes, on the other hand, can only be defined in terms of their social relationship to other classes, or in more precise terms, by their location within the social relations of production. (*1980: 177*)

Thus, he argues, occupational aggregations cannot produce 'classes', and his own empirical work has used especially gathered survey data to locate individuals within his successive class schemes: 'The basic strategy I have used . . . has been to elaborate the ways in which class relations are embodied in specific *jobs*, since jobs are the essential "empty places" filled by individuals within the system of production' (Wright 1989: 277).[8]

Individual jobs are then located within Wright's class scheme, which has been derived from explicitly Marxist principles. Notions of control and exploitation within the social relations of *production* are central to

Wright's analysis (it should be noted that he has consistently maintained a distinction between his own approach and Weberian approaches to the measurement of social class, which he characterizes as being grounded in *market* relationships). In developing the first version of his scheme, he argued that the social relations of production can be broken down into three interdependent dimensions: (a) social relations of control over money capital, (b) social relations of control over physical capital, and (c) social relations of authority – that is, control over supervision and discipline within the labour process (1980: 24). One of Wright's major preoccupations has been to give an empirical account of the 'middle class', or 'nonproletarian employees', in contemporary capitalist societies. Braverman (1974) had argued that the growing stratum of employees such as supervisors, or lower managerial and administrative workers, had a 'foot in both camps' (that is, bourgeois and proletarian), in that it both 'receive[s] its petty share in the prerogatives and rewards of capital, but . . . also bears the mark of the proletarian condition' (1974: 407). Wright's initial solution to this paradox was to develop the concept of 'contradictory class locations'. Such jobs were said to represent positions which are 'torn between the basic class relations of capitalist society'.

Wright's first starting-point was from the three basic positions within class relations in capitalism; the bourgeoisie, who are characterized by their economic ownership, and exercise social control over both the physical means of production and the labour power of others; the proletariat, who are characterized by neither ownership nor control – even of their own labour-power – which is in fact purchased by the bourgeoisie; and the petty bourgeoisie, who own and control their means of production even though they do not control the labour-power of others. To these basic class positions Wright added three contradictory locations: (a) managers and supervisors, who, even if they do not legally own the means of production, nevertheless exercise *de facto* control over both the material means of production and labour-power; (b) semi-autonomous employees who, even if they do not own or control the material means of production, nevertheless retain control over their own labour-power, and (c) small employers. This set of class positions is brought together in figure 1, which shows that individuals are located within the 'class map' according to the extent to which they possess economic ownership, control, autonomy – or lack of it – within the process of production. Specific information on these topics has been gathered via large-scale sample surveys carried out by Wright and his collaborators (Wright 1985, appendix II).

Wright's first class scheme was subject to a number of theoretical criticisms which eventually resulted in a recasting of his original model. Most fundamentally, Wright came to the opinion that his original class

Production assets

Organization assets

Skill/credential assets

	Owners of means of production	Non-owners [wage labourers]		
		+	**0**	**–**
Own sufficient capital to hire workers and not work	1 Bourgeoisie	4 expert managers	7 semi-credentialled managers	10 uncredentialled managers	+
Own sufficient capital to hire workers but must work	2 small employers	5 expert supervisors	8 semi-credentialled workers	11 uncredentialled supervisors	0
Own sufficient capital to work for self but not to hire workers	3 Petty Bourgeoisie	6 expert non-managers	9 semi-credentialled supervisors	12 Proletariat	–

Source: Wright (1985:88)

FIGURE 2 *Wright's second class map*

map had not, as he had argued, provided an analysis of the Marxist account of *exploitation* within capitalist relations of production but, rather, had merely given a descriptive account of *domination* (Wright 1985: 56–7). Domination is, of course, a significant aspect of class relations but it may be viewed as essentially epiphenomenal – that is, as a consequence of exploitative class relationships, rather than their cause.

Wright's solution to this theoretical problem was to develop the work of John Roemer, who had applied game-theoretic principles to Marx's analysis in order to give an account of exploitation. Wright summarizes Roemer's basic strategy as follows:

> The basic idea of this approach is to compare different systems of exploitation by treating the organization of production as a 'game'. the actors in this game have various kinds of productive assets (i.e. resources such as skills and capital) which they bring into production and which they use to generate incomes on the basis of a specific set of rules. The essential strategy adopted for the analysis of exploitation is to ask if particular coalitions of players would be better off if they withdrew from this game under certain specified procedures in order to play a different one. (*Wright 1985: 68*)

If a group would be better off by withdrawing from the first game, and entering into an alternative game (and their previous partner would be worse off as a consequence), then exploitation can be said to be taking place under the conditions of the original game.

In his development of the analysis of exploitation (rather than domination), Wright distinguishes four types of assets, the unequal ownership or control of each of which forms the basis of different types of exploitation. These are: labour-power assets (feudal exploitation), capital assets (capitalist exploitation), organization assets (statist exploitation) and skill or credential assets (socialist exploitation). No actually existing society ever consists of a single form of exploitation, and thus, empirically, classes with particular assets may be simultaneously exploited through one mechanism of exploitation but exploiters through another mechanism. Through this complex chain of abstract reasoning, therefore, Wright develops a further 'class map' reflecting relations of exploitation, rather than domination (see fig. 2).

As can be seen from figure 2, the number of Wright's classes has increased from six to twelve. The major difference between Wright's earlier and later approaches, however, is that whereas the presence or absence of work autonomy was central to the identification of significant 'contradictory' class groupings in Wright's first scheme, this element is absent from the second version. Rather, such groupings are now identified through their possession of organizational assets, expertise and credentials. It has been pointed out that this development of Wright's analysis has a close parallel in Weberian approaches to the identification of the individual's 'class situation'; as such assets clearly differentiate groups 'according to the kind of services that can be offered on the market . . . and will thus have an impact on individual "life-chances"' (Rose and Marshall 1986). Wright would reject such suggestions. His arguments, however, make it clear that his continuing commitment to a Marxist class scheme stems from his primary commitment to Marxist theory as an organizing theoretical framework, which he claims is still 'the most coherent general approach to radical, emancipatory social theory' (Wright 1989: 322).

Rather like Goldthorpe's, therefore, Wright's class scheme has to be evaluated in the context of his work as a whole – although the theoretical elaboration of his scheme has occupied a significant place within this corpus. Besides the empirical evaluation of his own approach to social class against other strategies of operationalizing the 'class structure' (particularly the 'productive labour' definition employed by Poulantzas – Wright's conceptualization, unsurprisingly, proved to be superior) Wright's aim has been to test empirically a number of basic Marxist assumptions. Thus, for example, he has, like Goldthorpe, been highly critical of liberal analyses concerning the class trajectory of 'industrial societies'. Wright and Singlemann (1982) have used empirical data classified by Wright's class categories (mark I) in an analysis of the American occupational structure which appeared to demonstrate that, contrary to Blau and Duncan's optimistic assumptions, relating to occupational 'upgrading', the American class structure was undergoing a process of 'proletarianization'. Their evidence suggested that Braverman's thesis of the 'deskilling' of the labour force could be sustained at the macro-level. Within given economic sectors there was 'a systematic tendency for those positions with relatively little control over their labor processes to expand during the 1960s and for those positions with high levels of autonomy to decline' (1982: 198). These tendencies had been to some extent masked by the growth of semi-autonomous employment, particularly in the state sector, but they predicted that this would be checked by a decline in state employment given the growing 'fiscal crisis' of the state.

However, in a later paper (Wright and Martin 1987) which draws upon further evidence (and uses class categories mark II), Wright argues that, contrary to the predictions of his earlier argument: 'In terms of the working class . . . the 1970s were a period of relative *de*-proletarianization . . . In no case is there any evidence that the prolonged stagnation of the 1970s generated a tendency for the proportion of managers, supervisors and experts within sectors to decline . . .

these results [run] consistently counter to our theoretical predictions' (1987: 16). Indeed, all of the evidence points in the *opposite* direction: 'The implication of these analyses, then, is unmistakable: the results are more consistent with what we construe to be the post-industrial society thesis than the traditional Marxist proletarianization thesis' (1987: 18). Wright does not as a consequence reject Marxist analysis. The globalization of capitalist relations, he argues, suggests that national units of capitalism are not necessarily representative of capitalism as a whole and, in any case, such internationalization means that there will be a tendency for managerial class locations to expand more rapidly in the core capitalist countries and proletarian positions to expand more rapidly in the Third World. In any case, he suggests that the extent of the incompatibility between Marxist and liberal theories of industrial development may have been overdrawn; as the effects of the material conditions posited in postindustrial theory can, using his revised class framework, be described in class terms.

Wright also uses comparative data drawn from Sweden and the United States to develop his arguments relating to class structure and politics. The long tradition of left-corporatist social democracy in Sweden has shaped not only the 'class' (that is, occupational) structure, as compared to the United States, but has also, perhaps paradoxically, resulted in a heightened salience of 'class thinking' and thus class attitudes which are more polarized. Thus he is careful always to stress that the effects of class structure are mediated by politics. To the extent that Wright indulges in political prescription, it is perhaps paradoxical that his comments are very similar to those of Goldthorpe (who, it will be remembered, suggests that the interests of the 'mature' working class in Britain would be best served by some version of 'left democracy'), in that he states that 'the heart of the positive struggle for socialism is radical democracy' (Wright 1985: 287). Thus despite their very different theoretical orientations and strategies of analysis, it would seem that Wright and Goldthorpe might be in broad political agreement on a number of contemporary issues.

Conclusions

This chapter has reviewed a number of different strategies (or classification schemes) through which the structure of employment in industrial societies may be divided in order to produce statistical aggregates which are then labelled 'social classes'. Many such schemes are largely descriptive in their intentions – that is, they provide a convenient measure of the broad contours of structured social inequality in late twentieth-century capitalism. They also supply a (somewhat rough and ready) indication of 'lifestyle' and associated social attitudes. Different schemes have been used in a wide variety of social science and other contexts – for example, research on social policy, market research, research on voting behaviour and social mobility. The range of different theoretical and practical applications for which different class schemes are utilized suggests that it is not possible to identify particular schemes which are 'right' or 'wrong'; rather, different schemes are more or less appropriate for particular tasks. Nevertheless, sociologists have at times appeared to be reluctant to accept such theoretical and methodological plurality, and there have been extensive arguments about which particular scheme is 'superior' – arguments which extend across a range of different issue areas. For example, Marshall et al. (1988) have compared in some detail the Registrar-General's, Goldthorpe's, and Wright's class schemes. It is difficult, however, to see what is actually gained from this exercise, as the class schemes in question were devised for different purposes and on the basis of different (implicit and explicit) theoretical assumptions.

Employment-derived class schemes have also been used to provide evidence for theoretical debates – for example concerning the nature and future trajectory of 'industrial societies' (Wright and Singlemann 1982; Wright and Martin 1987), or to test Marx's and Braverman's arguments concerning 'proletarianization' (Rose et al. 1987). This chapter has drawn particular attention to the class schemes associated with the development of the theoretical programmes of class analysis of Goldthorpe and Wright. These programmes were generated as part of a widespread critique within sociology of approaches to the study of society which emphasized order, rather than conflict, within the stratification system and employed subjective and/or intuitive occupational rankings in its 'class' analyses. Relational schemes, in contrast, attempted to capture the underlying divisions and conflicts within capitalist industrial societies.

Both Goldthorpe and Wright have been engaged, in the 1970s and 1980s, in extensive programmes of empirical research to which their (rather different) definitions of 'class' are central. Their respective energies have produced a considerable quantity of published materials, and associated debates, which merit separate books in themselves (indeed, such volumes have appeared: Clark et al. (1990); Wright (1989). Such productivity may be seen as admirable, but one of its consequences is that the increasing statistical sophistication of one 'school' (Goldthorpe), and the theoretical elaborations of the other (Wright), have rendered the focus of the debates increasingly inaccessible to the sociological community in general. However, despite the claims of both Wright and Goldthorpe to have developed approaches which identify, empirically, the actualities of class relations in a Marxist or

Weberian sense, it will later be argued at some length that, in reality, approaches to class analysis deriving from the structure of employment can never provide *uncontaminated* empirical measures of 'class'. Other factors besides class processes – in particular 'ascribed' features such as gender and ethnicity, as well as specific national factors – will all have significant effects on the levels of power, material reward, and so on accruing to particular jobs, as well as on the kinds of persons recruited to them.

Nevertheless, there is a widespread assumption within the social sciences that 'class' is described by the occupational structure – indeed, 'class structure' and 'occupational structure' are often taken to be synonymous. This convention stems from the practice established by turn-of-the-century statisticians such as Stevenson of dividing up the population into unequally-rewarded occupational orders or 'classes'. Stevenson was engaged in a debate with eugenists, not Marx or Weber, and it is not surprising, therefore, that such 'class' schemes as the Registrar-General's should correspond only fortuitously to their theoretical concerns. However, this convenient assumption (class structure = occupational structure) can cause problems for the unwary, or those not versed in the finer details of relational class schemes. In the next chapter, therefore, we will examine these and other criticisms of the diverse project of 'class analysis' as a whole.

Notes

1 As an illustration of this anomaly, Nichols points out that in the British *Classification of Occupations*, 1951, the 'capitalist, the 'business speculator', and the 'landowner' were lumped into the same residual category as the 'expert' (undefined) and the 'lunatic (trade not stated)'!

2 For the purposes of Goldthorpe's subsequent research on social mobility, the seven categories were extended to ten. This was a consequence of: (a) separating out agricultural workers in classes IV and VII, and (b) further distinguishing between those with and without employees in class IV.

3 Blau and Duncan were at pains to emphasize the fact that their general findings were not applicable to the black population, and were very critical of the extent of structured racial inequality in the United States.

4 Goldthorpe (1987: 27). Ch. 1, 'Social mobility and social interests', provides an excellent account of the history and background of research and theorizing in the area of social mobility.

5 Glass's original enquiry has been subject to extensive criticisms which have argued, amongst other things, that it underestimated the actual extent of mobility. See Payne (1987: ch. 6).

6 One obvious example would be the case of the societies of what used to be referred to as the 'Eastern bloc'. For ideological as well as economic and

organizational reasons, such societies have been more likely to designate particular occupations as belonging to the 'working class', and the size of the non-manual category is correspondingly reduced. Thus if 'occupation' is taken as an index of 'class', the 'class structure' of Eastern bloc societies is quite different from that of Western societies, although they are both 'industrial' societies (Parkin 1972; Goldthorpe 1967).

7   The debate relating to Wright's corpus as a whole is extensively reviewed in Wright (1989).

8   In fact, Wright's distinction between 'occupation' and 'class' as reflecting the distinction between 'technical' and 'social' relations of production cannot be sustained, as many occupational titles encompass 'social' relationships. For example, 'managers and administrators' constitute a Major Group within the Standard Occupational Classification (UK).

4

Problems of Class Analysis

Introduction

Chapter 3 has considered a range of different strategies developed within sociology and the social sciences for the measurement of the 'class structure' via the structure of employment. A feature of all such approaches is that the identification of the class structure may be treated as analytically and empirically separable from the question of class action. Many such measures (for example, the Registrar-General's social class classification) are descriptive schemes devised for social policy purposes rather than as a contribution to debates in theoretical class analysis. However, the question of the most appropriate measure of social 'class' became a central issue for an important debate within postwar Anglo-American sociology: 'consensus' versus 'conflict' approaches. It was argued that normative functionalism had laid an unwarranted emphasis on integration and consensus, thus obscuring the very real conflicts that characterized industrial capitalist society. The stability and (apparent) cross-national similarity of occupational rankings had been interpreted as a manifestation of this supposed consensus, as well as providing an empirical demonstration of the 'industrial society' thesis. In contrast, those sociologists who stressed the significance of social conflict emphasized the need to develop measures of social *class*, rather than descriptive measures of occupational inequality. Thus in the 1970s and 1980s there were developed sociological measures of the structure of employment which, in contrast to 'gradational', status or 'commonsense' schemes, purported to reflect, theoretically, the structure of actual class *relations* in capitalist societies. Two major empirical programmes of 'class analysis' – those of Goldthorpe and Wright – have been developed using such schemes.

Theoretical, relational class schemes have been constructed on the assumption that the underlying processes identified by particular class theories are systematically reproduced within the structure of employment and occupations. The occupational order does indeed bear the imprint of class processes. However, whatever the class theory informing the initial scheme (that is, whether Marxist or Weberian), in practice it is impossible to arrive at an 'uncontaminated' measure of 'social class' deriving from the structure of employment. As Bourdieu has argued: 'the property emphasised by the name used to designate a category, usually occupation, is liable to mask the effect of all the secondary properties which, although constitutive of the category, are not expressly indicated' (1986: 103). These other properties include characteristics such as gender, age and race, as well as other factors such as 'social standing', 'culture' or 'locality'. Thus 'class analysis' has always incorporated the study of the interaction of class with these other properties.

Occupational-class schemes may be used to carry out this task – empirical indicators representing the properties may be straightforwardly compared with occupational class, using cross-tabulations or other statistical approaches. However, these 'other factors' enter into the very structuring of employment relationships themselves. Thus an important strand within class analysis has focused primarily upon the formation and structuring of social classes, upon the manner in which employment relationships are constituted and upon the circumstances in which employment-related groups emerge.

Empirical researchers investigating the structuring of class and stratification categories have usually employed methodologies other than the construction and manipulation of large data sets. In particular, they have used the case-study approach. The case study has been described as 'a way of organizing social data so as to preserve the unitary character of the social object being studied . . . it is an approach which views any social unit as a whole' (W. J. Goode and P. K. Hatt, cited in Mitchell 1983). Case studies relating to class processes have been carried out at the micro-level of the occupation or work group – as in, for example, Burawoy's (1979) participant observer study of lathe operators 'making out' in the machine shop of Allied Corporation. A case study, however, may also be carried out at the macro-level – as in, for example, Thompson's study of the 'making' of the English working class. Indeed, many socio-historical studies of class and stratification might be regarded in this light.

Within sociology, therefore, there have been developed a range of different approaches to the investigation of the class structure and class processes, from descriptive accounts of inequality to the investigation of occupational status and the development of theoretical class schemes, as well as sociological and socio-historical accounts of the processes of class structuring. However, the idea of 'class' is also of considerable significance for debates concerning politics and society more generally, and these debates have been reflected within class analysis in sociology. Indeed, it is often difficult if not impossible to separate the sociological from the political debates – as in, for example, Heath et al.'s (1991) extensive explorations of the relationship between occupational 'class' and voting behaviour. In recent decades there have been a number of economic, social and political changes in Western societies, which have apparently challenged the usefulness of the diverse enterprise of 'class analysis' as a whole.

Changes in the structure of work and employment

Since the end of the Second World War, the expansion of capitalist industrialism has had important consequences for the international division of labour. The industrialization of South East Asia has been accompanied by the decline of heavy manufacturing in the West, the United States 'steel belt' has become a 'rust belt' and in Britain, once-dependent single-industry localities in South Wales and the North-East have ceased to manufacture this most basic commodity of 'industrial society'. Other major industries, such as shipbuilding, have suffered a precipitate decline in the level of worldwide demand, whilst that construction which remains is predominantly in countries such as Korea. Postwar expansion in the West had seen the rapid growth of manufacturing to meet the demand for consumer goods – notably vehicles – but increasing competition and the saturation of home markets has also led to a marked decline, particularly in Britain, in these industries. The postwar boom was already coming to an end by the 1960s, but the worsening of the economic crisis, exacerbated by the world oil price rises of the early 1970s, led to a further collapse of manufacturing industry in the West.

Throughout the 1970s, governments in Britain – particularly Labour governments – had attempted to grapple with the worsening economic situation through a further extension of the broadly 'corporatist' bargain which had been consolidated during the period of postwar expansion. This had involved the adoption of Keynesian policies of state economic management – a policy of full employment, which governments attempted to maintain by controlling demand through taxation and other fiscal policies – in combination with increased levels of state provision of education, health, and welfare.[1] In 1974, the Labour government in Britain entered into a 'social contract' with the trade union movement, in which the unions agreed to regulate the wage demands of their members in exchange for an increased right to participate in the shaping of government policies. These policies were not successful in stabilizing the economy, and inflation continued to rise, as did rates of unemployment – a phenomenon which was given the suitably unpleasant title of 'stagflation'.[2] They culminated in the 1979 'winter of discontent', during which public-sector workers, whose wages had declined sharply as a consequence of the 'social contract', went on strike.[3] The Conservative government which was then elected pursued policies in sharp contrast with those of the 'social contract'. Industries in decline were no longer protected, and government 'intervention' in the economy was restricted to attempts to control the money supply. Trade unions were excluded from access to state power – indeed a full-frontal attack was mounted on their position, and legal rights (such as those embodied in the Trade Unions and Labour Relations Act 1976) they had achieved during the 1970s were simply removed. Under the influence of neo-liberal economic theories the Conservative government spearheaded a return to 'market forces' in the regulation of economic affairs, which involved the transferring to the private sector of state monopolies such as gas and telephones, the increasing 'privatization' of welfare, the application of 'quasi-market' principles to those areas remaining within the state's orbit (such as schools, universities and hospitals), and the promotion of individual entrepreneurship.

The impact of this attempt to move away from the 'welfare state deal' in Britain in the 1980s will be further examined in chapter 6. For the moment, the significant fact to note is that these policies contributed further to the headlong collapse of manufacturing, together with a sharp rise in unemployment. Employment in manufacturing declined by 3 million between 1971 and 1988, from 8 to 5 million employees. New jobs were created during the economic restructuring of the 1980s, but these were largely in the service economy, which increased form 11.6 million employees in 1971 to 15.2 million in 1988. This rapid decline in employment in manufacturing, therefore, which has taken place in most Western economies, has resulted in a further decline in those occupations which have by convention been described as 'working-class'. The decline in working-class employment has also been associated with the erosion of working-class communities (for example, in coalmining areas), an increase in individualism, etc. The decline in manufacturing employment in the West has also been a decline in mass, large-scale production – what remains has simply gone elsewhere.

These changes have been described as a move from 'Fordist' to 'post-Fordist' methods of production and labour organization (R. Murray 1989; Sabel 1982). 'Fordism', it is argued, was characterized by large-scale mass production of cheap, uniform commodities, the detailed division of labour, and extensive hierarchical organization of productive activity. Hence the label 'Fordist', which describes the system of mass, assembly-line production of cars developed by Henry Ford in the United States during the early decades of this century. It is the system of production in manufacturing which Braverman described as the 'degradation of work in monopoly capitalism'. 'Post-Fordism', in contrast, is supposedly characterized by flexible production techniques on smaller, dispersed sites. The emphasis is on product variety and rapid response to consumer demand – in contrast to Henry Ford's famous statement that customers could have any colour car they wanted – as long as it was black. The extent to which a real move in the direction of 'post-Fordism' has actually occurred has been widely contested (Sayer 1989), as has the real import of 'flexibility' – it has been argued, for example, that 'flexibility' is a euphemism for increased intensity of labour exploitation and the employment of low-skilled and disadvantaged labour in part-time and temporary work (Pollert 1988). However, although the actual extent of 'flexibilization' and 'post-Fordist' organizational forms may be empirically disputed, it is important to recognize that these debates are not only, or even primarily, concerned with changes in the world of work itself. Commentators such as Harvey have stressed that: 'Postwar Fordism has to be seen, therefore, less as a mere system of mass production and more as a total way of life' (1990: 135). Mass production is associated with mass consumption, buttressed by the state's regulation of the economy. The capacity to plan and regulate national economies rationally, which seemed to have been achieved in the West during the long period of economic growth after the Second World War, is the apotheosis of 'Fordism'.

Economic expansion, followed by economic decline in the West, has been accompanied by other significant changes in the world of work. The period of 'Fordist' expansion was one of rising working-class affluence, and greater protection of employment brought about by the 'welfare state deal'. It was argued in the 1960s that, as a consequence, work was becoming less of a 'central life interest' (Dubin 1956; Zweig 1961) for the majority of the population; and, moreover, that the working classes were becoming more 'middle-class' in their attitudes and outlook. Goldthorpe et al. (1969) carried out an empirical examination of this thesis of 'embourgeoisement'. Although they found that there were still real differences in the attitudes and behaviour of their 'working-class' and 'middle-class' respondents, their results nevertheless confirmed that the 'affluent worker' had become more home-centred and concerned with domestic consumption. The significance of 'work' which was not employment has also been emphasized by Pahl

(1984), who argued that the capacity for 'self-provisioning' was a crucial area of difference amongst working-class households. The recession of the 1980s meant that long-term unemployment affected increasing numbers of people, early retirement became more common, young people spent longer in full-time education – or were simply failing to find work. Work as employment was becoming scarce, and in any case technological change had massively reduced labour inputs in many industries. It was argued, therefore, that not only had the working class declined, but that work (as employment) was becoming less important in people's lives. Thus Offe argues the need to 'break with the idea that the sphere of work has a relatively privileged power to determine social consciousness and action' (1985a: 133).

However, for a significant category of people – women – employment was becoming considerably *more* important. In all of the OECD countries, women's employment has grown rapidly since the Second World War – particulary since the 1960s (Paukert 1984). This rise was almost entirely accounted for by an increase in the employment of *married* women. The recession of the 1970s and 1980s was not accompanied by any great decline in women's employment – indeed, many of the service-industry jobs which were created as a consequence of economic restructuring were low-level 'women's jobs'. Women's continuing participation in the formal economy has also been accompanied by both the rise of 'second-wave' feminism and an improvement in their levels of academic and work-related qualifications, and we should expect, therefore, that women will increasingly achieve higher-level positions within employment. The emerging structure of employment in the West at the end of the twentieth century, therefore, is not only service-based but increasingly feminized.

These rapid changes in the structure of employment and unemployment over the last twenty years present a number of difficulties for class analysis. The decline of manufacturing 'working class' and the expansion of 'white-collar' service occupations might appear to signify an expansion of the 'middle classes' – as theorists of 'industrial society' had anticipated (Mayer 1963) – but a number of factors militated against a too-easy adoption of this view. In particular, could the same criteria of occupational class classification be retained given the very considerable changes that had taken place in the nature of 'work' itself, as well as in the people doing it? Could routine service-sector employment really be described as 'middle-class'? These kinds of arguments were given added force by the arguments of Braverman (1974), who argued that an inherent tendency towards the routinization and 'deskilling' of work accompanied all aspects of capitalist employment. These tendencies, he argued, would result in the ultimate deskilling, and thus the 'proletarianization', of lower-level white-collar and even managerial work. The 'upgrading' of the occupational structure, therefore, was more apparent than real. The employment of women presented particular problems. Many women, for example, were in lower-level clerical jobs, but as these were usually of the dead-end variety, were they 'middle-class' occupations?

Changes in the structure of work and employment, therefore, have in the late twentieth century presented a number of difficulties for established sociological approaches to 'class analysis', in the area of occupational classifications as well as in arguments concerning the significance of 'work', and thus class-as-employment. These changes have also been accompanied by important political developments.

Class and politics

'Class' is a central concept within the Marxist theoretical framework; it has, therefore, always had a central place in the political discourse of socialists and Marxists. As far as the left is concerned, it is unlikely that the 1980s will be remembered with affection. It was an era which began with the electoral defeat of reformist socialism in both the United States and Britain (although some have argued that the possibilities of socialist co-operation have been enhanced through institutions such as the EC; see Bottomore 1991) – and ended with the apparent dismantling of existing regimes in the majority of the self-proclaimed state 'socialist' countries in the Eastern bloc. There were and are, of course, many on the socialist left who had always maintained that the centrally planned regimes of the Soviet Union were not in fact 'socialist', but nevertheless, even such critical socialist analyses have suffered from 'guilt by association' as discredited regimes crumble apace.

A powerful subtext in these debates is that the 'failure of the left' is also a failure of socialist theory; that socialists have remained encumbered for too long by the trappings of outdated ideologies which required revision and updating in the light of 'New Times'.[4] The major thesis associated with such arguments, which reflects the economic changes discussed above, is that the decline of mass production, and with it a mass labour force, has led to the declining significance of the (mass, male) 'working class' and thus of class *politics*. The political parallel of mass production was Keynesian economics in combination with varying degrees of centralized planning and organization; when such political accommodations finally collapsed at the end of the 1970s the vacuum was filled by the neo-liberal 'return to the market' which has further fragmented class politics. Thus 'class', at least in its now-obsolete mass manual, male working-class dimensions, is of declining significance in 'New Times', and must be replaced by a new emphasis on ecological and feminist issues, a concern for internationalism together with a move away from authoritarian centralism, and a recognition of the centrality of consumption, rather than outdated 'productivism' (Hall and Jaques 1989; 11–12).

'Post-Marxists' such as Laclau and Mouffe (1985, 1987) have developed a critique of what they describe as classical Marxism which emphasizes the discursively constructed nature of human society; 'discourse' replaces 'ideology' as a central concept in 'post-Marxism'.[5] Marxist theory and its development stands accused of 'essentialism' and 'dualism', and in arguments which echo those of 'New Times' theorists Laclau and Mouffe also challenge the primacy given to 'class' in classical Marxist theory: *'There are* interests, but these are precarious historical products which are always subjected to processes of dissolution and redefinition. What there are not, however, are *objective* interests, in the sense in which they are postulated in the "false consciousness" approach' (1987: 97). Thus the working class has no privileged role in the anti-capitalist struggle, and other radical anti-capitalist social movements such as environmental groups, not linked to any particular position in the social structure, will assume importance (1987: 104). In contrast to what they perceive as the essentialism and economic reductionism (or 'monism') of classical Marxism, Laclau and Mouffe suggest that oppositional struggles in fact only emerge when the democratic discourse becomes available, when ideas of liberty and equality become humanly *possible*. This occurred, they suggest, at the moment of the French Revolution, which began the 'democratic revolution'. The absolute power of 'the people' was asserted, thus introducing 'something truly new at the level of the social imaginary' (1985: 155). The *ancien régime*, which had rested upon a perception of society in which individuals appeared fixed in differential positions, and was justified by the logic of the divine will, at this point in history received its fatal blow.

Not surprisingly, there have been substantial responses to Laclau and Mouffe's 'post-Marxist' arguments from left theorists who have maintained that classes, and class action, remain central to Marxist political thought (Geras 1986; Wood 1986). Wood argues that Laclau and Mouffe's analysis of 'classical Marxism' rests upon a caricature which effectively reduces Marxist theory to an economically and technologically over-determined 'straw person'. 'Democratic discourse', she argues, is *constituted* by class conflict, rather than being its source, and there was a long history of class conflict *before* the French Revolution. In contrast to Laclau and Mouffe, Wood emphasizes the *social* (rather than 'discursive') origins of political movements.

Within left-oriented political debates, therefore, some have dismissed a concern with 'class' as 'outdated productivism'; others still maintain its historical centrality. Within political sociology, contemporary debates have also emphasized the significance of the development of the 'New Social Movements' identified above by Laclau and Mouffe which, according to Offe (1985a) have 'transformed the boundaries of institutional politics'. Offe describes the 'old politics' – that is, the major political issues in Western Europe from the immediate postwar years until the early 1970s – as being centrally concerned with issues of economic growth, distribution and security. In 'New Times' language, the 'old politics' corresponded to the politics of Fordism. Although the old politics was marked by a considerable degree of consensus – on the desirability of economic growth, of welfare provision, and so on – distributive conflict organized politics along broadly 'class' lines; parties of the unionized working class competing with bourgeois parties which included both the old and elements of the 'new' (that is, lower-level white-collar) middle class. However, the accommodative basis of the old politics has been challenged by both the New Right, as well as by the growth of New Social Movements, which include the peace movement, ecological movements, human rights and feminist movements.

The neo-liberal New Right is highly critical of the extent of state involvement characteristic of the 'old politics', which it saw both as acting as a brake upon economic recovery and as eroding the base of individual responsiblities and undermining civil society. New Social Movements are similarly critical of the state's capacity to resolve the major problems which they identify, but, Offe argues, they seek not to 'roll back' the state, or 'reprivatize' civil society but to *transform* political action through the development of a non-institutional politics which will bring about permanent changes. The feminist slogan 'the personal is political' may be used to describe this approach to political action, which is also characterized by relatively non-hierarchical modes of organization, mass protests and, often, direct action.

New Social Movements, Offe, argues, represent a significant break with class politics. The bases of their organization do not correspond to socio-economic classes, or their corresponding left/right ideologies, but 'is rather coded in *categories* taken from the movements' issues, such as gender, age, locality etc., or, in the case of environmental and pacifist movements, the human race as a whole' (Offe 1985a: 831; my emphasis). Class, in the sense of socio-economic status, is related to New Social Movements, however, in that much of their membership is drawn from the 'new' new middle class – that is the educated, socially aware elements of the middle class who grew up within the economic security of the old politics and found employment within the institutions it created (that is, in administration, health, education, etc.).

The 'new' new middle class may be distinguished from the 'old' new middle class of lower-level white-collar workers. Such groupings have politicized, not on behalf of a class, but around the wider issues addressed by New Social Movements: 'New middle class politics, in contrast to most working class politics, as well as old middle class politics, is typically the politics *of* a class but not *on behalf of* a class' (1985a: 833).

This summary of recent changes and commentary has had a focus on the last two decades. However, the political significance of 'class' is in fact an issue that has been extensively rehearsed since well before the beginning of 'New Times'. It should be remembered that in capitalist societies, 'class politics' has rarely, if ever, been reflected in the *mass* mobilization of the working class. In Britain in the nineteenth and into the twentieth century, for example, the working class has been split by craft and sectionalisms which were reflected in the organization of the trade union movement. The working class can hardly be said to have been indifferent to matters of consumption in the nineteenth century, as is evidenced by the growth of working-class domestic consumption and indeed a culture of domesticity, particularly amongst the skilled working class, during the Victorian era (Gray 1976; Crossick 1978).

Many of the developments summarized above – such as the expansion of 'middle-class' occupations, and the apparent decline or absence of working-class conflict – have been in process throughout the twentieth century. In particular, they have long been a source of criticism of, and perplexity within, Marxist theory. For example in the 1930s Klingender (1935) argued, using Marxist terminology, that low-level white-collar employees such as clerks and shop assistants were 'falsely' conscious of their 'true' class situation, and the apparent reluctance of the working class to fulfil its historic role has been seen as a problem from the earliest days of socialism. In the earlier decades of the twentieth century, revolutionary socialists such as Rosa Luxemburg emphasized above all the importance of the spontaneous, self-emancipatory efforts of the working class in the achievement of its objectives (that is, the revolutionary transformation of society), whereas others such as Lenin and Kautsky argued that revolutionary intellectuals and the Party had a crucial role in leading the working classes to socialism – they could not achieve this on their own account.

These kinds of issues, however, are also problematic for *non*-Marxist class analysis. Changes in the structure of employment have raised similar problems of placement and allocation – where are women located within the 'class structure', how should occupational-class schemes deal with the burgeoning 'new middle-class' occupations? The question of class action has always been a contentious issue in sociology. Thus class analysis has not just been criticized as a

Marxist enterprise, but also because the very concept of 'class' is seen as somehow redundant in the context of late twentieth-century industrialism.

These criticisms will be examined under three broad, and inter-related, headings. First, the location of individuals and (often newly emerging) groups within the class structure – the problem of where to put people. Second, the problem of the failure of class action, particularly working-class action, to materialize, as well as more general arguments concerning the declining significance of 'class politics'. Third (and following from the two previous points), there is the question of the declining significance of 'class' – both relative and absolute.

Where to put people

The problem of where to draw class boundaries has been most acute for those authors whose initial or primary focus has been on the class structure. As far as those approaches which focus on the occupational structure are concerned, the situation is rendered even more complex on account of its fluid and ever-changing nature, as economic and technological developments create new occupations whilst others decline in numerical importance or even disappear altogether. This discussion of where to draw boundaries and locate individuals will focus on two issues which have achieved particular prominence: first, the question of the 'middle classes'; and second, the classification problems raised by the substantial increase in the paid employment of women.

The 'middle classes'

An important feature of expanding non-manual employment is its extreme heterogeneity. Lower-level non-manual employment shares many features traditionally associated with manual work (close supervision, routinization, low rates of pay, etc.), whereas higher-level non-manual jobs are often associated with the dominant structures of wealth and power. As far as lower-level jobs are concerned, the issue has often been whether or not they should be located within the 'middle' or 'working' class (or associated with the 'bourgeoisie' or 'proletariat'). The expansion of higher-level jobs has been associated with debates concerning the rise to prominence of a 'new' class – often described as the 'service' class.

In the *Communist Manifesto*, Marx and Engels apparently made a confident prediction concerning long-term occupational developments in capitalist societies: 'Society as a whole is more and more splitting up into two great hostile camps, into two great classes directly facing each other: Bourgeoisie and Proletariat' (1962: 35). Elsewhere in Marx's work there is ample evidence that he was fully aware of the empirical existence, and probable expansion, of 'middling' occupational groups (Rattansi 1985). Nevertheless, the statement above by Marx and Engels has been widely interpreted as a prediction that there would be an expansion of 'proletarian' (or 'working-class') occupations as capitalism developed. Thus the growth of non-manual occupations has always been seen as problematic for Marxist analysis. They were a discomfort not only because the levels of material reward of the expanding 'middle-level' labour force hardly corresponded to the proletarian condition,[6] but also because, even at the lower levels of white-collar employment, such workers showed little identification with the proletariat and indeed often seemed to be at some pains to distinguish themselves from it.

Lockwood's (1958) influential work directly engaged with Marxist arguments. He argued that although clerks and manual workers might share a common status as propertyless employees, the *consequences* of their employment status were not identical and, indeed, varied as between different categories of white-collar workers. (At the time of Lockwood's research bank clerks, for example, were regarded as the 'aristocracy' of white-collar labour, having superior wages and promotion prospects as compared to other categories of clerk.) Using the Weberian concept of 'life chances', Lockwood argued that the 'work' and 'market' situation of the clerk was superior to that of the manual worker, and that they could not, therefore, be said to share the same 'class situation'.

Lockwood's work has been an important element in the development of a 'neo-Weberian' approach having a pronounced structural emphasis (Goldthorpe 1987), in which the differences in the 'market' and 'work situation' of particular occupational categories have been used as the basis upon which to allocate occupations to 'classes'. The question of where to put the middle classes is not particularly difficult as far as a market-oriented Weberian approach to class classification is concerned, as skill differences will, like property, shape life chances in the market and produce a diversity of 'class situations'.

Structural Marxists have also attempted to identify the objective location of the increasing mass of non-proletarian workers (or 'agents') within the social division of labour. Poulantzas argued that the bourgeoisie may be unambiguously identified as those who own the material means of production, but besides legal ownership, he also identified the significance of *possession*, that is, 'the capacity to put the means of production into operation' (1975: 19). Thus managers may be said to be carrying out the functions of capital even if they do not legally own the means of production, and their class location may be identified with that of the bourgeoisie. State functionaries may be similarly identified, as in a capitalist state they 'manage' on behalf of capital. The 'new' petty bourgeoisie, however, are non-productive wage labourers who cannot, therefore, be included in the working class and who, moreover, indirectly participated in the political and ideological domination of the proletariat.[7]

Wright's class scheme was developed in a critical dialogue with Poulantzas's work. Unlike Poulantzas, Wright argues that the position of many lower-level white-collar employees is objectively 'proletarian'. In developing this argument, the influence of Braverman's *Labor and Monopoly Capital* (1974) was crucial. Wright has employed first, the notion of contradictory class locations, then asset exploitation, in order to locate various middle groupings within the class structure. His procedures have been described in some detail in the previous chapter and will not be repeated here. His work may be seen as one of the more sustained of a number of different attempts by Marxist theoreticians, which came to prominence during the 1970s, to identify 'correctly' the class location of the burgeoning numbers of non-manual employees. A feature of all such accounts was an emphasis on the essential ambiguity of such class locations; for example, Carchedi (1975: 51) argued that such a worker who performs 'both the global function of capital and the function of the collective worker . . . is therefore both the labourer (productive and unproductive) and the non-labourer and . . . is both exploiter (or oppressor) and exploited (or oppressed).

As far as the upper levels of non-manual employment are concerned, an important strand in the debates concerning their location has derived from the Austro-Marxist Karl Renner's identification of the 'service class'. This concept has been developed by both Goldthorpe (1982, 1987) and Lash and Urry (1987); see also Abercrombie and Urry (1983). Goldthorpe's 'service class' incorporates occupations at the upper levels of the occupational structure, which he identifies as having characteristic 'work' and 'market' situations incorporating autonomy, the exercise of delegated authority, and the security of a bureaucratic career (1982: 169). As we have seen in the previous chapter, Goldthorpe argues that the expansion of this class has constituted 'a primarily conservative force within modern society, so far at least as the prevailing structure of class inequality is concerned' (1987: 341).

Lash and Urry, however, suggest that the development of the 'service class' has been a destabilizing element in capitalist society. Although they include similar occupational groups to those identified by Goldthorpe in their discussion of the service class, their approach to 'class analysis' is quite different from that of Goldthorpe (Crompton 1992), and has a primary focus on the active structuring of classes and class relations – the nature of the occupational structure is the end point, rather than the starting-point, of their analysis. Their work is explicitly informed by a 'realist' approach (see chapter 2 above). Thus the advantaged position that the service class has achieved is seen as being an outcome of the realization of its causal powers, and it is these processes which have contributed to the disorganization of capitalism. The service class, they argue, grew out of a struggle between already-existing capital and nascent managerial groupings. The service class services capital through meeting three functions: to conceptualize the labour process (and thus facilitate 'deskilling'); to control the entry and exercise of labour power within the workplace (that is, management), and to orchestrate the non-household forms under which labour power is produced and regulated (education, health, welfare, etc.). Initially, the developing service class had an interest in the growth of 'organized' capitalism, that is, a 'Fordist' capitalism characterized by centraliza-tion, large firms, mass organizations (such as trade unions), state planning, and so on. However, the growing service class subsequently contributes to the 'disorganization' of capitalism, as the members of this class struggle to protect their own interests as well as playing an active role in the generation of New (and non-class) Social Movements. The state becomes overloaded with the demands of their fragmented interests and thus further disorganized.

Parkin (1974) has also emphasized the significance of struggle (or 'action') in the identification of class boundaries, using the Weberian concepts of exclusion and 'closure'. Social closure refers to any pro-cess by which groups try to maintain access to social resources, and limit the access of others to them. Thus successful professionals, for example, both claim unique access to certain areas of employment and limit occupational access by requiring particular credentials. In their more bureaucratic forms, such credentials will be formal, university (or similar), qualifications, but exclusion can also incorporate status or prestige characteristics (for example, being the 'right type' or 'one of us') and, historically, has included ascribed characteristics such as gender and race. Strategies of exclusion are countered by solidaristic strategies of *usurpation*, where the excluded group struggles to acquire the privileges of the excluding group – through, for example, trade-union and/or political struggles. According to Parkin, 'class' bound-aries occur where strategies of exclusion and usurpation (solidarism) meet each other. Parkin's strategy of class differentiation is explicitly *processual*; indeed, through a focus on action, his approach seeks to avoid an 'attributional' approach in the determination of 'who goes where'. Thus in the case of lower-level white-collar workers, for example, Parkin would argue that it is not their non-manual status (or by extension, aspects of their 'work' or 'market' situations) which is of most significance, but rather the strategies by which they 'lay claim to and seek to justify rewards under changing material conditions' (1974: 15). He suggests that such workers are characterized by the fact that they engage in *dual* strategies of both exclusion (that is, credentialism) as well as solidarism (that is, trade-union activity).

The emphasis on action in Parkin's conceptualization means that although his extension of Weberian concepts has supplied numerous insights into the analysis of the *behaviour* of particular categories and occupational groups, it has not been particularly helpful as far as analyses of the (occupational) class structure as a whole are concerned. Indeed, Murphy (1984, 1986) has criticized Parkin's analysis of closure as moving too far in the direction of action, culminating in a completely non-structuralist, collective-action conception of class. However, in complete contrast to Parkin, structural Marxist responses to the 'problem of the middle classes' have focused almost entirely on the 'correct' location of these groups within the structure of employment, and have paid no attention to action whatsoever.

This discussion of the 'middle classes' has identified a number of different issues. These include, first, the question of how a class boundary should be drawn between these and other (usually working-class) groupings. Second, there is the question of whether particular groups should (or should not) be allocated to the 'middle class', and the appropriate criteria to be employed. Both of these topics have consequences for a third – the putative class interests and political allegiance of the middle class(es), and the role of these class(es) in the past and future development of capitalist societies. Recent work on the growth of the middle classes has also argued that their development has been crucially affected by the growth of consumer capitalism and a corresponding preoccupation with 'lifestyle'; this topic will be explored at some length in chapter 7.

The 'woman problem'

It is simply not possible to separate the question of the class position of women from the feminist critique, developed within sociology following the growth of 'second-wave' feminism in the 1960s. As feminists have argued, sociology, in common with the other social sciences, treated the social world – in particular, the 'public' sphere of paid employment, class and politics – as if it were gender-neutral, whereas it is, in fact, profoundly structured by gender differences. In the particular instance of class analysis, abstract class theories such as those of Marx and Weber had not considered gender – although

Marx's collaborator, Engels (1940), had written extensively on the issue. As far as measures of the occupational 'class structure' were concerned, an empirical convention had emerged where a woman was allocated the same class position as that of the male 'head of household'. This convention, albeit unconsciously, reflected the predominant division of market and domestic labour between the sexes characteristic of the mid-twentieth century, where the male 'breadwinner' went 'out to work' whilst women retained the primary responsibility for the domestic sphere.

It might be argued, therefore, that the conventional 'male model' of the occupational class structure simply reflected the *de facto* predominance of men within the structure of employment. For example Giddens wrote that: 'Given that women still have to await their liberation from the family, it remains the case in the capitalist societies that female workers are largely peripheral to the class system' (1973: 288). This convention, however, could not be sustained, given the continuing increase in women's employment which has taken place since the Second World War, together with feminist arguments which brought to prominence the reality of the gendered division of labour in both the public and private spheres of social life (Stacey 1981).

Thus when a major national investigation of the British class structure was published in the early 1980s (Goldthorpe 1980; 2nd edn 1987), it was subjected to extensive criticism on the grounds that it focused entirely on men, women only being included as wives. Goldthorpe has continued to defend the correctness of his empirical and theoretical stance, although he has more recently modified his original position in adopting, with Erikson, a 'dominance' strategy, in which the class position of the household is taken as that of the 'dominant' occupation in material terms – whether this occupation is held by a man or a woman (Erikson and Goldthorpe 1988). Nevertheless, the class position of women remains a highly contentious issue (Goldthorpe 1983, 1984; Heath and Britten 1984; Stanworth 1984; Crompton 1989).

It will be argued that much of the discussion relating to the proper 'class' location of women within the occupational structure may be described as a pseudo-debate. Within the position that Goldthorpe has taken up and is concerned to defend, his arguments are logically correct. Thus the initial charges of 'intellectual sexism' concerning Goldthorpe's work were somewhat misleading and have, indeed, served to deflect attention from the more serious limitations of his approach to 'class analysis'. His strategy, described in the last chapter, may be summarized as it relates to women as follows:

1　Class analysis starts with a structure of positions – that is, the Goldthorpe class scheme described in chapter 3.

2   The degree of *demographic class formation* which has taken place within this structure is then established empirically – that is, the extent to which classes are identifiable as collectivities whose members are associated with particular sets of positions over time. Thus the family (household) is the unit of class analysis, and patterns of social mobility are crucial to the identification of these collectivities ('classes').

3   The extent of *socio-political class formation* can then be determined – that is, the degree to which the classes so identified manifest similar lifestyles, patterns of action, socio-political attitudes, and so on.

Therefore:

4   As the family is the unit of 'class analysis', then the 'class position' of the family can be taken to be that of the head of the household – who will usually be a male. Thus arguments concerning the extent to which women are disadvantaged within the structure of employment merely serve to prove his point. As women's employment does not usually provide the main household income, the male head of household strategy is appropriate. Far from being a case of intellectual sexism, his approach actually recognizes the discrimination which women suffer.

5   To incorporate women's employment on the same terms as men's would obscure the pattern of demographic class formation. Many women work in lower-level white-collar jobs ('Intermediate' class locations in Goldthorpe's class scheme), and to incorporate their occupations would result in the generation of 'excessive' amounts of spurious social mobility which would confuse the issue considerably.

6   In respect of socio-political class formation, his empirical evidence has demonstrated that a woman's 'conjugal' class is in general more significant than her 'occupational' class in determining her socio-political attitudes. This finding gives further support to his overall strategy.

Goldthorpe has always assumed that discussions of 'class analysis' are encompassed completely within the particular approach that he has developed, and thus arguments and evidence which fall outside this may be safely discounted. In his exchange with Leiulfsrud and Woodward (1987), for example, the qualitative evidence they offer on the nature of conjugal roles in 'cross-class' families is dismissed as 'impressionistic' and 'just not adequate' (Erikson and Goldthorpe 1988). (Leiulsfrud and Woodward had argued that occupational class disparities within the household were reflected in gender roles – for example, who should stay at home with a sick child.) Rather, he seeks to reject their case using *aggregate* data, which demonstrate that: 'while a significant association exists between wife's class and wife's social imagery, a further significant association exists between *husband's* class and wife's imagery *and that this latter association is much stronger than the former'* (1988: 548; emphasis in original) – that is, he demonstrates his case via a finding corresponding to (6) above.

Nevertheless, the increase in women's employment presents serious difficulties for occupational-class schemes in general. A number of major problems may be identified, many of which relate to the persistence of occupational segregation (that is, the concentration of women and men into disproportionately 'female' and 'male' occupations). First, there is the problem of occupational sex-typing. The status, rewards, association with authority and so on (the 'work' and 'market' situation) of particular occupations has been determined historically (and in a downward direction) by the fact that they are 'women's' occupations, that is, according to presumptions about the nature of the likely incumbent, rather than according to the class processes structuring the occupation, its job content in a 'technicist' sense, and so on. A classic example of this process of sex-typing is to be found in the example of the secretary or 'office wife'. In Britain, the all-female profession of speech therapy is paid less than professions requiring a similar level of qualification and experience (Crompton and Sanderson 1990). The reality of occupational sex-typing has recently been legally recognized in 'equal-value' legislation. Thus it is just not the case, as Lockwood has argued, that 'it is the position of an occupation within some hierarchy of authority that is decisive for its status and not the sex of the person who happens to be in it' (1986: 21).

In any case, most occupational-class schemes (both 'commonsense' and 'theoretical') have been developed with reference to the structure of *male* employment. Thus they differentiate only poorly between women's jobs – a recent study of the British occupational class structure, for example, revealed that 39 per cent of women, but only 6 per cent of men, were in Goldthorpe's class III. Men were much more evenly distributed through the 'class' structure, the greatest concentration being the 23 per cent in class VII (Marshall et al. 1988: 74).

As well as changes in women's employment, developments in family and household structures have generated considerable difficulties in the application of occupational-class schemes. Goldthorpe's strategy of taking the (male) head of household as the unit of (class) analysis caused such a furore at least in part because it seemed to fly in the face of the empirical increase in female-headed households – which itself is associated with changing social mores in respect of matters such as divorce and non-married parenthood. At the empirical level, the 'unit of analysis' problem is probably best treated as a practical question (Duke and Edgell 1987; Marshall et al. 1988). In certain situations – for example, in labour-market and employment contexts – a woman's 'own' occupational class situation is probably the most appropriate measure to use. In respect of other factors – such as, for example, voting behaviour and social attitudes – there is a considerable amount of empirical evidence to the effect that 'household class' might be a more useful indicator. To use a simple example, a low-level female clerical worker married to a bricklayer is considerably more likely to vote Labour than a woman in a similar job who is married to an insurance manager – both women, however, would on an individual basis be in Goldthorpe's 'Intermediate' class. As with our discussion of the middle classes above, however, the discussion of the 'class' location of women concludes again with the question of attitudes, imagery and action – and it is to this problem of class analysis that we now turn.

The failure of class action

The question of the 'correct' location of an individual (or, more usually, a group) within the class structure has often been associated with the (implicit or explicit) assumption that class interests may be identified corresponding to their structural location, and likely class action then derived from these interests. This reasoning, therefore, moves from structure → consciousness → action (Pahl 1989). It might be thought to be a characteristically Marxist progression, but it is *not* specific to Marxist authors. For example, Erikson and Goldthorpe (1988) identify the need to investigate the conditions under which a 'class in itself' becomes a 'class for itself', that is, 'the conditions under which individuals who hold similar class positions do actually come to define their interests in class terms and to act collectively – for example, through class-based movements and organizations – in their pursuit' (cited in Müller 1990). Goldthorpe's analytical reasoning from class structure → demographic class formation → socio-political class formation reflects this linkage of structure → consciousness → action, but he regards this linkage as contingent, rather than inevitable.

In chapter 2, we saw how establishing the linkages between 'structure' and 'action' was not just a problem for class analysis in sociology, but for the social sciences more generally. One of the most influential critiques of the failure of class action, however, has been directed specifically at Marxist class theory and its development within sociology. Lockwood (1981) argues that Marxism's 'weakest link in the chain' (a phrase borrowed from Lenin's dictum that a chain is only as strong as its weakest link) lies in the inadequacy of Marx's theory of action, which, he argues, is basically utilitarian in inspiration. Thus in the Marxist account the capitalist is a 'rational miser', but the proletariat is expected to achieve a 'higher-order' rationality or reason – that is, to perceive that short-term advantage (for example, gains achieved in competition with other proletarians) will not necessarily lead to the long-term objective of socialism. Marxism explains proletarian deviations from rational action as being either 'irrational' – that is, due to ignorance, or error, as in the case of 'false consciousness'; or 'non-rational' – that is, as a consequence of ideological domination which results in the dominance of 'inappropriate' alternatives (for example, religion or nationalism) to socialist beliefs. Marxism, argues Lockwood, lacks the conceptual tools with which to consider non-rational beliefs and action systematically. Far from recognizing this as a problem, recent Marxist theorists have gone in the *other* direction. Here Lockwood is extremely critical of French structural Marxism as well as sociologists, such as Wright, who were influenced by it. Such debates, Lockwood argues, have not addressed the question of action at all but have instead become a controversy over objective 'places' in the class structure.

Similar criticisms of the Marxists' failure to give an account of action had already been developed in Pickvance's (1977) critique of the application of structuralist Marxist concepts in the field of urban sociology, in which 'the social force appears from the social base at a wave of the magic wand of organization' (p. 179). However, these criticisms, which are well taken, have been directed at a particular variant of Marxist analysis. There are also those who would consider themselves 'Marxists' – such as, for example the work of E. P. Thompson (discussed in chapter 2) – to whom it would be very difficult to apply these strictures.

Both Lockwood and Pickvance have directed their criticisms at the deficiencies of the structuralist-Marxist account of action, at the failure to make the links in the structure → consciousness → action chain. Both argue that insights drawn from Weber's work are appropriate for making these links, as Weber places value-orientations at the *centre* of his account of social action. The status order is a central element in a Weberian approach to social stratification. It might seem paradoxical, therefore, that non-Marxist sociologists have also been criticized for their failure to treat adequately the question of class action.

Thus Hindess has developed an extensive critique of Goldthorpe's approach to social class, arguing that it is reductionist, and that: 'Like the Marxism he rejects, Goldthorpe effectively reduces social elements of political life to products of an underlying social reality' (Hindess 1987: 93). Hindess argues that: 'classes are not social forces at all, and . . . they never have been' (1987: 8). 'Classes' are not actors, and they cannot act. Class analysis – and he is here referring to abstract conceptions of class as major social forces that arise out of fundamental structural features of society, together with the theoretical, 'relational' class schemes derived from these conceptions – gives no account of the *mechanisms* whereby parties, unions and so on can be said to act in terms of class interests. Rather, class analysis *asserts* the existence of a link between structural location and class interests, without demonstrating its existence.

Pahl's polemical account develops a similar critique of 'class analysis'. He argues that in sociology, 'class' has been used unproblematically to give an account of 'structure' in the structure → consciousness → action chain, but as the 'links in the chain' between structure, consciousness and action have not been identified, then 'class as a concept is ceasing to do any useful work for sociology' (1989: 710). However, it may be argued that the force of Pahl's argument is undermined by the fact that he fails to take account of the complexity of the different approaches to 'class analysis'. Pahl's rejection of the use of 'class' to describe an abstract force which explains political and social change rests uneasily alongside his enthusiastic endorsement of E. P. Thompson's approach to class analysis (1989: 717), given that Thompson's objective has been to demonstrate the relevance of class for our understanding of history. In fact, it may be suggested that Pahl's major target, which his discussion does not specifically identify, is the development of the tradition of 'class analysis' based upon the application of theoretical, relational class schemes – that is, the work of Goldthorpe and Wright (Crompton 1991). As has been described above, these authors do begin with the presumption that the starting-point of 'class analysis' lies in the identification of the class structure. Consciousness and action are then assumed to derive from this. Wright asserts that such progression is systematic, Goldthorpe, following Weber, makes no such assumptions and treats class action as contingent. Goldthorpe may therefore defend his approach from critics such as Hindess and Pahl on the grounds that they have imputed a determinism to his arguments which is simply not there (Goldthorpe and Marshall 1992).

However, neither Marxists nor non-Marxists working in the field of class analysis have provided a theoretically robust account of the analytical move between class 'structure' and consciousness/action. As another contributor to the debate sparked off by Pahl's polemic has argued (and as we have seen in chapter 2), such arguments reveal a much more deep-seated malaise in sociology – and the social sciences in general. Mullins (1991) argues that the sociological analysis of the social forces producing change – whatever these might be – are themselves seriously underdeveloped: 'there is little understanding of various social forces, such as class and consumption . . . [there] are gross deficiencies in sociological theory, since most of what is called theory is not theory, but a mix of critique, philosophy, history and taxonomies' (1991: 119). A 'general theory of action' has not yet been achieved. There is no dominant theoretical paradigm in sociology which might provide a comfortable prop (as did, briefly, normative functionalism in the 1950s), for the sociologist's analysis and explanation of social structure and action. However, sociology's *de facto* reliance on an eclectic mix of middle-range theory and historical insights, it may be suggested, does at least reflect the complexity of the phenomena under investigation.

Alternative sources of social identification and action

Two related strands of argument may be identified in respect of debates concerning the significance of non-class factors for identify and action. These are first, the *relative* significance of 'class', as compared to other sources of social differentiation, in the structuring and perpetuation of social inequality. Such factors are often ascribed, rather than achieved, and include 'traditional' or conventional distinctions deriving from gender, ethnicity and age, as well as nationhood and 'citizenship' (see chapter 6). Second, it has been argued that 'class' is of declining significance as a source of social identity in late capitalist societies. The focus of class-based organizations, such as trade unions, and class-based political parties has been increasingly upon issues related to distribution rather than matters relating to control and autonomy within the process of production itself. Thus access to, and the maintenance of, *consumption* have become the major issues contended for by different groups – and consumption claims do not relate neatly to class categories. Indeed, they may play their part in transforming class categories. For example, once organized labour has achieved basic rights and market protections, then they may be characterized (and indeed, may think of themselves) as 'taxpayers' rather than as a particularly deprived or 'class' category (Bauman 1982: 168).

The question of gender has already been discussed in relation to the location of women within the occupational class structure. However, this particular aspect of the debate might be viewed as something of a side issue as compared to the larger questions which the revitalization of feminism raised for class theory in general. 'Patriarchy' – the domination of women by men – was held to be more significant than 'class' in shaping women's situation. Some feminist writers have argued that the bases of patriarchy are largely ideological, rather than material. For example, Mitchell (1975) used psychoanalytic concepts in combination with those of structuralist anthropology in order to argue that patriarchal ideology is deeply rooted in human culture. However, much of the feminist debate from the 1960s onwards was conducted in a dialogue with Marxism, and the question of the relationship between gender and class was seen as of central significance.

For example, the 'domestic labour debate' (Seccombe 1974) was an attempt to locate women's labour, and thus the nature of their exploitation, within a Marxist analysis of the capitalist mode of production. Engels (1940) had differentiated between the bourgeois family, where the wife received board and lodging in return for the production of legitimate heirs to bourgeois property, and the proletarian family, where both husband and wife were exploited through wage labour. This materialist analysis was widely interpreted to imply that the 'liberation' of women lay in drawing them into wage-labour relationships, whence both men and women could subsequently transform their proletarian condition. However, as feminists argued, this analysis ignored women's domestic work, as well as the social and ideological domination of women. Marxist theorists of 'domestic labour' attempted to demonstrate that women's labour in the domestic sphere made a contribution to the generation of surplus value, and thus the exploitation of women could be identified as an element in specifically *capitalist* production relationships.

These arguments have not proved particularly persuasive or long-lasting (Molyneux 1979). However, a broadly materialist account of women's oppression within capitalism is still influential (Barrett 1980; 1988), but it is not one which attempts to reduce the nature of women's oppression to the workings of the capitalist system (as the 'domestic labour' analysis had done). Rather, the object of these authors has been to identify a material system of patriarchy which articulates with capitalism. Hartmann's (1981) initial statement of 'dual systems' theory has been extremely infuential in setting the terms of this debate: 'Capitalist development creates the places for a hierarchy of workers, but traditional Marxist categories cannot tell us who will fill which places. Gender and racial hierarchies determine who fills the empty places.' Thus 'patriarchy' is being described as a system equivalent or similar to 'class' in shaping the occupational structure, and women are seen as suffering a double disadvantage – by virtue of their sex, as well as in their employment.

The material disadvantages of women in respect of employment have already been described in our discussion of occupational segregation. Women have been concentrated in less well-paid, sex-typed occupations; disadvantaged in the labour market as a consequence of their domestic and childrearing obligations; and, until relatively recently, excluded by men from access to many of the better-paying and more prestigious occupational roles (Walby 1986; Crompton and Sanderson 1990). The material *consequences* of the social position of women are so great that they cannot be denied; an important question for class analysis, however, is whether male/female differentiation is also a significant *source* of collective, and persisting, social identity and action.

Lockwood has argued that it is not. As gender relations are usually heterosexual, they are cross-cut by class and status relations; thus the economic and associational relationships between men and women are highly fragmented. There are thus 'powerful objections to the claim that gender relations are macrosocial phenomena of the same order as classes and status groups' (1986: 15). These kinds of argument would be disputed by many feminists (Walby 1988, 1990). The introduction of Equal Opportunities legislation in many industrialized countries has furnished a context in which women, as women, may pursue the material advantage of their sex, and they have not been reluctant to do so (Equal Opportunities Commission 1990). National campaigns such as those associated with the women's refuge movement, and abortion legislation, have also united women as a group – although it must be conceded that these issues have divided, as well as united, them (but is there unity amongst the 'working class'?). It should be recgnized that, in the changing circumstances of late twentieth-century capitalist industrialism, gender and sexuality are emerging as coherent focuses of social organization.

It has been argued that ethnicity and 'race' are similar phenomena to gender in that the patterns of social discrimination and disadvantage with which they are associated are *socially*, rather than biologically, constructed (Barrett 1980; 1988). The persistence of discrimination on racial grounds has been extensively documented, and the point need not be laboured here (Jenkins 1988). However (and in some contrast to gender), race and ethnic organization *has* for long been a significant focus of organized social identity. Ethnic divisions may at times have been advantageous to capital – for example, in the creation and maintenance of a supply of cheap and flexible labour – but capital did not create these divisions. They cannot be simply regarded as epiphenomena of class processes.

Thus there are significant sources of social differentiation, which have material consequences for the structuring of inequality, which cannot be simply reduced to the workings of class processes. These criticisms have been paralleled by the argument that, although 'class' may have had some relevance as an explanatory concept in the nineteenth century, it is declining in significance as far as late twentieth-century industrial societies are concerned. The significance of 'class' as a basis of political organization has also been challenged. Collective action is increasingly organized on a 'non-class' basis; 'social movements' (including feminism) have assumed more significance than class politics (Turner 1986: 89–90). Many of these arguments have focused on the significance of *consumption*, or 'modes of life' (Offe 1985a).

Unfortunately, arguments relating to consumption have tended to reflect the confusion of debates and evidence which has increasingly characterized class and stratification analysis. It will be suggested here that three interrelated, although different, dimensions may be usefully identified. These are, first, the growing emphasis on the cultural significance of consumption in both the *construction* of collective or class identities and the maintenance of positions of advantage and disadvantage. Second, there is the debate within urban sociology in Britain concerning the significance of consumption sectors for a range of behavioural and attitudinal factors, including voting behaviour. Third, there are a broader set of arguments relating to the importance of consumption as a *focus* for collective action in late twentieth-century industrial societies, and the consequences of this for 'class' identities. As we shall see, these debates tend to be associated with different methodological approaches to the study of class and stratification processes.

The first set of arguments emphasizes the growing significance of consumption in the everyday concerns of individuals and families. Whereas 'class' or occupation may have been a significant source of social identity and action during a period in which work was for the majority insecure, arduous and absorbed the greater part of the day (and lifetime, given the generally shorter life expectancy which prevailed); this is no longer the case. Not only is work less invasive as far as the individual is concerned, and people have more time to consume, but also, as material living standards have risen, so the facility for consumption has expanded. As Pahl has put it: 'If the symbol of the nineteenth century city was the factory chimney, the equivalent symbol at the end of the twentieth century in Europe and North America is surely the shopping mall' (1989: 718–19). Many of the arguments relating to the significance of consumption, therefore, suggest that more of an emphasis should be given to the cultural, rather than the economic, construction of 'class', and class identity, in the 'postmodernist' capitalist consumer societies of today. These debates will be explored in chapter 7.

In Britain, arguments relating to the significance of consumption have also been of considerable importance within the 'new urban sociology'. Saunders (1987) has developed a 'sociology of consumption' which he offers as an alternative to the 'sociology of production', or 'class':

> a major fault line is opening up in countries like Britain between a majority of people who can service their key consumption requirements through the market and a minority who remain reliant on an increasingly inadequate and alienative form of direct state provision. This division, arising out of the social relations of consumption, is, it is argued,

becoming as if not more significant than the more familiar class divisions. (*1987: 290*)

The major consumption cleavage which Saunders identifies is between, on the one hand, those whose incomes, housing needs, as well as transport, education, and health requirements, are met by the state and, on the other, those whose needs are met by the purchase of such services in the private market. It has also been argued that this shift has been reflected in the phenomenon of 'class dealignment' in voting behaviour – in particular, the decline in the Labour share of the working-class vote. These arguments will be examined in subsequent chapters. Saunders has also been extremely critical of what he perceives to be a 'left-wing' and 'Marxist' bias in British sociology; a bias which he also sees as reflected in both the 'realist' approach ('there are, as far as I know, no examples in contemporary social science of non-Marxist realist work'; 1987: 361) as well as the attachment to the 'class' concept. He is critical of 'realism' (particularly in urban sociology) because it accords explanatory primacy to causes which can only identified theoretically and are therefore immune to empirical testing: 'realism', he argues, is 'a revised and more subtle form of Althusserianism' (1990: 360).[8] Thus Saunders strenuously rejects the utility of the 'class' concept, a rejection which includes Weberian, as well as Marxist, sociologists:

> resources today are allocated not only on the basis of market power, but also by a political logic determined by the exercise of state power. Yet the significance of this change has not generally been recognized in theories of social stratification, for whether Marxist or Weberian, they continue to employ essentially nineteenth-century ideas to analyse late twentieth-century conditions. (*1987: 319*).[9]

As we shall see in chapter 7, the empirical contours of the debate concerning 'consumption-sector cleavages' have been largely shaped by the terrain marked out by occupational-class analysis. That is, the explanatory power of 'occupational class' on the one hand, and 'consumption sector' on the other, has been systematically investigated in relation to a number of attitudinal and behavioural factors.

In contrast, the third set of arguments relating to consumption which has been identified above have drawn upon broader socio-historical analyses of societal developments. Authors such as Bauman (1982), Lash and Urry (1987) and Offe (1985a) have all argued that the emphasis on distributive issues, which became, increasingly, the focus of organized class action during the twentieth century, has culminated in the increasing dominance of consumption issues within contemporary political debates. Such arguments have a long pedigree. In the 'Eighteenth Brumaire' Marx (1962a) described Louis Bonaparte's use of 'liquor and sausages' (p. 333) in order to gain support for his manoeuvrings in mid-nineteenth-century France; Sombart's (1906) commentary on the United States noted that 'All socialist utopias have come to grief on roast beef and apple pie', and during the 1960s boom in the West after the Second World War, the 'affluent worker' (Zweig 1961) was similarly held to be preoccupied more with consumption than class identities. (These disparate arguments, it may be noted, have all tended to focus on the lower or working class.)

After the Second World War, it is argued, the conditions of the postwar boom were sustained by (amongst other factors) a class compromise which in fact rested upon the organized power of the male, full-time, permanently employed working class. This class compromise rested upon a structure of welfare benefits and employment protections which could only be met through continuing economic growth. It was, however, inherently an unstable compromise and, as described in the first section of this chapter, the system became increasingly incapable of meeting the demands placed upon it, such as maintaining an 'expected' level of wage increases without too much erosion of profit margins. In addition, new obstacles to growth, such as the demands of the 'Third World', and the fragility and finite nature of environmental resources, began to emerge; the crisis subsequent upon the massive rise in the world price of oil in 1973 encompassed both of these issues (Bauman 1982). However, largely because of the economic, technological and labour-force changes which have been described at the beginning of this chapter, the rhetoric of 'class' no longer provided a framework through which opposition to the effects of the economic crisis (rising unemployment, welfare cuts etc.) could be generated. This is in part because of the globalization of capitalism itself. Lash and Urry (1987) argue, for example, that corporatist compromises – such as that attempted within the framework of the 'Social Contract' in Britain in the 1970s – can only take place within the framework of the nation state. With the internationalization of capitalism, the state begins to lose control over important economic processes. The homogeneity of working-class organizations is further fragmented by the single-union and company agreements sought by international capital – such as, for example, those between the Electricians and the Murdoch empire following the transfer of the Murdoch newspapers to Wapping, or the single-union agreements between Japanese car manufacturers in Britain and the Amalgamated Engineering Union (AEU) (now Amalgamated Engineering and Electrical Union).

Such arguments, therefore, suggest that the language of 'class' no longer corresponds to either the organizational capacities, or the primary concerns, of the late capitalist labour force:

> the spread of new powers . . . typical of consumer society . . . is . . . a 'de-civilising process'. Passions, self-indulgence, entertainment are cleansed of disgrace . . . The new powers are articulated in terms of self-identity . . . etc. . . . and none of these articulations has a room for the traditional oppositions. (*Bauman 1982: 180*)

These kinds of argument rest upon extensive historical analyses of the development of industrial societies in the West. Their in-depth evaluation is outside the scope of this book, although we will be returning to a number of these issues in subsequent chapters. There is a simple but important point, however, which should be briefly stated. Even if commentators such as Bauman and Offe proved to be broadly correct in their assertions that 'class' is losing, or has lost, its capacity to act as a source of collective identity and organization, the *work* that people do is nevertheless likely to remain as the most important indicator of their 'life chances' and patterns of material advantage and disadvantage more generally. Employment-based class schemes, therefore, will continue to describe the considerable extent of material inequalities, in capitalist societies and these inequalities will, to varying degrees, be reproduced across the generations. Thus those working within the occupational or employment-aggregate approach to class analysis will be able to continue to demonstrate the association between 'class' – as they have defined it – and a range of other factors, and thus to assert the continuing significance of 'class' in the late twentieth century. These arguments, however, represent only one particular approach to 'class analysis', and cannot, therefore, be realistically expected to resolve conclusively the many issues raised by the range of debates within class theory and analysis as a whole.

Conclusion

This chapter has examined the manner in which different class theorists have attempted to grapple with the implications of the many changes in twentieth-century Western industrialism. As we have seen, these responses have not always been particularly convincing. Is 'class', therefore, as Saunders and Pahl have argued, an irrelevance in the late twentieth century? Has sociology lost its way and become but a victim of its political preferences? It will be argued that neither of these arguments can be sustained. However, if the class concept is to retain its utility in sociological investigation, it is necessary to achieve rather more by way of understanding of its definition and scope than is at present the case, and this will be the aim of the next chapter.

Notes

1 This historical period has been described as one of 'Butskellism'; a term derived from the surnames of two 'moderate' party leaders of the contemporary left and right – Hugh Gaitskell and R. A. B. Butler.

2 It may be suggested, however, that the legislation which accompanied the 'social contract' – notably in respect of Equal Pay, and Sex Discimination and Equal Opportunities legislation, has proved to have far-reaching social consequences in extending 'citizenship' rights to these categories.

3 Private industry had not participated in the corporatist deal, and wages in the private sector had risen sharply as a consequence of inflation.

4 An influential political account has been developed by intellectuals associated with the journal *Marxism Today*. It should be noted that although *Marxism Today* was officially a journal of the Communist Party in Britain, many of the contributors have never been members of the Communist Party and the journal was in any case from its inception associated with the right-wing, 'Eurocommunist' faction within the party. It should therefore be seen as a forum for left intellectuals, rather than Communist Party members.

5 'The idea of a world organized through a stable ensemble of essential forms is the central presupposition in the philosophies of Plato and Aristotle. The basic illusion of metaphysical thought resides precisely in this unawareness of the historicity of being. It is only in the contemporary world, when technological change and the dislocating rhythm of capitalist transformation constantly alter the discursive sequences which construct the reality of objects, that the merely historical character of being becomes fully visible' (Laclau and Mouffe 1987: 97).

6 For example, DeVault's (1990) careful study of turn-of-the-century Pittsburgh demonstrates that white-collar wage levels – even in quite modest jobs – were generally higher than those of the manual jobs available at the time.

7 This is only the briefest of summaries of Poulantzas's arguments relating to this topic, which are extremely complex. However, the influence of his work has declined considerably, and it would not be justified to devote the amount of space to their exposition which a full account would require.

8 This point raises important questions relating to the philosophy of science. These will not be explored here (see Chalmers 1982 for a readable introduction to the topic for a non-philosopher). The position being taken in this book is that whereas it is incumbent upon the social scientist to provide empirical data and explanations, the theory-dependence of important (observational) categories in the social sciences, particularly in

respect of 'class', means that comprehensive falsification – which is often a major objective of empirical testing – is not a possibility. It might be noted that Saunders would share with Goldthorpe a commitment to the primacy of empirical testing.

9   There can be little doubt of the strength of Saunders's feelings on this issue: 'Those social analysts who insist on continuing to view the late-twentieth-century world through the blinkers of nineteenth-century social theories will increasingly be at a loss to make sense of the changes going on around them' (1990: 336).

5

Rethinking 'Class Analysis'

Introduction

The argument which will be developed in this chapter is that the most fruitful way forward, as far as class and stratification analysis is concerned, is not to attempt to mount a defence of 'class analysis' as a whole, but to begin by recognizing the diversity of the different approaches within it. The major theoretical dichotomy in the field of class analysis has been conventionally viewed as being that between Marxist and Weberian approaches (McNall et al. 1991: 1). However, in the course of the preceding chapters, a number of other dichotomies, methodological as well as theoretical, have emerged relating to the study of class and stratification. These dichotomies should not be regarded as representing impermeable boundaries between different approaches, but nevertheless, their identification is a useful heuristic device for the exploration of class and stratification analysis.

In chapter 1 an underlying difference of emphasis was identified between, on the one hand, the use of 'class' as a straightforward descriptive term to indicate the contours of material and social inequality – most usually, through the identification of aggregates of employment or occupations – and, on the other, the use of the term to suggest entities which correspond, in some manner, to the structures and relations of power and advantage which have produced these inequalities. As far as the latter use of the term is concerned, descriptive employment or occupational aggregates might be held to give some kind of empirical indication of these entities, but not necessarily to describe them in any exact sense. However, class analysts such as Goldthorpe and Wright *have* attempted to provide theoretically sophisticated measures of the structure of employment which, it is

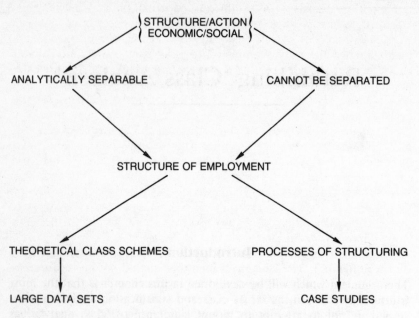

FIGURE 3   *Dichotomies in class and stratification analysis*

argued, also describe 'classes' empirically as structures of power and advantage.

Resting upon these differences of emphasis is a further set of distinctions. First, a distinction may be drawn between, on the one hand, those sociologists whose work reflects an analytical separation between (class) 'structure' and (class) 'action' and, on the other, those who treat 'structure' and 'action' as a unity. The latter assume structure to be activity-dependent, so that, empirically, class structure cannot be treated separately from class consciousness or action. These rather different methodological stances have been taken by both Marxists and Weberians. Second, within the broader tradition of stratification analysis, the significance of non-economic factors for social differentiation has been emphasized to a greater extent than within class analysis. The extent to which social or cultural, as contrasted to economic, factors should be taken into account in the identification of social classes – and, indeed, whether 'economic' and 'social' factors can be analytically separated – is a further dichotomy which may be identified. A feature common to all class and stratification analysts who seek to explain, rather than simply to describe, material and social inequalities is that identifiable groups are regarded as emerging from the predominant relationships of production, distribution and exchange in capitalist industrial societies. A distinction may be drawn between Marxist approaches, which emphasize the significance of production, and Weberian theorists, who lay more of an emphasis on life chances in the market. Besides property, therefore, employment relationships in capitalist industrialism have been regarded as the major locus within which 'classes' can be identified. Those assuming the analytical separation of 'structure' and 'action' have developed theoretical, relational class schemes which may be mapped on to the structure of employment. These schemes may be either Marxist or Weberian, and those working within this approach to 'class analysis' have often worked at the macro-level, applying advanced statistical techniques to large data sets. In contrast, those regarding structure as activity-dependent have tended to focus upon the *processes* of occupational and class structuring, and their empirical work has involved some variant of the case-study approach.

A schematic representation of a number of these dichotomies is shown in figure 3. The categories identified should not be regarded as describing coherently differentiated approaches to class and stratification analysis, rather the figure represents an organizing strategy for the identification of different tendencies within this diverse field.[1] Indeed, it may be argued that the immediate objectives of the different approaches identified are in fact complementary – for example, the categories of theoretical class schemes cannot be formulated without recourse to case-study evidence. 'Market' and 'work' situations, for example, are key elements governing the location of occupations within Goldthorpe's class scheme. However, we can only assess the nature of the 'work' situation of a particular occupation within the organizational context – which can only be investigated through some variant of the case-study method (Crompton 1990a).

Nevertheless, a failure to recognize this *de facto* diversity of approach has often led to pseudo-debates. By 'pseudo-debate' is meant that class theorists may be arguing on the basis of very different definitions of basic concepts, such as 'class'. It can also refer to significant differences between the protagonists in their underlying theoretical and methodological assumptions regarding the nature of social science investigation – for example, between those who treat structure and action as a unity, and those who regard them as analytically separable. These differences, however, are often left implicit rather than made explicit. Thus arguments about the continuing significance (or otherwise) of 'class' have often taken the form of arguments concerning the continuing strength of the association between occupation (or job) and a variety of attitudinal and behavioural factors. That is, class is equated, in a relatively unproblematic fashion, with occupational or employment aggregates – or, to put the matter in a slightly different fashion, the 'employment-aggregate' approach is implicitly taken to represent 'class analysis' as a whole. Additionally, often no distinction is made between the different class schemes which are available. For example, Pahl, in developing his case relating to the growing significance of 'consumption', rather than 'class', suggests that this is demonstrated by the fact that market researchers now prefer 'lifestyle' to 'class' measures (1989: 714). Thus 'class' is being taken to be adequately described by occupational or job measures – indeed, *any* such measure. Similarly, arguments concerning the political significance of class have been conducted through an examination of the statistical association between occupational class categorizations and voting intentions and behaviour. Trenchant critics of class analysis such as Saunders have used this kind of evidence to demonstrate the declining significance of class.[2] Conversely, defenders such as Marshall and his colleagues have argued, on the basis of data which demonstrate a fluctuating, but not consistent, association between occupational class(es) and voting patterns that: 'Social class and social class identities are no less salient today than during earlier periods commonly acknowledged as being characterized by "class voting"' (1988: 260).

All too often, arguments concerning the relevance of 'class' fail to distinguish between 'commonsense' and 'theoretical' class schemes – even amongst those working within an employment-aggregation approach to class. As Saunders points out, for example, Dunleavy's arguments concerning the significance of consumption sector have been empirically demonstrated 'using both the advertising industry's grading scheme and neo-Marxist class theory (!)' (Saunders 1990b: 221). Heath and his colleagues have argued for the superiority of the (theoretical) Goldthorpe class scheme over the more commonly used dichotomous (or commonsense) measures in the analysis of patterns of voting behaviour in Britain (Heath et al. 1991; Sarlvik and Crewe 1983). They argue that the Goldthorpe class categories have greater construct validity – that is, the Goldthorpe class measure is closer to the underlying theoretical term ('class') than the simple manual/non-manual division of the psephologists. These arguments have been reinforced by comparing the strength of the association between the categories identified by the different schemes and the phenomena they purport to explain (voting behaviour).[3] Heath et al. are surely correct to argue that occupational-class measures should be modified in order to reflect the transformations of the occupational structure; put simply, it should be recognized that the old or conventional manual/non-manual boundary is outdated. They are therefore right to adopt a measure which reflects the differentiation within the category of non-manual occupations. Debates concerning the utility of the measure, however, do not conclusively demonstrate the relative significance of 'class' (by which is meant occupation) to late twentieth-century politics (by which is meant voting).

The extent to which occupation is related to vote *is* a significant issue. However, the strength of the association between occupation and voting intention does not constitute sufficient evidence with which to resolve the much larger debates concerning the significance – or otherwise – of class identities and action in contemporary societies. It will be argued in the next section that 'classes' and class processes cannot be adequately analysed through employment or occupational aggregations alone. The explanatory power of the 'class' concept rests in the assumption that classes are regarded as significant social collectivities. Social collectivities can only be fully investigated in their context, and must therefore be studied in relation to the institutions and organizations which articulate their claims – trade unions, political parties, and so on. This requires a methodological approach extending beyond that of survey analysis.

However, another source of pseudo-debate occurs when evidence and data regarded as valid within the context of a particular approach to 'class analysis' are not regarded as legitimate within another. For example, we have already seen in chapter 4 that, in respect of debates relating to women and class analysis, Goldthorpe would only accept as relevant evidence deriving from large-scale data sets, and ethnographic and/or case-study data would be rejected as inadequate. Similarly, Rose et al. (1987) have argued that ethnographic or case-study evidence which apparently demonstrates the 'deskilling' or 'proletarianization' of supervisory employees cannot be accepted in its own right, but has to be assessed against the evidence of large-scale survey data. These arguments assume that the 'class' concept *is* adequately conceptualized through the application of 'theoretical' or 'relational' class schemes to the occupational order – an assumption which, as we shall see, is highly problematic.

Debates and disputes within class analysis, therefore, are often characterized by an extensive borrowing and mixing of evidence and arguments from different approaches, with the unfortunate result that the protagonists are often to be found talking past, rather than to, each other. A common feature of pseudo-debates in class analysis is that they often stem from a major, if unacknowledged, dichotomy within the field – between, on the one hand, approaches which take 'classes' to be occupational or employment aggregates and, on the other, the socio-historical investigation of the processes of class structuring and their consequences. Thus, in a fairly straightforward fashion, a wide range of theoretical debates within class analysis have been treated as capable of being resolved by the correlation of attitudinal and other variables against occupational- or employment-class aggregates. This would be a viable strategy if such aggregates *did* actually represent 'classes' in a theoretical sense, or if there were general agreement as to the empirical definition of the class concept – but neither of these conditions applies. The sociological convention of treating occupational or employment aggregates as 'classes' has had, and continues to have, many fruitful applications, but it has also been a major source of confusion.

The problematic nature of employment 'class'

In contemporary industrial societies, occupation is an extremely powerful indicator of an interrelated network of social advantage and disadvantage. The appropriateness of various measures of employment class, as compared to other indices of social differentiation, is open to discussion (Marsh 1986). It is not being suggested that we should abandon the use of such schemes. The empirical association between measures of employment class and structures of inequality and 'life chances', as well as between employment class and aspects of social attitudes and behaviour, is of continuing significance to sociologists (and not just sociologists; neither political parties nor advertisers, for example, are exactly indifferent to who votes for whom or who buys what). However, if evidence relating to employment aggregates is to be used in wider theoretical debates relating to the significance of 'class' in society and politics, then we have to be confident that these aggregates do, indeed, represent 'classes' in a Marxist and/or Weberian sense – that is that they represent real entities with identifiable interests and capacities to act. The frequency of the assumption that this *is* the case has been reinforced by the theoretical claims of authors such as Goldthorpe and Wright; but are they, in fact, valid?

There are a number of good reasons for arguing that even the most sophisticated variants of employment-based class schemes do not represent theoretical 'classes' in this sense. Such schemes have always been susceptible to the criticism that their procedures have allocated particular jobs or occupations to the 'wrong' categories. The 'unpacking' of Wright's class categories, for example, reveals a number of apparent anomalies. His 'semi-autonomous' category was found by Marshall and colleagues to include 'everyone from lawyers and doctors, on the one hand, to hospital orderlies and fork lift truck drivers, on the other. And . . . there are a number of cleaners, caretakers, and domestic helpers in the group' (Marshall et al. 1988: 51). In short, this evidence highlights the simple fact, long familiar to sociologists of work and employment, that actual employment situations are structured by many other factors besides capitalist production relationships. In the particular case of work autonomy, work *context* is of considerable significance. Many jobs which might be thought to be objectively 'working-class', such as milk roundspersons, or park keepers, nevertheless allow their occupants considerable autonomy on a day-to-day basis – and indeed, there is evidence that some workers actively seek out this kind of employment (Blackburn and Mann 1979). Marshall and his colleagues have argued that Goldthorpe's class scheme is superior to Wright's. However, Goldthorpe's scheme, like Wright's, involves the aggregation of non-comparable jobs and occupations – particularly within the 'service class' – whose 'work' and 'market' situations, as well as their political attitudes, are very different from each other (Savage 1991).[4]

Variations in work context are not the only factors structuring work and occupations. As we have seen, the occupational structure is also segmented by gender and race. It is not the case, as Hartmann (1981) has argued, that 'capitalism creates a structure of empty places' and then 'gender and racial hierarchies fill the places'; the 'places' themselves have often been actively created as gendered occupations. Occupational organizations, such as trade unions and, more particularly, professional bodies, can act so as to change the relative ranking of particular occupations. In short, the occupational structure is fluid, is socially constructed by a variety of other factors besides 'class' processes, and 'no individual sociologist can claim to have found the philosopher's stone which, on being applied to any [employment] situation, will produce 24-carat "classes"' (Crompton 1991: 112).

Thus 'market' and 'work' situations, as well as power and organization assets, skills and credentials (the criteria through which individuals are allocated within Goldthorpe's and Wright's class schemes), are in fact shaped by a number of factors including cultural, spatial and technical contexts, wider political processes, and the gender, race and age of the likely occupant of the position in question. In addition, both Goldthorpe and Wright are susceptible to the more general criticism that the employment aggregates (or 'classes') they identify do not in themselves constitute class *actors*, and that the account each provides of the processes whereby aggregate 'structures' are transformed into 'actors' is inadequately specified.[5]

Nevertheless, the class structure = occupational structure equation is deeply entrenched in sociology. As we have seen, debates concerning the utility of employment class as a measure have often been confused with arguments concerning the utility of 'class analysis' in general. This tendency has been exacerbated by Goldthorpe's and Wright's claims to have developed strategies of class analysis which reproduce empirically this elusive concept. As all-encompassing approaches to class analysis, however, their strategies must be counted as heroic failures. Goldthorpe and Wright may be viewed as the leading practitioners of a distinctive sociological approach to class analysis which was developed during the 1960s and 1970s. The impetus for this approach, as has been described in previous chapters, came from the use of theoretical accounts of 'social class', drawn from the work of Marx and Weber in order to develop theoretical, relational employment classifications which described the 'class structure' – as we shall see, it was considered particularly important to distinguish between 'class' and 'status'. These accounts were then operationalized through the large-scale sample survey, a method of research whose capacities were enormously enhanced by the advent of computers and electronic data processing. This approach brings together, within a single framework, the theoretical analysis of social class with the empirical analysis of class inequalities and class structures. It is an approach with tremendous promise, but also severe limitations. As we have seen, there are insoluble difficulties in the identification of 'class' independently of the other factors which structure employment relations, and the nature of the links between class structure and class consciousness or action cannot be sufficiently explored through survey data. Both Goldthorpe and Wright are clear that the concept of 'class' refers to social *relationships*, but these relationships cannot be adequately grasped through approaches which rest, in the last instance, on the aggregation of individual attributes (Ingham 1970).

Both Goldthorpe and Wright, therefore, as well as those involved in the debates surrounding their work (such as Marshall, Saunders and Pahl) might be described as being engaged in discussions of 'long-term developments in the employment structure'; 'the inheritance of occupational inequality' or 'the relative significance of "occupation" as a variable in attitudinal research' rather than as delivering the final word on social-class analysis. For example, when Saunders writes that: 'It is often thought that the British class system is closed and rigid, but we have seen that this is not the case' (1990a: 130), what he actually means is: 'Although some have argued otherwise, the extent of mobility within the occupational hierarchy in Britain is actually quite high.'

Goldthorpe and Marshall (1992) have in fact noted the limited nature of their claims in a defence of their position. 'Classes' are explicitly defined as 'employment relations', and the approach to 'class analysis' they represent is described as a research programme within which a range of theories may be formulated and empirically assessed. As detached scientific observers, they claim no commitment to any particular theory or theories of class, or of history.[6] The question of class consciousness and action is regarded as contingent. As evidence of the successes of their research programme they cite: establishing the commonalities of relative social fluidity (and thus occupational mobility) in advanced industrial societies; demonstrating the empirical link between occupational class and educational inheritance; and showing the persisting association between occupational class and voting behaviour. As they argue, 'class analysis in our sense may well then appear as a far more limited project, intellectually as well as politically, than in its Marxist form' (1992: 15). A variety of protagonists are identified by Goldthorpe and Marshall in their defence of their position, including Pahl, Saunders, Offe, Holton and Turner. They are correct to point out that many of their critics have not fully comprehended their own particular approach to 'class analysis' – although some of their 'critics' (Offe 1985, Holton and Turner 1989) have not, in fact, directly engaged with their work and are clearly working with a very different conception of 'class analysis' to the occupational-aggregate approach they favour (this might be described as an example of pseudo-debate). Indeed, Goldthorpe and Marshall's defence of their own position has the perhaps unintended consequence of excluding from consideration a whole range of approaches to 'class analysis' which differ from their own. In particular, those approaches which have focused directly upon the processes of class structuring, or class formation, are not considered.

One of the major targets of their anti-Marxist arguments is Wright. Wright is explicitly committed to the empirical development of Marxist class analysis, and is therefore committed to a particular theory of class and of history. Wright has recently reaffirmed his commitment to a Marxist position:

> the Marxist tradition . . . continues to provide . . . the most comprehensive and compelling theoretical framework within which to understand the possibilities for and obstacles to emancipatory social change . . . The choice between Marxist and Weberian concepts of class . . . is not . . . a choice between concepts with equal theoretical standing . . . the choice . . . is not between two theories of society, but between a theory and a nontheory. (*1989: 319–20*)

The ultimate incommensurability of the theoretical assumptions underlying these two different approaches (those of Goldthorpe and Marshall and of Wright) to 'class analysis' suggests that, despite the underlying similarity of their methodological approach, an empirical resolution of the issues which divide them is simply not possible.[7]

Nevertheless, it must be counted as a major strength of the employment-aggregation approach to class analysis that its results are amenable to empirical test and assessment. Even though Wright is operating within a very different theoretical framework to that of

Goldthorpe and Marshall, for example, Wright's work still represents the major attempt to provide a 'repertoire of Marxist class structure concepts capable of effective deployment in concrete, micro-level analysis' (1989: 346). In response to theoretical and empirical criticisms, he has developed a complex range of concepts which, he suggests, are applicable to the analysis of 'class' at different levels of abstraction – and these solutions may be judged as more or less appropriate in respect of particular empirical investigations (Edgell and Duke 1991). Moving away from the specifics of Wright's and Goldthorpe's work, the utility of the occupational aggregational approach to class analysis for the investigation of structured social inequality, and the effectiveness of social policies devised in respect of such inequalities, can hardly be doubted.

It is being argued here, therefore, that employment-based measures are useful, but by no means comprehensive, indicators of class inequalities and class relations. One obvious difficulty as far as their utility as a measure of inequality is concerned is that employment is not a reliable indicator of wealth holdings. Gender is another important aspect of inequality which is not adequately captured by existing schemes. The persistence of occupational segregation means that many such schemes, which were initially constructed in relation to the structure of male employment, do not reflect the reality of women's paid work. In addition, the lifetime participation in the labour market for most women in Western industrial societies is rather different from that of men, being characterized by features such as part-time work and periods of withdrawal from paid employment.[8] It is somewhat problematic to allocate an employment-based 'class situation' to non-employed women, or part-time workers, and the occupational class of the household, or 'main breadwinner', has often been used a way round this problem.

A number of other practical strategies have also been suggested to accommodate these difficulties. Studies of women's employment, such as, for example, the Department of Employment's *Women and Employment* survey (Martin and Roberts 1984) have devised occupational scales specifically for women. Other researchers have used data relating to the 'market situation' of women's occupations to derive gender-specific occupational class schemes (Dale et al. 1985).[9] However, for as long as structured variations in the nature and pattern of male and female employment persist, it is unlikely that a single scale can be devised which encompasses both men's and women's work.[10]

Employment-based class measures, therefore, cannot encompass all aspects of structured social inequality. Even in their most refined theoretical versions, they cannot distinguish effectively between 'class' and 'non-class' sources of employment structuring. The methodology of employment-aggregate class analysis is also not particularly well suited to the exploration of the links between structure and action. It can provide macro-level estimates of attitudes and identities which might be assumed to be associated with 'class' in its broadest sense, but it cannot throw much light on the workings and trajectories of the 'political movements and parties', or 'their ideologies, programmes and strategies' which are the actual bases of political mobilization (Goldthorpe and Marshall 1992).

In fact, in part because of the weaknesses described above, theoretical, relational occupational/employment class analysis has not been particularly flexible in its response to contemporary economic and social developments.[11] We have seen that Goldthorpe's approach to class analysis is not particularly well suited to the exploration of the impact upon the class structure of the increasing employment of women. In respect of the growing significance of consumption, employment-based class analysis has been confined to arguments which evaluate the significance of occupational class against consumption-sector variables (chapter 7 below). It has not addressed itself directly to the consequences that an enhanced capacity for, and growing preoccupation with, consumption might have for patterns of social differentiation in the late twentieth century. In the last section of this chapter, it will be suggested that this is a consequence of the sharp distinction which has been drawn between 'class' and 'status' in employment-based class analysis. Nevertheless, employment-aggregation approach(es) to the analysis of class and inequality have been associated with significant empirical work, and a variety of strategies have been developed relating to schemes of occupational and employment classifications and their applications, which might go some way towards meeting the criticisms reviewed above.

The continuing relevance of employment class

It has been emphasized throughout this book that 'class' has always been used as a descriptive term in relation to patterns of social inequality, and there can be no question that employment-based measures – of all kinds – remain essential for the investigation of structured social inequality. Empirical research using occupational-class schemes has and continues to be carried out in order to assess the impact of social policy. For example, such research has demonstrated the (relatively) limited impact of government reforms which have been designed to moderate the impact of structured occupational inequality in areas such as education. After the Second World War, the 1944

Education Act instituted free secondary education for all school-children in Britain. However, secondary education was organized in a tripartite system of grammar, technical, and secondary modern schools which were not of equal academic standing. It was demonstrated that there were significant occupational *class* biases in the selection of children at the age of eleven (proportionately more middle-class children were selected for grammar schools, more working-class children allocated to secondary moderns), even when measured intelligence was held constant (Douglas 1964). In 1962, the Robbins Report on higher education recommended changes designed to tap the underdeveloped 'pool of ability' in British society, and as a consequence there was a massive expansion of university and post-secondary education. However, as Halsey has argued, empirical research (deriving from the same sample as that used for the Oxford Mobility Survey) demonstrated that: 'The familiar picture . . . emerges, as with educational expansion generally, that though the fastest *rates* of growth almost always accrue to the working class, the greatest absolute increments of opportunity go to the service class' (Halsey et al. 1980; Halsey 1988: 188, 291). Thus whereas the proportion of working-class children at university had tripled as between the 1913–22 and 1943–52 birth cohorts in the sample, this has represented an increase of 0.9 per cent to 3.1 per cent, whereas the proportion of the 'service class' going to university had increased from 7.2 per cent to 26.4 per cent (these data relate to men only). Thus although the data reveal evidence of a long-term trend in the direction of greater educational opportunity (Halsey 1988; Marsh and Blackburn 1992), the educational reforms committed to increasing the 'openness' of British society seem to have met with only moderate success.

This demonstration of empirical associations between inequality and occupational-class measures could easily be extended – examples might include evidence relating to infant mortality, children's reading capacities, as well as many others. There can be little doubt, therefore, that occupational class retains its utility as a measure of inequality, as well as likely 'life chances'. The central role of occupational-class analysis in the British 'political-arithmetic' tradition should not be abandoned. Even if, as theorists such as Offe (1985a) have argued, 'work' has become less centrally important in the lives of individuals (and this claim is open to dispute), the work individuals do remains the most significant determinant of the life-fates of the majority of individuals and families in advanced industrial societies.

The claims which have been advanced on behalf of theoretical, relational approaches such as those of Wright and Goldthorpe should be modified (indeed, Goldthorpe and Marshall's (1992) defence of their position suggests that this has already taken place, as they are careful to make no theoretical claims whatsoever!). Nevertheless, this work also includes substantial empirical achievements. We have already described Goldthorpe's work on social mobility, which, together with that of his colleagues associated with the CASMIN project, has demonstrated conclusively the significance of *structured* occupational inequality, and its persistence through generations. Comparative work using a standard measure of occupational class has enabled sociologists to assert with some confidence the nature of the circumstances which contribute to different mobility experiences; that is, we have now a considerably enhanced understanding of the under-lying *causes* of social mobility. Recent work using a modified version of Wright's class scheme has explored empirically the nature of the impact of public expenditure cuts on attitudes – showing quite con-clusively, for example, that it has been public-sector managers who have been most politicized by these policies (Edgell and Duke 1991).

Testing and refining measures of employment class

Chapter 3 identified three different categories of employment-based class schemes. 'Commonsense' schemes, such as those of the Registrar-General or market researchers, are hierarchical, continuous scales, as are occupational-prestige scales. In contrast, it has been emphasized that the third type of measure (theoretical class schemes) claim to represent the actualities of class *relations*, that is, occupations and jobs are allocated to categories according to their relationship to other classes, rather than because they possess more or less of a particular quality, such as income, education or prestige. In statistical language they are therefore categorical rather than hierarchical or continuous measures – although this has been disputed.

In practice, however, the three different types of employment-based class measures are characterized by a broad similarity of actual occupa-tional placements, in that professional and managerial occupations are at the 'top', and manual and unskilled occupations at the 'bottom'. It has been important to emphasize the difference between measures of occupational class in order to grasp the very different theoretical objectives of the sociologists who have developed them; for practical purposes, however, the empirical findings associated with the different measures are often very similar.

This point may be illustrated by a comparison of voting intentions using the same data classified by the Registrar-General's, Goldthorpe's, and Wright's class classifications (table 1). The distributions within the three sections of the table are by no means identical, but the general direction of employment-class voting intentions is the same in every

Table 1 Voting intention by class: Essex sample (percentages)

I Registrar-General's classes

	1 Professional etc.	2 Intermediate	3N Skilled non-manual	3M Skilled manual	4 Partly skilled	5 Unskilled
Conservative	43	46	49	28	28	22
Labour	14	22	23	50	45	53
Alliance	38	23	19	16	15	17
Would not vote	7	9	9	6	12	7
	(100)	(100)	(100)	(100)	(100)	(100)
N:	42	283	247	317	178	58

II Goldthorpe's classes

	I Higher-grade professional; managerial	II Lower-grade professional; managerial	III Routine non-manual	IV Small proprietors self-employed	V Supervisors technicians	VI Skilled manual	VII Semi- & unskilled manual
Conservative	53	47	41	55	38	19	25
Labour	17	24	27	14	35	62	51
Alliance	23	23	20	20	21	12	17
Would not vote	8	7	12	12	6	7	8
	(100)	(100)	(100)	(100)	(100)	(100)	(100)
N:	106	208	210	102	100	141	267

III Wright's classes (mark I)

	Bourgeoisie	Small employers	Petty bourgeoisie	Managers and supervisors	Semi-autonomous workers	Workers
Conservative	67	66	48	44	39	29
Labour	13	11	15	26	29	47
Alliance	8	15	24	23	26	15
Would not vote	12	8	13	7	5	9
	(100)	(100)	(100)	(100)	(100)	(100)
N:	24	53	71	308	127	551

Source: G. Marshall et al. (1988), tables 9.3; 9.7.

case. For example, 53 per cent of Registrar-General class 5, 51 per cent of Goldthorpe class VII, and 47 per cent of Wright's workers would vote Labour.

For many practical purposes, therefore, research carried out using different schemes will be broadly comparable, and in many instances, the use of a 'good enough' occupational classification will suffice – indeed the relevant data may not be available in any other form. The relatively 'permissive' attitude to employment-based class measurement which is being advocated here does not imply, however, that particular if class schemes cannot be judged as more or less adequate, or as more or less suitable in particular research situations. However, there is often no single 'correct' measure, nor even a 'best buy' among the class schemes available. Some schemes are more appropriate for researching some empirical situations than others. A study of women's employment, for example, would utilize a measure sensitive to the specifics of women's occupations; studies of children's educational achievements will perforce use some kind of 'household' measure of occupational or employment class. Nevertheless, disputes still persist over which class scheme is 'best'. Sometimes, this is expressed as a basic methodological question concerning validity – that is, the extent to which the occupational or employment-class measure is indeed associated with the class-related attribute – income, education, voting behaviour, for example – which it is supposed to be measuring. Heath et al.'s arguments for the superiority of Goldthorpe's class scheme for the analysis of voting behaviour is an example of this kind of reasoning.

The strategy of using the strength of the association between occupational or employment-class measures and class indicators such as income and education in order to evaluate the utility of different schemes has also been employed by those who have consistently argued that a rather different version of an occupational scale is sociologically more appropriate than existing occupational schemes. Stewart and his colleagues have spent over two decades devising and refining the Cambridge occupational scale. This scale has been constructed, not through a process of allocating occupations to groups on the basis of the investigator's theoretical judgements, or the rankings allocated by survey participants or other 'experts', but via the analysis of the occupational friendship choices of their respondents. The Cambridge group argue that their scale is unique in that it attempts to incorporate the *socially constructed* nature of human reality.[12] Thus they argue that:

> One of the most important points about the scale is the way in which its construction was able to meet the criteria for genuine measurement, something which does not simply make it technically superior but also

gives it a much firmer theoretical foundation. Other approaches have
had to rely on some prior conceptualisation of the very concept they are
seeking to establish. (*Prandy 1990: 629–30*)

They are careful not to describe the Cambridge scale as a measure
of 'social class'; and they reject the Weberian distinction between
'class' and 'status', arguing that their scale encompasses both material and social dimensions of inequality. Stewart and his colleagues
argue that Weber's distinction between 'class' and 'status' is neither
useful nor necessary; that material and social advantage are indivisible
concepts (1980: 28).[13] Their conception 'is one of stratification
arrangements that involve differences in generalised advantage (and
disadvantage) and hence in life-style and in social interaction related to
level of advantage and life-style' (Prandy 1990: 635). In developing the
argument for the superiority of their scale as a technical measure,
Prandy compared a grouped version of the Cambridge scale with the
three-version grouping of the Goldthorpe class categories. He was
able to show that the grouped version of their scale performs better
in demonstrating the association between income, education, voting
intention and social mobility than the three-category version of the
Goldthorpe scale. This evidence thus provides further arguments
against the claims of 'theoretical' occupational-class schemes to
have identified homogeneous groups, or 'distinguishable collectivities'
('classes') which have a reality which distinguishes them from other
groups ('classes'), as within-group homogeneity is shown to be stronger
when using the divisions of a *continuous* scale than a categorization
devised on the basis of sociological theory and knowledge.

Although there have been a number of recent advances in the
methodological and statistical manipulation of occupational or employment based class schemes, therefore, the very real differences in the
theoretical preconceptions of those who devise and use them implies
that questions as to the utility and suitability of particular schemes will
continue to be the focus of a lively debate. Pawson (1989, 1990)
has attempted to move such arguments on to a different plane. He
notes that, despite the fact that different measures of occupational or
employment class contain implicit (and different) theories about class
formation, they nevertheless give very similar results across entire
ranges of class indicators – as has been illustrated in table 1, for
example. He argues, therefore, that there should be a wholesale move
from a 'verificatory' investigative strategy (that is which class measure
provides the strongest empirical association with indicator X) to an
'adjudicatory' strategy. This would involve empirical testing not on the
familiar ground of the predictive validity of different occupational and
employment class measures, but rather through the *creation of points
of intersection between rival theories* (Pawson 1989: 255).

Pawson models his adjudicatory strategy on that first developed by Wright (1985). Wright was concerned to evaluate his exploitation-centred model of employment class against Poulantzas's productive-labour definition (Poulantzas, it will be remembered, had argued that 'unproductive labourers' were key elements in the 'new petty bourgeoisie'). Wright argued that: 'All things being equal, all units . . . within a given class should be more like each other than like units in other classes *with respect to whatever it is that class is meant to explain*' (1985: 137; emphasis in original). He thus created a simple cross-tabulation of his and Poulantzas's definitions of 'working-class' and 'middle-class wage earners' which produced two 'agreed-upon' cell categories of undisputed 'working-class' and 'middle-class' occupants, and two disputed categories;[14] in these Wright's and Poulantzas's definitions would have allocated individuals to different classes. The 'adjudication' takes place by determining whether the characteristics of the disputed categories are closest to those of the 'agreed-upon' working or middle class. Wright's process of adjudication finds that in the disputed cases his original occupational class categories are closer in their characteristics to the agreed-upon version, and he thus concludes that his class categorization is superior to that of Poulantzas.

Pawson develops Wright's arguments to suggest an ambitious programme whereby different theories may be developed so as to identify points of intersection at which such adjudications may take place, on the basis of the same data. Such a programme, however, would require especially-gathered data which can be used to express rival theories:

> What I am talking about is very large-scale collaborative research in which the data are collected in such a way that existing concepts and operationalizations can be repeated alongside those of any rival hypotheses that the investigator wants to add to the adjudication process. The crucial point is for research to follow a *programme of reproducing and transforming conceptual schema*. (*1989: 283; emphasis in original*)

As Pawson recognizes, such a strategy would be extremely expensive, and would require a level of national and international co-operation not often present in social science research. It is doubtful, therefore, that his suggestions will be found to have provided a final solution, but they do serve to illustrate a possible strategy whereby the use and application of employment-based class schemes may be further refined and developed.[15]

This kind of work, therefore, is an important sub-area within class analysis which has been characterized by a number of significant theoretical and methodological advances. However, it may be argued that its very strength and sophistication has also contributed to mis-understandings and misapprehensions which have been somewhat counter-productive within the context of 'class analysis' as a whole. The focus of such research on the large-scale sample survey has, willy-nilly, incorporated an emphasis on quantification and measurement which has tended to downplay the significance of individual and collective human action within real social contexts. The conduct of such research has often appeared to be 'methods-driven' to the extent that the relative outsider, even within the sociological community, has simply lost any sense of what is going on. The claims of some of its practitioners to have identified 'social classes' within the occupational structure has also contributed to an over-identification of 'class analysis' with occupational measurement.

Bringing status back in

One of the major objectives of those who have developed theoretical, 'relational' approaches to employment-based class analysis has been to distinguish their measures from prestige or status scales. In chapters 2 and 3, an account has been given of the manner in which, after the Second World War, sociologists who were actively developing the 'conflict' approach in the field of class and stratification theory and research sought to distance themselves from the prevailing tradition of stratification research in the United States. This tradition was represented in the many-volume *Yankee City* series, which drew upon anthropologically inspired community research which began in 1930 (Warner 1963). Warner defined 'social class' as follows:

> By social class is meant two or more orders of people who are believed to be, and are accordingly ranked by the members of the community, in socially superior and inferior positions. Members of a class tend to marry within their own order, but the values of the society permit marriage up and down. A class system also provides that children are born into the same status as their parents. A class society distributes rights and privileges, duties and obligations, unequally among its inferior and superior grades. (*1963: 36–7*)

Rather than studying 'social classes', as he had claimed, Warner had in fact been investigating the prestige order. In fact, Warner's definition emphasizes the cultural, rather than the economic, construction of class and corresponds more closely to the commonsense definition of 'class' in ordinary usage. Theoretically informed sociologists were at considerable pains to dissociate themselves from this approach and, following Bendix and Lipset, were emphatic as to the importance of the Weberian distinction between 'class' and 'status'.

Thus in his defence of his version of 'class analysis' against feminist critics, Goldthorpe (1983) laid much emphasis on this distinction between the 'American' and the 'European' traditions of class analysis:

> In the mainstream American literature the dominant . . . form of stratification [is seen] in terms of *social status*: that is, as resulting from the differential evaluations of family units that are made by 'the community' . . . the term 'social class' [is used] where European writers would be more likely to use that of 'status groups'. (*Goldthorpe 1983: 466*)

Similarly, when he came to develop his Marxist 'class map', Wright also drew a sharp distinction between the status or prestige order and the analysis of occupational *class* (Wright 1979; ch. 3 above). He has argued that as status bears no relation to production, it has no place in class analysis (Wright 1985: 79).

Economic 'class' factors (such as the nature of market demand, the extent and nature of control and authority relationships) *are* analytically seperable from 'prestige' factors in the structuring of employment. However, in practice, it is exceptionally difficult to draw a clear distinction between 'class' and 'status' at the level of jobs and employment. That these two aspects are inextricably intertwined is demonstrated, for example, by the considerable extent of empirical overlap between 'class' and 'status' (or prestige) occupational classifications.

The sharp distinction drawn between class and status in the development of theoretically-informed empirical measures of 'social class' has had a number of consequences, not all of which have been positive. These arguments have had a tendency to identify status with *prestige* or social ranking. However, prestige is only one dimension of the complex status concept, and it may be suggested that the attention given to this dimension has tended to overshadow the exploration of the other aspects of status. Additionally, the desire to separate class from status empirically has also tended to deflect attention from the investigation of their interrelations.[16] However, it will be argued that status relates to the overall structuring of inequality along a number of different dimensions.

In previous sections of this chapter we have reviewed the practical difficulties, deriving from the many-faceted structuring of employment relations, of developing a precise theoretical measure of 'class'. We have also explored some of the limitations of the employment-aggregate approach – for example, the problems raised by the increase in women's paid employment, and the difficulties imposed by the methodology of the large-scale sample survey in providing any systematic account of class consciousness and action. These issues have generated lively academic debates, but those not directly involved might consider that they have made only a modest contribution to our understanding of recent social and political changes. For example, arguments relating to 'class dealignment' in the patterns of voting behaviour in Britain may have been effectively critiqued by demonstrating the continuing association between working class occupations and non-Conservative voting, but these findings do not illuminate what some might consider the larger issue of the long-term diminution of the 'working class' itself. Within sociology, the employment-aggregate approach to 'class analysis' has been described as 'hegemonic' (Savage et al. 1992). The argument of this chapter has not been that this approach should be abandoned, but rather that its limitations should be recognized. This kind of work *must* be complemented by approaches to *social* class analysis which, rather than seeking to distance themselves from the status concept, are premissed upon the interrelationship of the 'economic' and the 'social'. In addition to the investigation of employment aggregates, and equally significant for the understanding of class and stratification, is the study of the *processes* of the active structuring of occupations and groups. Work in this area has been both 'Marxist' and 'Weberian' in its theoretical inspiration, but has been different from the occupational-aggregation approach in respect of its methodology as well as its assumptions about the nature of social reality. Much empirical work in this area has been recently associated with a 'realist' approach – which has maintained a simultaneous emphasis on both 'structure' and 'action'. Rather than being based upon the large-scale sample survey, these investigations of class structure and action have utilized, above all, the *case study*. We will return to these arguments at the end of this chapter, but first we will briefly indicate how an approach which stresses the interrelatedness of class and status might illuminate a number of important issues.

The Weberian concept of status has a number of different dimensions which have not always been clearly identified by those who have used it (see chapter 2 above). It will be argued that the status concept may usefully be considered to have three dimensions: (a) to refer to prestige groupings or consciousness communities; (b) more diffuse notions of 'lifestyle' or 'social standing' (these two aspects will obviously overlap to a considerable extent); and (c) non-market-based claims to material entitlements or 'life chances'. The first aspect of the status concept identified above – prestige groupings – is, as we have seen, the aspect from which 'theoretical', employment-based 'class analysis' sought to differentiate itself most sharply. Such groupings are here described as *consciousness communities*: 'In contrast to classes, *status groups* are normally communities' (Gerth and Mills: 186; emphasis in original). 'Community' in this sense need not necessarily imply residential propinquity. Not surprisingly, Warner's *Yankee City* provides a good historical example of these kinds of linkages:

> When George Washington made his grand presidential tour of the new nation . . . he came not only as the Father of his Country and leader of all his people, but as a visiting Virginia aristocrat . . . when he arrived in Yankee City he was entertained in the great houses of the town by people who knew him as an equal. (*1963: 15*)

'Community' in this sense describes associational groups sharing common cultures (Crompton 1987). The material wealth and power of those in the 'great houses' indicates their dominant *class* situation; such groupings, however, also maintain their dominance through the manner in which they deploy their *cultural* resources. In a recent book, Scott (1991) has documented the manner in which the British ruling class is reproduced through a network of social activities including private London clubs, the residual activities of the London 'season', attendance at major sporting and social events, and so on. The British public schools, as well as Oxbridge, also serve to inculcate the kind of 'correct' behaviour which is likely to facilitate recruitment to superior positions: 'Without any need for a consciously intended bias in recruitment, the established 'old boys' sponsor the recruitment through their networks of contacts of each new generation of old boys' (1991: 117). Status as prestige, therefore, plays a central role in the processes of class formation and reproduction. In a later chapter, we will explore Bourdieu's notion of 'cultural capital', which examines these processes in some detail.

The ruling-class 'consciousness communities' briefly described above are clearly associated with a distinctive lifestyle, as Weber argued: 'In content, status honor is normally expressed by the fact that above all a specific *style of life* can be expected' (Gerth and Mills 1948: 187; emphasis in original). Whereas 'class' is concerned with the production of goods, status is concerned with their consumption. This has been described by Turner (1988: 66) as including 'the totality of cultural practices such as dress, speech, outlook and bodily dispositions'. 'Lifestyle' categories need not necessarily correspond to consciousness communities (although they might reflect an aspiration to join them). The notion of 'lifestyle' is thus clearly linked to consciousness communities. However, the topic of consumption and its relation to class and stratification also raises a broader range of issues. As we have seen in the last chapter, rising living standards in the West have brought issues relating to consumption into sharper focus, and it is increasingly argued that an investigation of consumption-related concerns should replace an outdated 'productivism' in class and stratification analysis. Although these arguments will by no means be taken on board in their entirety, consumption in this broader sense – to include issues such as, for example, the consumption of the environment and the construction of self-identities – may be seen to have an impact on class and stratification systems. Besides the role of specific lifestyles in the reproduction of established groupings, therefore, 'lifestyle' in this broader sense may be seen as contributing to the emergence of newly differentiated groups, and supplying new focuses for the articulation of interests and concerns. In particular, these issues are argued to be central to the emergence and identification of the 'new middle classes', a topic which will be explored at greater length in chapter 7.

The third aspect of the status concept which may be identified is its use to describe non-market-based claims to material entitlements or 'life chances'. Thus the term may be used to describe pre-industrial 'estates' in contrast to 'classes', or the traditional claims of a particular caste grouping. Weber described status situation, in contrast to the economically determined class situation, as 'every typical component of the life fate of men that is determined by a specific, positive or negative, social estimation of *honor*' (Gerth and Mills 1948: 187). Even in contemporary capitalist societies, the occupational order is socially, as well as economically, structured. An instance which has already been explored at some length is that of gender. Occupational segregation means that the 'life fates' associated with particular occupations have been crucially affected by the gender of the likely occupant. The occupational order is also shaped by explicit status claims. One example would be that of professionalism. Many professional groups (such as doctors, or lawyers) rest a part of their claim to material rewards on their undertaking *not* to exploit their skills to their full market advantage, and to practise 'institutionalized altruism' in respect of their clients (Crompton 1990a).

One of the most frequently employed uses of the concept of status as entitlement, however, has been in T. H. Marshall's development of the concept of *citizenship*.[17] As we shall see in the next chapter, Marshall has described the development of social citizenship – that is, the right of all 'citizens' to services such as education and benefits such as those provided by the welfare state – to be one of the most important developments to affect stratification systems in the twentieth century. The analysis of the interrelations between 'class' and 'citizenship', therefore, provides another potentially fruitful way forward for class and stratification analysis.

Large-scale, aggregate-level 'class analysis' in sociology, as in the work of Goldthorpe and Wright, has sought systematically to exclude considerations of 'status' from its investigations. In this book it is being suggested that an explicit recognition of the *interrelationship* of class and status is also necessary. It is further being argued that a particular methodological approach will also be required. Large data sets and sample surveys have had, and continue to have, a central place in empirical investigations of the 'class structure'. However, it has been argued that the investigation of the processes of class structuring – which will include the examination of aspects of status – requires an alternative methodology. Similarly, although large data sets may provide useful attitudinal data relating to topics such as class consciousness, the dynamics of the processes and organizations which shape this consciousness can only be explored using a methodology which views the social unit (the neighbourhood, the trade union, the workgroup, the political party) as a whole – that is, the case study. In the concluding section of this chapter, it will be argued that, in fact, there already exists a rich tradition of empirical research in class analysis which has explored the interrelationship of class and status, and that this research has, indeed, employed the case study as its predominant method of investigation.

Many recent empirical investigations of class processes which have employed the case-study method have been carried out by sociologists who have self-consciously embraced a 'realist' approach to their empirical work (Bagguley et al. 1989; Savage et al. 1992). However, the methodology of the case study is not specific to realism. Indeed, it may be argued that the case study still remains as the bedrock of empirical investigation in the social sciences, despite the fact that, as a research method, it has been variously dismissed as unscientific, capable only of generating, not testing, hypotheses, prone to bias and arbitrary interpretation, and so on. The methodological issues raised by these criticisms are complex. They will therefore be simply stated as follows. (a) The case-study approach should not be taken as synonymous only with qualitative methods, or ethnography. A case study may be quantitative, as was, for example, the early investigation of the 'Affluent Worker' by Goldthorpe et al. Case studies of particular occupations have also frequently incorporated extensive programmes of interviewing and the quantitative analysis of interview data – as, for example, in Newby's study of agricultural workers. (b) Case studies are in fact the *only* method whereby collective action may be explored in its context; they facilitate theoretical/logical thinking and thus *causal* explanations. Often, cases are judged on their 'typicality', but, as Mitchell (1983) has argued, they should be judged on the basis of the validity of their analysis, rather than their typicality. In any event, case studies are not immune to empirical evaluation. Besides the relatively orthodox strategy of replication, the theoretical reasoning developed in the context of a particular case study may be subjected to empirical scrutiny through a process of comparison, particularly cross-national comparisons (Pickvance 1992). These points are made in order to emphasize that to advocate the method of the case study should not be taken to imply a recourse to mere description, or to abandon any attempt at the rigorous investigation of the topics at issue.

Conclusion: the interrelationship of class and status

Criticisms of 'class analysis' have been directed at many of its wider theoretical assumptions, particularly the linkages of structure → consciousness → action. It has been argued, however, that these kinds of criticism are not peculiar to the claims and objectives of 'class analysis', but reflect wider problems concerning theoretical explanations offered by sociologists of both social change and future societal developments. It would not be sensible, however, to put into effect an empirical moratorium until the necessary theoretical advances have been achieved. Large-scale employment-based class analysis, as in the work of Goldthorpe and Wright, can demonstrate the association between employment aggregates and attitudinal clusters. This approach assumes the possibility of an analytical and empirical separation between 'class structure' and 'class action'. The investigation of the processes of class articulation and organization through case studies of their occupational, organizational and locality contexts confers a more direct and immediate understanding of these processes – as in, for example, Brown and Brannen's (1970) study of shipbuiding workers, which described how the traditional craft loyalties which prevailed in the shipbuilding industry in the 1970s effectively segmented what might otherwise have been anticipated to be 'traditional proletarian' (Lockwood 1966) images of society. Those who have not separated 'structure' and 'action' in their approach to 'class analysis' have focused on the manner in which classes have deployed their 'causal powers' in the processes of class formation – as in, for example, Lash and Urry's account of the emergence of the 'service class'. Their 'realist' approach might currently be a fashionable label for the historical and case-study approach in class analysis, but in fact there is an established sociological and historical tradition of enquiry employing these methods.[18]

This research has also provided a wealth of information relating to status – in its various dimensions as discussed above – as well as class. Lockwood's (1958) study of clerical workers charted the historical decline in the status of the male clerk, and the *Affluent Worker* series (1969) which was directed by Goldthorpe and Lockwood studied the economic, normative and relational dimensions of class amongst affluent workers in Luton. The relational dimension, it may be suggested, corresponds broadly to the 'consciousness-community' dimension of status as described above – only in the case of the 'affluent workers', it is not the ruling class, but the working class, which is reproducing itself through its particular social practices. Earlier work, often influenced by anthropology and within the tradition of community studies, had also identified particular status groupings in British society; for example, the distinction between the 'roughs' and the 'respectables' within the working class (Klein 1965), and Stacey's analysis of local status systems in the English market town of Banbury (1960); the work of Warner and his colleagues in the United States has already been discussed. Even when the major focus of the case study has ostensibly been on 'class' – as in, for example, Willis's study of working-class youths (1977) – the lifestyles associated with specific class trajectories have been essential components of the theoretical argument.

It has been stressed that status is a multifaceted concept. Thus it incorporates both economic – that is, non-market-derived claims to entitlements – as well as cultural aspects, such as prestige. It may be used to analyse, for example, the material impact of citizenship claims and struggles, as well as to explore the cultural developments which have been associated with the changes in the occupational order with the development of 'consumer capitalism'. Has the welfare state deal associated with the growth of citizenship, for example, created an 'underclass' which represents a qualitatively new social phenomenon? (This will be examined in chapter 6 below.) Have the occupational changes associated with the development of the 'service economy' been associated with the development of a cultural plurality which might radically transform conventionally established class boundaries? Such arguments have been associated with the currently fashionable emphasis on 'postmodernism', in which cultural form (or lack of it) appears increasingly as the motive force for human action. These debates will be explored in chapter 7.

One of the major arguments of this chapter has been that the empirical study of occupational class as identified, within the structure of employment, by various class schemes, is only one approach to 'class analysis' within sociology – albeit a very important one. It is an approach which has a number of difficulties and weaknesses stemming from both the fluidity and the multiple structuring of the occupational order as well as the difficulties of making theoretical and empirical linkages between 'structure' and 'action'. The study of occupational class within sociology has been complemented by a long tradition of contextual analyses which have explored the effects of 'class' within particular occupations, organizations and localities. The significance of 'associations, locality-based groups and networks' has not been ignored within class analysis, even though Pahl has suggested otherwise (1989: 719). The existence of these kinds of studies has been stressed as part of the more general argument that, as with many critical arguments relating to 'class analysis' in sociology, it proves to be the case that particular issues – such as 'lifestyle' – which are presented as having been 'ignored', 'not taken seriously', or 'demonstrating the irrelevance of class analysis' have, in fact, already been explored in some depth. History may indeed always repeat itself but, as sociologists, we should be able to learn from it.

Notes

1   For example, as we shall see later in this chapter, Stewart and his colleagues, who have strenuously argued for the indivisibility of the 'economic' and the 'social', have developed measures which have been applied to large data sets.

2   Although it is paradoxical that Saunders's own data demonstrate that the association between occupational class and voting remains stronger than that between voting and house tenure – the particular aspect of consumption with which he has been primarily concerned (Saunders 1990b 262). Defenders of occupational class-analysis such as Marshall (1991) have not been slow to point his out.

3   Marshall and his colleagues prefer Goldthorpe's class scheme in their analysis of voting behaviour and intentions because the Goldthorpe 'classes' better clarify the relationship between class and voting than the occupational classification used by Crewe, and voting intentions and behaviour show a stronger association with the Goldthorpe 'classes' than the Wright 'classes': 'no further reference will be made to Wright's class frameworks in the course of this chapter, since direct comparison with Goldthorpe's neo-Weberian categories shows that the former are less useful than the latter for the explanation of voting behaviour. Applying analysis of variance techniques to the data we find that the F ratio for Goldthorpe classes is significantly higher than those for either of the Wright classifications in the case of both Labour and Conservative voters' (Marshall et al. 1988: 236).

4   Goldthorpe has always recognized the extent of the diversity of the occupations grouped within his class scheme, but would argue that never-theless the utility of his classification is confirmed by his further evidence relating to mobility boundaries.

5   In the case of Wright, his procedures are susceptible to the criticisms of the Marxist theory of action developed by Lockwood (1981), reviewed in some detail in ch. 4 above. Goldthorpe has maintained an explicit commitment to an 'action approach' in sociology. However, as Johnson (1990) has argued, in practice the roots of class action in Goldthorpe's

account of 'class analysis' are reduced to outcomes of the pattern of social mobility – i.e. 'demographic class formation': 'Goldthorpe's . . . argument . . . slides inexorably from a claim that mobility must be seen to have some significance for class action to a position in which . . . mobility takes on the role of prime cause. Once we link this with Goldthorpe's claim that mobility-induced class conflict is central to social change, then we are close to straightforward prime-factor theory, in which action is assumed to be reducible to mobility experience' (p. 391).

6 This position is difficult to maintain, however, given that, as we have seen, Goldthorpe's class scheme (their favoured variety) has been constructed according to explicit theoretical principles. It might still be argued by Goldthorpe and Marshall that they demonstrate no partiality in their choice, in that the Goldthorpe scheme is subject to the same rigorous examination as any other. However, given that these exercises are also of their own devising, it is not surprising that their scheme performs 'best'.

7 See, however, Pawson's arguments reviewed later in this chapter. Goldthorpe has also argued, following Popper, that disagreements may be resolved empirically via a sophisticated version of 'falsificationism'.

8 Although flexible employment patterns are a common feature of women's employment, the form this takes manifests important cross-national variations. See Jenson et al. (1988); Crompton et al. (1990).

9 The practical suggestions made by Dale and her colleagues are not being criticized here. However, the logic of the argument being pursued in this book suggests that the title of their article, 'Integrating women into class theory', is rather misleading. A better description would be: 'Integrating women into occupational class analysis'.

10 Prandy (1991) has claimed that the Cambridge scale, which is based upon friendship choices, does provide such a measure.

11 In respect of Goldthorpe and Wright in particular, the sources of rigidity are rather different. The role played by social mobility in the identification of the Goldthorpe 'classes' means that he is constrained to assume that occupations remain in a similar 'class' location over time. Wright is constrained by his commitment to Marxist theory, which makes it difficult for him to incorporate factors – such as gender – lying outside the scope of the original theory.

12 This gloss on the theoretical position of the Cambridge group may be justifiably criticized as inadequate and misleading. Their theoretical position, in fact, is one which does not admit of a disjunction between the 'natural' and the 'social', and a recourse to 'action' explanations deemed to be examples of 'explanatory failure' (Holmwood and Stewart 1983). They would certainly not concur with the rather simplistic dichotomies which have been used to organize the arguments in this textbook (which is not a work of social theory).

13 This rejection depends upon a particular interpretation of the Weberian concept of 'status': 'We do not believe in the Weberian distinction of classes, which are formed in the rational pursuit of interest in the context

of the market, from status groups which rest upon successful claims to special esteem and develop bases for collective identification and action in economically non-rational conventions of consumption and behaviour' (Stewart et al. 1980: 28). This distinction may indeed be problematic in relation to the occupational order in particular – it is, indeed, virtually impossible to separate 'class' from 'status' in the ranking of occupations, and later in this chapter the argument will be developed that the attempt to maintain this distinction may have been counter-productive for stratification research as a whole. However, studies of the occupational order may be seen as only one dimension of class and stratification analysis, and the heuristic distinction between 'class' and 'status' as distinguishable bases of allocation in modern societies (although not, perhaps, clearly identifiable groups) may be defended as essential to our understanding of stratification processes in modern societies.

14   In fact, as Wright's exploitation-centred definition had three classes within the range, and Poulantzas's only two, the actual table has six cells. This detail, however, would substantially complicate the present exposition, and the interested reader is referred to Wright (1985: 137ff) and Pawson (1989: 269ff), for further discussion.

15   Marshall and Rose have carried out this process of adjudication with the Essex data, and conclude that 'Goldthorpe's theory certainly better explains class identification and voting intentions than does that of Wright' (1990: 265).

16   Marshall et al. do provide a suggestive mapping of the interaction of class and status (1988: 199). However, their substantive discussion is concerned to demonstrate the continuing salience of 'class' – as they define it.

17   It may be noted that T. H. Marshall's ideas on citizenship developed out of his earlier work on professionalism; see Crompton (1990a) for an account of this.

18   It is somewhat paradoxical that Marshall, whose subsequent work has been concerned almost entirely with such large-scale occupational-class analysis, should have argued in 1983 that in respect of the investigation of class consciousness 'research energies and resources should be channelled in the direction of intensive, longitudinal ethnography, in which the different aspects of consciousness are located firmly in the context of class practices – everyday work at the factory, leisure time at home and in the club . . . and conceptualized at the outset as inherently dynamic phenomena . . . such research provides a more suitable *alternative* to the large-scale survey' (1983: 290–1). The apparent contradiction in first advocating one type of research, then embarking upon another, has been discussed at some length by one of Marshall's collaborators (Rose 1988). He argues that (a) the initial evidence required by the Essex team was 'extensive rather than intensive', and therefore required a large-scale sample survey; and (b) that, in any case, Marshall had reconsidered his approach to the whole problem of class consciousness as a result of his survey endeavours (see also Goldthorpe and Marshall 1992). Point (a)

above refers to a practical requirement relating to the research process, and cannot be disputed. Point (b), however, refers to the fact that 'class consciousness', according to the Essex researchers, should now be seen as an attribute of *collective* actors, and should therefore be 'seen in terms of organisations rather than individuals' (p. 28). Such organizations would be political parties, trade unions etc. It is difficult to see how this conclusion (whether valid or not) can be used to justify survey research in itself. If class action should now be seen in terms of organizations rather than individuals, then the proper focus of empirical investigation is the organization – and the study of organizations, of course, requires the deployment of case-study analysis.

6
Citizenship and Entitlements

Introduction

In the previous chapter, it was noted that, in particular within the employment-aggregate approach to class analysis, considerable efforts have been made, by both Marxists and Weberians, to draw a distinction between, on the one hand, aggregates representing economic 'classes' and, on the other, 'status' or prestige aggregations. However, it was emphasized that 'prestige' is only one dimension of the status concept, which has also been used to describe patterns of consumption or 'lifestyles', as well as claims to entitlements which do not rest upon power in property or the market. In this chapter, we will explore the interaction of class and status in respect of this latter dimension. Class and status power represent different claims to material resources, and Weber suggested that they existed in a cyclical relationship: 'When the bases of the acquisition and distribution of goods are relatively stable, stratification by status is favoured . . . Epochs and countries in which the naked class situation is of predominant significance are regularly the periods of technical and economic transformations' (Gerth and Mills 1948: 193–4). However, it has been stressed that, even in circumstances in which access to property and the market – that is, class situations – are the major determinants of material circumstances, non-market and non-property factors – that is, the social and moral claims associated with status – are nevertheless of persisting significance. Traditional evaluations associated with gender, race and age all affect levels of remuneration in contemporary societies, for example. In this chapter, we shall see that class-based organizations have actively pursued status claims – most particularly, in respect of the development of social citizenship. The pursuit of status equalization by disadvantaged groups such as women and ethnic minorities has also had a substantial impact on the stratification order.

In the first chapter of this book, we emphasized the fictional nature of the 'pure' capitalist market society. A 'market society' is an ideal type, rather than a description of any actually existing societal form. In reality, no society exists or persists in the absence of some kind of regulation, and the market is by itself insufficient as a regulator of capitalist industrialism. As Polanyi has argued: 'To allow the market mechanism to be sole director of the fate of human beings and their natural environment . . . would result in the demolition of society' (1957: 73). In a capitalist market society, sources of regulation which afford some protection for the individual may be found in aspects of pre-capitalist or 'traditional' societies which have persisted into the modern age – we may mention, for example, structures of family or kinship obligations or, more contentiously, Hirsch's (1977) identification of the 'moral legacy' of religious doctrine. There are also contemporaneously forged institutions which have been developed in order to check the free play of market forces. These would include, for example, trade unions and occupational associations, but foremost amongst these institutions is the modern form of the status of citizenship.

At the beginning of the 1990s, 'citizenship' is emerging as an important concept in the political programmes of both left and right political parties. In Britain, both Conservative and Labour have produced their variants of a 'citizen's charter'; theoretical and ideological supports are provided by corresponding ideologues (Andrews 1991; Plant and Barry 1990). 'Citizenship' is a term which denotes full and participating membership of a nation state, that is, it does not necessarily incorporate all persons resident within a given territory. In the ancient world of the Greek city states, for example, the term was reserved for free adult males alone; women, slaves (including debt slaves), foreigners and the young were excluded from participation in the *polis*. In the modern world, South Africa, for example, still stands as an example of a national territory in which the majority of the population are effectively denied full civil rights, and in Germany, even the German-born children of *Gastarbeiter* are not, in law, full 'citizens'. We should also remember that in a number of advanced Western industrial societies women have for much of the twentieth century been denied full civil and political rights – in France, for example, women were not enfranchised until after the Second World War.

Citizenship implies both rights and duties: rights against the arbitrary exercise of state power, as well as duties in respect of the state's activities. Thus the citizen has the right to hold private property, the state has the right to levy taxes. As far as stratification analysis is concerned, a crucial aspect of citizenship is that it cannot be marketed; it is not a commodity but rather denotes a particular aspect of the social *status* of the individual or group. Sociological analyses of the concept have been dominated by T. H. Marshall's 'Citizenship and social class' (1963), an account which Lockwood has described as 'the only work of post-war British sociology which . . . bears comparison with, and stands in a direct line of succession to those classical texts which mark the origins of modern sociology' (1974: 363).

T. H. Marshall and the development of the concept of citizenship

Marshall's brief text derives from lectures delivered in 1949, published in 1950. His major thesis is that the basic equalities which in contemporary Western industrialized democracies are shared by all 'citizens' serve to both reduce and make legitimate the persisting inequalities of (capitalist) social class. In an oft-quoted phrase, he asserts that: 'in the twentieth century citizenship and the capitalist class system have been at war' with each other (1963: 87). Marshall identifies three elements of modern citizenship: civil, political and social. Civil citizenship describes those rights necessary for individual freedom – 'liberty of the person, freedom of speech, thought and faith, the right to own property and to conclude valid contracts, and the right to justice'. Political citizenship refers to the right to participate in the exercise of political power, which in contemporary societies corresponds to universal suffrage, without such restrictions as property qualifications, and the right to hold political office. These two aspects correspond, broadly, to the liberal ideal of citizenship. To these basic rights of the individual Marshall added a third dimension, social citizenship, which he described as 'the whole range from the right to a modicum of economic welfare and security to the right to share to the full in the social heritage and to live the life of a civilized being according to the standards prevailing in the society' (p. 74). These rights, he argued, are associated with the development of the institutions of the modern welfare state.

Marshall developed his arguments through an analysis of recent British history. Chronologically, civil rights in England began to be established in the seventeenth century and were largely accomplished by the eighteenth century, during which equality before the law was established and the last elements of servile status were abolished, leaving individuals free to enter employment, to make contracts, to change employers, and so on. Political rights were progressively attained by increasing numbers of the population during the nineteenth century, although full political citizenship for adults, including women, was not achieved until the twentieth. The major achievement of the twentieth century, however, lay in the development of the welfare state and the growth of social citizenship. Another important development spanning the nineteenth and twentieth centuries was the growth and legal recognition of trade unionism, which Marshall describes as a 'secondary system of industrial citizenship parallel with and supplementary to the system of political citizenship' (p. 98).

The major contribution of citizenship to class abatement lies in its social dimension. The incorporation of social rights into the status of citizenship creates a universal right to real income which is not proportional to the market value of the claimant. The rights of social citizenship incorporate:

> no longer merely an attempt to abate the obvious nuisance of destitution in the lowest ranks of society. It is no longer content to raise the floor-level in the basement of the social edifice, leaving the superstructure as it was. It has begun to remodel the whole building, and it might even end by converting a skyscraper into a bungalow. (*pp. 100–1*)

In short, the rights of social citizenship make a significant contribution to 'the modern drive towards social equality' (p. 73).

Marshall's analysis of citizenship has been tremendously influential. However, Marx (1843) had already expressed his objections to the real value of modern democratic, or bourgeois, citizenship (that is, individual freedom, universal suffrage, and equality before the law). Of what significance are these individual rights, he argued, in class-divided societies in which individuals do not have the *practical* ability to exercise them? Political equality can accommodate itself all too easily to structural inequalities in the distribution of wealth and power, and yet these systematically undermine any formal equality in rights. Indeed, he argued that these 'bourgeois freedoms' were both necessary to the development of capitalist society and served to perpetuate it; by declaring distinctions based on birth, rank, education and occupation to be 'non-political', the state effectively sanctions these inequalities. In a similar vein, left critics of Marshall's thesis argued that the development of the welfare state had signified, not class abatement or amelioration but, rather, the necessary strategies of the capitalist state in response to the changing requirements of the capitalist mode of production – an interpretation supported by structuralist Marxism's identification of education and welfare systems as 'ideological state apparatuses'. In this view, for example, educational provision (for

Marshall a central component of social citizenship) would be viewed not as an element of class abatement but, rather, as a channel through which capitalism acquires the kinds of employees it requires (Bowles and Gintis 1976).

In some contrast to these left critics, others saw in Marshall's arguments a more positive and indeed optimistic account of the integration of the working class into capitalist society through the development of citizenship and the subsequent decline of class and class conflict (Bendix 1964). Such interpretations had a strong parallel with the 'optimistic' liberal perspective on the development of industrial societies which has been described in previous chapters; for example, in Blau and Duncan's assertion that with industrialism there would develop a society in which individual attainments would more or less match individual abilities. The equal status of citizenship, it was suggested, would make a significant contribution to this equalization of opportunities.

Recent discussions of Marshall have highlighted the ambiguities, and some of the deficiencies, of his original account. Before we proceed to an examination of these arguments, however, it would be useful to attempt to resolve, in brief, the differences in the current party political uses of the concept. On the political right, there is a considerable emphasis upon the *duties* of the citizen, through the notion of 'active citizenship'. 'Active citizenship', through such schemes as neighbourhood watch, voluntary social service, and so on, might also be seen as a part of the right's strategy of moving away from the state's provision of welfare services, which were seen by Marshall to be central elements of 'social citizenship'. The 1991 Conservative 'citizen's charter' also seeks to further empower the individual in respect of large, public-service bureaucracies – for example, in instituting a system of payment to passengers to compensate them for the late arrival of trains. Drawing upon Offe's analysis, briefly discussed in the last chapter, these elements within the Conservative citizen's charter might be seen as efforts to 'reprivatize' conflicts and issues which are not properly dealt with by means of public authority (Offe 1985b: 819).

Recent debates on the social democratic political left have also argued that the question of individual freedom is central to socialist, as well as to right-wing politics. We may recall, for example, the 'New Times' criticism of socialism's over-identification with 'productivism' and 'classism'; this has been linked, by authors such as Laclau and Mouffe with the necessity for socialism to have a strong commitment to the deepening and expansion of individual freedoms (1985: 176ff). A recent commentary states this case succinctly: 'It is liberty rather than equality that socialists now turn to with enthusiasm, with personal freedom given greater prominence in most left agendas . . . than the redistribution of wealth' (Andrews 1991: 12). Recent events in Eastern Europe, it might appear, serve to strengthen these kinds of arguments, as the ideology of centrally planned, redistributive state socialism has been rejected via popular protests in which demands for individual liberty are prominent. However, the political left's perspective on citizenship also incorporates a commitment to collectivism, through the strengthening and consolidation of the health service, education, and other social benefits, that is, of the rights of social citizenship as described by Marshall.

To return, therefore, to the debates initiated by Marshall's work: a number of critical themes have emerged even amongst commentaries that have been basically favourable to his analysis. These are, first, that Marshall's account was somewhat ethnocentric and, second, that it provided an over-optimistic, evolutionist model of the development of citizenship. The first point of criticism must surely be accepted, as Marshall's discussion focused only on the English case. Both Mann (1987) and Turner (1986, 1990) have contributed comparative socio-historical analyses of the development of civil rights, political rights and welfare entitlements in different nation states. These accounts are also critical of the evolutionism implicit in Marshall's scheme, as they suggest that in particular national circumstances the development of rights may not follow the trajectory suggested by Marshall – in late nineteenth- and early twentieth-century Germany, for example, civil and social citizenship advanced faster than political. Such historical discussions are important for our comprehension of the general character of citizenship, but of more immediate concern to our present discussion is the relationship of citizenship to stratification systems.

As we have seen, Marshall argued that citizenship and the class system were at war with each other. Marshall did not go to great lengths to spell out his conceptualization of 'class', but it is reasonable to assume that he was describing the structure of market-related inequalities characteristic of capitalism, as well as the social differentiations associated with them (Barbalet 1988). Thus citizenship not only blunts the edge of market inequalities by 'creating a universal right to real income which is not proportionate to the market value of the claimant' (Marshall 1963: 100), but also promotes an awareness of the common situation of all 'citizens' which overrides, or at least reduces, the consciousness of social differences. Thus the identification of citizenship by Marshall, Lockwood argues, provides the 'clearest and most cogent' answer to the question which was raised by Durkheim: 'namely, what is the basis of the "organic solidarity" of modern societies?' (1974: 365). Lockwood argues that citizenship has emerged as a central element in the *modern* status order, in contrast to the status order of the feudal era which capitalism eventually dissolved, and which was based upon legally sanctioned *inequalities*, rather than the common rights of all 'citizens'.

Dahrendorf (1988) has developed Marshall's arguments in his description of the conflict between 'provisions' (economic growth and material plenty) and 'entitlements' (citizenship rights) as 'the modern social conflict'. This conflict has arisen and persists, Dahrendorf argues, because a certain degree of inequality is required to stimulate economic growth. However, the claims of 'provisions parties' are consistently challenged by 'entitlements parties', not least because the process of the development of 'citizenship' is far from complete: 'In the world at large ... barriers of privilege remain the key issue. Citizens have not arrived, they have merely gained a new vantage point in the struggle for more life chances' (1988: 47).

Dahrendorf's discussion serves to highlight another aspect of the relationship between class and citizenship which has gained considerably in emphasis since Marshall's initial formulation. To describe class and citizenship as 'at war' with each other suggests conflict, but the suggestion that this leads to class abatement suggests also the long-term reduction of class conflict. This was certainly the interpretation put on Marshall's work by some of the earlier commentators making use of Marshall's framework (Halmos 1970). More recent commentaries, however, have tended to stress the inevitability of the persistence of conflict. Indeed, it is clear that Marshall himself saw that 'the basic conflict between social rights and market value has not yet been resolved'. This argument has been extended, however, by those who have stressed not only the continuing nature of the conflictual relationship between citizenship and class, but also the *origins* of citizenship in class conflict (Giddens 1982b).

Giddens argues that Marshall failed to emphasize that citizenship rights have not come about through some natural process of evolution – even though this process may have been stimulated by such massive shocks to the system as, for example, war, as Marshall recognized – but only through the process of *struggle*: 'In my view it is more valid to say that class conflict has been a *medium of the extension of citizenship rights* than to say that the extension of citizenship rights has blunted class divisions' (Giddens 1982b: 174; emphasis in original). The right to vote had to be fought for, and the extension of social citizenship may be seen as the outcome of the political aspirations of the enfranchised working class. Similarly, the rights of workers to organize in trade union activity are not best conceptualized as the more or less inevitable extension of civil citizenship – as 'economic civil rights' or 'industrial citizenship', as Marshall described them – but had to be fought over and were bitterly contested by the ruling class. Indeed, the institution of trade union rights was (and is) interpreted by liberal ideology as being in basic conflict with the individual rights of civil citizenship. The erosion of trade union rights which has been a feature of Conservative government policy in Britain over the last decade has often been carried out under the banner of the sacrosanct nature of individual freedoms – as in, for example, the right not to belong to a union and the abolition of the 'closed shop'. Recent historical developments such as these reforms of trade union legislation, as well as policies directed at the dismantling and 'marketization' of the institutions of the welfare state, have also led authors such as Giddens to emphasize, in some contrast to Marshall, the essentially fragile and contested nature of modern citizenship. In our brief examination above of 'right' and 'left' political perspectives on the nature of citizenship, and the rights and duties associated with it, we can indeed see that citizenship is not to be regarded as a stable or permanent outcome of the development of modern industrial societies.

Authors such as Giddens (1982b) and Mann (1987), therefore, have emphasized the role of class conflict in the development of citizenship – whether citizenship is viewed as the outcome of working-class struggle or ruling-class strategy. Turner (1986), however, although similarly regarding the development of citizenship as the outcome of struggle and conflict, has emphasized above all the significance of *non-class* social movements in its genesis. As we have seen in our previous discussions, 'social movement' is a somewhat imprecise descriptive term which has increasingly been used to identify forms of collective organization which self-consciously seek to change or defend some feature of a society, which possess a distinct ideology, but which are not tied to any specific class or locale (as are, for example, class-based political parties or nationalist movements). As we have seen in the last chapter, Offe (1985b) has identified 'new social movements' as highly significant in the context of the 'new politics', and as being concerned with issues such as ecology and the built environment, peace and human rights – particularly feminism (although there are those who might balk at the identification of feminism as 'new').

Much of Turner's argument relating to the inadequacy of 'class' as an explanatory variable in the description of the evolution of citizenship stems from his observation that the ethnocentric nature of Marshall's original formulation renders it inappropriate for the analysis of the development of citizenship in modern societies which lack a feudal past, or where the final transition from the past had been violently achieved by dramatic events such as defeat in war. As well as class conflict, therefore, Turner emphasizes the significance of war and migration to the development of citizenship. Migration is of significance both in the case of migrant societies such as those of the United States and Australasia, as well as the role of rural – urban migration in breaking traditional ties and obligations within the nation state. War not only has the impact of speeding up indigenous processes of the development of citizenship (for example, it is widely acknowledged that in Britain the extension of the franchise to women was justified with reference to their participation in the war effort during the First World War), but also may result in the imposition of democratic institutions, including citizenship, on defeated societies, as was the case in Japan after the Second World War.

These arguments of Turner's may be seen as simply extending Marshall's original account of citizenship's historical origins to incorporate the historical realities of cross-national variations, but he presses his case for the significance of non-class social movements in the development of citizenship beyond this. Indeed Turner criticizes class-based interpretations of the expansion of citizenship (such as those of Giddens and Mann) as reductionist, and argues instead that:

> the notion of social movement provides us with a valid approach when understanding the nature of citizenship within recent capitalist history . . . Social movements which aim to change society in the name of a generalised belief inevitably raise questions about the nature of participation in society and thus are inevitably movements about the rights of citizenship. (*1986: 89, 92*)

This conclusion has been contested by Barbalet (1988). However, it may be suggested that debates about whether 'classes' or 'social movements' are more (or less) important to the growth of citizenship are not particularly helpful, as, in reality, *both* have contributed significantly to its development – indeed, Turner himself would seem to be taking up this position in his more recent work (Turner 1988).

Marshall identified three aspects of modern citizenship; civil, political and social. Both the kinds of rights associated with these different dimensions, as well as their interrelationship, have, as we have seen, been extensively debated (Barbalet 1988). Leaving aside these complex issues, however, it is not particularly contentious to draw an important distinction between, on the one hand, civil and political citizenship, and, on the other, social citizenship. Civil and political citizenship obviously involve rights, but their institution does not *directly* involve or address distributive issues. Indirectly, of course, as the Marxist critique has argued with some force, these rights might be held to legitimize distributive (or class) inequalities by defining them as 'non-political'.

In contrast, social citizenship *is* directly concerned with distributive issues, in its guarantee of certain rights to material benefits which are associated with the status of 'citizen'. This is, after all, why Marshall and those who have followed his arguments have described citizenship and the class system as being 'at war' with each other. The significance of class conflict and struggle – whether actual or anticipated – in achieving the material gains associated with social citizenship cannot be disputed. It should also be recognized that besides the advancement of the status of citizenship, class-based distributive conflict has also been frequently associated with other status claims – as in, for example, trade union claims for a 'fair wage', or in seeking to perpetuate 'traditional' pay relativities such as those between the skilled and the unskilled (Marshall et al. 1988; Wootton 1955). The 'institutionalized altruism' of professional groupings may also be cited as an example of a status claim which has material consequences (Crompton 1989). Thus status claims have always been widely utilized in arguments concerning the distribution and legitimation of market inequalities, and one of the most important in modern societies is related to social citizenship. In this important sense, therefore (as well as in others), class-based groupings – understood as groups organized in relation to their position in the social division of labour – have shaped, and continue to affect, the definition of social citizenship.[1]

Social citizenship, therefore, attempts to mitigate the inequalities associated with the unequal distribution of private property and market rewards in class societies. In contrast, the institutions of civil and political citizenship served to ameliorate the *status* inequalities associated with traditional, pre-industrial societies. Indeed, it is paradoxical that the status claims of class-based organizations in market societies have actually contributed to the perpetuation of some of the traditional material inequalities associated with status – of which one of the most obvious is the systematic exclusion of women from access to education, and the better-paid and more prestigious occupations, by trade unions and professional organizations. As we shall see in our subsequent discussion, many of the 'rights' of social citizenship may be seen to consist in large part of social insurances which relate to the (male) citizen as an *employee*, rather than accruing to all citizens irrespective of whether they are male or female, black or white. Nonetheless, although it may be argued that the initial conceptualization of liberal bourgeois citizenship excluded many 'traditionally' defined as of inferior status – such as women – it has proved ultimately powerless to resist the claims for civil and political rights articulated by feminists and others. The written (and unwritten) constitutions of the major industrial nations remain formally committed to ideologies of universalism, and although it is true that such ideologies have frequently given way to expediency, it is a sociological fact that such ideologies exist and have frequently been used in arguments against the perpetuation of institutions which discriminate against particular groups. Turner is correct to emphasize that claims on behalf of these groups have often been pressed most powerfully not by classes, but by social movements.

Women and citizenship

We have seen that the main thrust of the socialist/Marxist critique of the real significance of civil and political citizenship is that these individual rights have little impact upon, and may underpin and legitimize, structures of material inequalities. Feminists have developed their critique of citizenship even further, arguing that it is not only the case that individual civil and political rights have had little effect on the material position of women, but also that 'citizenship' itself has been from earliest origins a *gendered* concept; and moreover one that has systematically excluded women.

In a powerful critique, Pateman (1988, 1989; see also Phillips 1990) demonstrates that the original social contract, as described in the writings of political theorists such as Locke and Rousseau, from the first excluded women as 'citizens'. Women were viewed as creatures of passion rather than rationality, lacking the capacities required to participate as citizens and indeed as capable of bringing considerable disorder into the public sphere. The rights of men over women were seen to be natural rather than political; the contract theorists rejected the legitimacy of paternal rights, but absorbed and simultaneously transformed conjugal, masculine patriarchal right. Thus men's domination of women within marriage was universally accepted. The 'fraternal social contract' therefore 'constitutes patriarchal civil society and the modern, ascriptive rule of men over women' (Pateman 1989: 43). Citizenship is fundamentally *gendered*, and although a supposedly gender-neutral category incorporates essentially masculine attributes and characteristics such as participation in warfare, long-term adult participation in economic life (employment), and so on. The concept of citizenship abstracted from the differences between men and women and as a consequence, one sex (men) became the norm.[2]

The material benefits of social citizenship, therefore, have had very different consequences for men and women. We have seen that social citizenship has been regarded as contributing to 'class abatement' because, amongst other things, the institutions of the welfare state include rights to real income which do not depend on the market value of the claimant. Thus the development of social citizenship has been seen as a response to a major dilemma of liberal democracy – the fact that the free play of the market will include losers as well as winners. Unemployment benefits, old-age pensions etc., may be viewed as rights to which citizen-employees who are not particularly successful in the competitive struggles of the market are entitled – but what of those who are regarded as incapable of full market participation? As a consequence, feminists have argued, women have been incorporated into the welfare state not as workers or citizens, but as dependants and welfare providers – more particularly, as wives and mothers. Thus welfare policies have often served to reproduce the patriarchal structures of family life.

For example, in Britain, the Beveridge Report (1942), which laid the foundations of the postwar welfare state, assumed that 'during marriage most women will not be gainfully employed'; married women were thus regarded as their husband's dependants, and exempted from unemployment and sickness benefit schemes. As Beveridge argued:

> The attitude of the housewife to gainful employment outside the home is not and should not be the same as that of the single woman. She has other duties . . . In the next thirty years housewives as mothers have vital work to do in ensuring the adequate continuance of the British Race and of British Ideals in the world. (*Cited in Wilson, 1977: 151–2*)

In the United States, a sharp separation is drawn between 'social security', where benefits are paid to those who have 'earned' them during working lifetimes (the 'deserving poor'), and 'welfare', or public handouts to the (undeserving) poor – many of whom will be unsupported mothers (Pateman 1989: 187).

The exclusion of women from civil and political citizenship, and the reproduction of patriarchal institutions via social citizenship, has from the first been resisted by feminists. As Mary Astell was asking at the end of the seventeenth century: 'If all Men are born free, how is it that all Women are born Slaves?' Thus from eighteenth century onwards, liberal feminists have been engaged in struggles to achieve the status of citizens for women. Characteristically, this struggle has taken the form of arguing that women are in no sense 'naturally' inferior, but have capacities equal to those of men, and should not, therefore, be debarred from full citizenship. However, as Pateman has argued, this liberal feminist strategy carries with it an apparently insoluble dilemma: if citizenship itself is defined in masculine terms, how can women become partners to a *fraternal* social contract?[3] One consequence is that women seeking equality have often been constrained to behave as surrogate men – for example, in not taking responsibility for the care of children, often by remaining childless. Historically, the 'career woman' has been assumed to have a career rather than a family, a condition which was imposed on many women in England by marriage bars (for women only) which persisted in many areas of bureaucratic employment until the late 1950s. The conflict between 'equality' (with men) and 'difference' (as women) is one which defies a neat theoretical and practical resolution even within contemporary feminism. (Feminist authors including Cockburn (1991) have stressed the importance of working within *both* frameworks.) This contradiction is reflected in the history of the feminist movement in Britain and the United States. Once the struggle for women's suffrage had been achieved, the feminist movement in both countries diverged between liberal 'equal-rights' and 'welfare feminist' activities. Welfare feminism supported protective legislation for women in employment, for example, whereas this was opposed by equal-rights feminists who argued that such legislation would hamper the struggle of women for equal opportunities in employment (Banks 1981).

There are no ready answers available to these difficult questions, although Cockburn has suggested that it is in practice possible to transcend the contradiction of equality: 'Men tell us "women cannot claim to be equal if they are different from men. You have to choose." We now have a reply. If we say so, as women, we can be both the same as you *and* different from you . . . What we are seeking is not in fact *equality*, but *equivalence*' (1991: 10). Thus although it may be conceded that the gendered nature of citizenship status renders its achievement problematic for women, this should not be allowed to obscure the fact that women's struggle for citizenship status has brought with it many benefits. What Walby (1990) has described as 'first-wave' feminism in Britain extended from 1850 to 1930. During this period, women acquired the right to vote, to control their own property, to enter (most) universities and professions, and to live independently of their husbands; that is, they achieved most of the elements of civil and political citizenship. Left critics of the hollow nature of civil and political equality have rightly stressed their compatibility with material inequalities; for women, the situation is compounded by the fact that, even when civil and political equality has been achieved, they have had to contend with both material and sexual inequalities – particularly in respect of employment.

Social citizenship, as we have seen, has been directly concerned with the reduction of material inequalities. The role of the class struggle in developing the institutions of social citizenship has been described above. Marshall described 'the basic civil right' in the economic field as 'the right to work' (1963: 77); Giddens and others have emphasized the political significance of 'industrial citizenship' (that is, the recognition of trade unions and the institutions of collective bargaining) in extending the boundaries of social citizenship. However, women have not, until recently, spent most of their adult lives as full-time employees, and indeed have often been denied 'the right to work' by the very institutions which existed to defend these rights on behalf of adult males. Thus whilst it is true that worker's organizations have struggled to establish rights to welfare, these frequently assumed the form of work-related social insurances such as unemployment benefits and pension rights. What is less often emphasized, moreover, is the role of women, as feminists, in the struggle to establish welfare rights not related to employment. The concerns of women with children and the family has resulted in a long history of specifically female concern with the establishment and development of welfare and human-service institutions – some specifically directed at women, others at the promotion of material supports for family life. Women such as Octavia Hill, Florence Nightingale, Marie Stopes, Eleanor Rathbone and many others have all made significant contributions to developments in health, housing and welfare legislation which established what Marshall described as social citizenship. In Britain, welfare feminists worked closely with the Labour Party, and Banks has argued that 'to a large extent we may see the welfare state in Britain as a product of an alliance between welfare feminism and the Labour Party' (1981: 174).

As the critiques of Pateman and others have demonstrated, there-fore, although the development of the welfare state has brought with it many material advantages for women, its institutions have also been developed in a manner designed to reproduce the patriarchal model of the 'male breadwinner', leaving the major domestic responsibilities to women.[4] Thus women are still the major providers of welfare – as low-paid workers in the public sphere and as unpaid workers in the private (Finch and Groves 1983). The reproduction of such patriarchal institu-tions became a major target against which the arguments of 'second-wave' feminism were developed.

As a number of recent historical discussions have stressed, feminism as a social movement has a long history (Banks 1981; Walby 1990). Nevertheless, it is possible to identify two exceptional waves of feminist activity: the first extending from the middle of the nineteenth century to the interwar period, the second from the 1960s until the present day.[5] Like the first wave, which had developed in association with the anti-slavery movement, the second also occurred at the same time as attempts to extend the boundaries of civil, political and social citizen-ship for racially excluded groups. In the civil rights movements and the associated growth of left politics during the 1960s, however, women once again found themselves relegated to typing, making the coffee, and providing moral support. Second-wave feminism, therefore, moved swiftly from a concern with equal rights towards a critique of the fundamentally 'gendered' nature of modern society, reflected not only in the separation between 'public' (male) and 'private' (female) spheres of activity, but also within the public sphere itself – as demonstrated, for example, in the extent of segregation by sex within employment. Thus during the 1960s and 1970s, there were important legislative gains related to equal pay and opportunities in Europe and North America, and during the 1980s, a significant shift beyond this in the direction of equal value. Equal opportunities relates to both equality of access and the absence of direct and indirect discrimination in employment (the latter would include, for example, the requirement to be geographically mobile in order to achieve promotion, a require-ment which would work against the circumstances of many women): equal-value legislation, however, is potentially much more radical in its impact. The principle of equal pay for work of equal value brings with it the necessity to re-evaluate the principles which have traditionally underpinned the relative ranking of occupations and the material rewards associated with them – and a major factor which has con-tributed to this ranking is, of course, that sex-typed 'women's' occupa-tions will be ranked lower than men's. In the welfare sphere itself, feminists have pressed for the material recognition of women's unpaid contributions – for example, for the right to payments for women caring for elderly dependants – as well as for the reform of the benefits system away from a structure which reproduced patriarchal family relations; these have, however, not been sufficient to prevent the feminization of poverty. Second-wave feminism, in an echo of the purity campaigns of the first wave, has also directed attention towards violence against women and their exploitation in sexual relations. Divorce and abortion law reform, together with the recognition of and protection from domestic violence, have been important elements in the struggles of women to achieve control over their own bodies. One outcome of these pressures has been that in recent court decisions in Scotland and England, the legal possibility of rape within marriage has been established, thus overturning the man's right of physical access, with or without her consent, to his wife's sexual services.

With considerable over-simplification, therefore, a major focus of the struggles of second-wave feminism might be viewed as the attempt to establish and extend the rights of civil and social citizenship on behalf of women. In so doing, as feminist theorists have argued, customary definitions of what constitutes civil society have been challenged, as has the relative ordering of work and occupations held by 'citizens' (Eisenstein 1981; Pateman 1988, 1989). Although many gains have been made on behalf of women, therefore, it still remains the case that many, perhaps the majority, of women are still second-class citizens. Thus Walby (1990), for example, has described the transition from the nineteenth- to the twentieth-century status of women as one from 'private' to 'public' patriarchy.

In the language of social stratification, it is true that women do not constitute a 'status group' (Lockwood 1986). Nevertheless, more or less concerted actions by feminists have, over the last one and a half centuries, served to enhance the relative status of women, both nationally and internationally. The gradual achievement of the different elements of citizenship by women has had an impact on the location of women within the stratification system, both individually and collectively. More women are entering higher-level professions and occupations, and in the arena of party politics, all of the major parties in Britain are acutely aware of the political significance of their stance on gender. It is important not to be complacent – Dahrendorf's comments to the effect that full citizenship has not yet arrived for the majority apply with particular force in the case of women – but it is equally important to recognize the changes that have taken place, and their implications for the structure of social stratification in advanced industrial societies.

Race and citizenship

There are a number of difficulties associated with the use of the term 'race' in sociology. The category was not included in the initial formulation of general theories of social inequality by nineteenth-century social theorists, and the nature of the conflict, exploitation and oppression which have been associated with and justified by 'racial' distinctions has made social theorists less, rather than more, likely to accept that they are rooted in any 'biological' difference. Investigations commissioned by organizations such as UNESCO have concluded that the human species had a single origin, and that although human groups could be classified on the basis of physical indices such as hair and skin type, such classifications had to recognize that there were considerable physical overlaps between one group and another.

One response to the rejection of the biological foundation of 'racial' distinctions has been to emphasize the significance of *ethnicity*, rather than race. This approach focuses upon the cultural differentiation of various ethnic groups; but, as Rex has argued, such an emphasis on 'difference' has a tendency to leave out of account the extent of the *inequalities*, rooted in oppression, coercion and exploitation, between ethnic groups. Rex, therefore, prefers to use the term 'race relations' to describe situations of particularly severe conflict and oppression in which it is not possible for an individual to leave the subordinate group, and which are justified by the dominant group in terms of some kind of deterministic theory – situations, in short, in which race and ethnicity are 'role signs' (Banton 1967) which lead to the assignment of positions in the overall system of exploitation (Rex 1986, 1987).

There is not the space here to go into the details of the history of European domination since the sixteenth century, which included booty capitalism, slavery, colonial exploitation and economic oppression and which has resulted in the widespread identification of blackness as a negative role sign. The harsh material realities of racism are not being denied; nevertheless, the fact remains that the systematic material inequalities and ascriptive distinctions which are associated with the physical marker of 'race' have come into conflict with the universalistic values of 'citizenship'.

In the British context, citizenship has acquired a particular significance in respect of race. The first generation of 'new Commonwealth' (that is, West Indian and Asian) immigrants who arrived during the 1940s and 1950s faced few legal restrictions; under the British Nationality Act 1948 they were allowed to enter Britain freely, to find work, to settle and to bring in their families. However, the increase in immigration during subsequent years led to growing social unease and to political agitation for controls. Thus the preferential status of Commonwealth immigrants in Britain has been whittled away by a succession of restrictive measures, culminating in the Immigration Act 1971, which restricted the right of abode to 'patrials', or persons having parents or grandparents who lived in Britain (a barely disguised measure to protect the rights of entry of whites from the 'old Commonwealth' of Australasia, South Africa and Canada); reinforced the conditionality of entry on having obtained employment; and reduced entitlements to bring in families. The recent history of immigration controls in Britain, therefore, has made the right to British nationality, and thus citizenship, a significant issue in the politics of race relations in Britain. It should be made clear, therefore, that the discussion of 'citizenship' that follows is largely concerned with blacks whose nationality is not in question – that is, black citizens of Britain and the United States.

Marshall's analysis of the development of citizenship rights has been widely employed in discussions of the unequal situation of blacks. This is not surprising, given that there is systematic empirical evidence that in Britain and America, by comparison with the white population, blacks have lower-level jobs, live in poorer-quality housing, are more likely to be unemployed and thus more likely to be benefit-dependent.[6] Although blacks may be citizens, therefore, the conclusion is inescapable that there exist systematic structural obstacles to the realization of their full citizenship rights. In the case of the United States, the origins of the black population in the institution of slavery is obviously a fact of considerable significance. The argument has often been made that in the case of the Northern States, successive waves of immigration from Europe, together with the open frontier to the West, facilitated individual mobility to an extent which restricted the growth of large-scale, overt class conflict during the nineteenth and early twentieth centuries. However, black migration from the American South has not been followed by any substantial immigrant flows from Europe, and the blacks have remained a ghettoized population at the bottom of the social hierarchy.[7] In 1965, Parsons described American Negroes as the 'prototypically disadvantaged category' within American society, and argued that their inclusion within American society depended for its success on the 'much more effective institutionalization of Marshall's social component of citizenship' (Parsons 1965: 736). Blacks had already organized in pursuit of citizenship through the Civil Rights movement of the 1960s, and even before this, the rulings of the Supreme Court had forced some desegregation in education and employment. Since the Civil Rights campaigns, however, Affirmative Action and Positive Discrimination – which have taken the form, for example, of black quotas in college education, special programmes for blacks, etc., may be seen as direct and interventionist attempts to 'effectively institutionalize the social component of citizenship'. The fact that these actions have met with only limited success should not be allowed to undermine their significance.

The situation in Britain is rather different. The black community has its origins in immigration rather than slavery – although the relevant point should be made that the black West Indian population is itself of slave origin, and the British were the major colonists in Africa and Asia. Rex (Rex 1986; Rex and Tomlinson 1979) has argued that black immigrants in Britain are at a disadvantage because, as recent entrants (and for a number of other reasons) they have been excluded from the British working class and thus the 'welfare-state deal'; like Parsons, therefore, Rex sees the material situation of the black community as stemming from blacks' lack of access to social citizenship, despite their formal possession of civil and political rights.

Rex (1986: 66) describes the 'welfare-state deal' as follows:

1 That workers shall have the freedom to engage in collective bargaining over their wages and conditions.
2 That the government shall take the responsibility for planning the economy in such a way that nearly full-employment is achieved.
3 That the best way of achieving this is through a mixed economy, so that both total free enterprise and total collective ownership are ruled out.
4 That workers in times of unemployment, ill-health and retirement will be entitled to a basic income paid for on the basis of compulsory insurance contributions by employers and workers.
5 That all people will be entitled to a basic standard of health, housing, education and other personal social services, the cost of which will be borne partly by general taxation.

Like Giddens, Rex regards the benefits of social citizenship as having been fought for and achieved through a process of class struggle. His account also incorporates the existence of Keynesian strategies in respect of the regulation of the national economy, as well as the Marshallian concept of social citizenship. As such, it assumes a particular mode of incorporation of the indigenous male working class which, it has been argued, has served to reproduce patriarchal structures in respect of the family and welfare institutions (Jenson et al. 1988). Nevertheless, Rex's analysis remains of value as it serves to illustrate the manner in which blacks have been excluded from the benefits of social citizenship in Britain during the immediate postwar period. Blacks were not at all prominent – as members or officials – in the trade union movement in Britain during the period when the unions had their greatest level of access to government – that is the 1950s to the 1970s. This relative lack of union protection, in combination with the extensive segmentation of the labour market, rendered the black population most vulnerable to unemployment. Access to local-authority housing (the major form of lower-class housing provision in the postwar period) depended upon length of residence; thus the immigrant population was at a serious disadvantage. The educational system is both highly competitive and residentially stratified, and minority children were as a consequence placed overwhelmingly in the worst sections of the worst schools. The 'authorities' in respect of the black population are drawn largely from the indigenous white population; racial harassment on the part of groups such as the police has contributed further to the marginalization of the immigrant community. For all of these reasons, therefore, Rex argues that the immigrant population (and its children) has been excluded from the 'welfare-state deal' struggled for by the British working class, and thus also from the benefits of social citizenship. As a consequence, Rex suggests that minorities of immigrant origin may be described as an 'underclass', 'who instead of forming an inert and despairing social residue, organize and act in their own "underclass" interest often relating themselves to colonial class positions' (Rex and Tomlinson 1979: 328).

Rex is careful to emphasize that the 'underclass' description does not apply to all blacks. An (increasing) minority have achieved both economic and social success, and Rex anticipates that, as the size of the relatively advantaged group within the immigrant community increases, so a process of assimilation will occur. His use of the term 'underclass', it should be stressed, differs from its more usual use to describe groups who have failed altogether to become economically self-supporting – as, for example, in Myrdal's (1962) description of the situation of the blacks in the United States. This use of the term, however, has become highly contentious, particularly in the light of right-wing arguments to the effect that, far from ameliorating class conflict, the effect of the development of social citizenship and the welfare-state deal has been to *create* an 'underclass' in advanced industrial societies.

Social citizenship and the 'underclass'

Our discussion so far has assumed that, despite a series of modifications and qualifications that should be entered in respect of Marshall's original arguments, social-citizenship rights have been widely achieved, and extended, in Western industrial societies. However, since the 1980s, social citizenship – understood as rights to welfare – has been under systematic attack from the political right. As Giddens and others have argued, citizenship rights should not be regarded as either somehow natural or permanent. It is not simply that welfare expenditure has been seen as 'too expensive' in a period of economic recession and lack of growth in Western economies – after all, left critics were predicting a 'fiscal crisis' of the state in the 1970s, O'Connor (1973). Rather, neo-liberal critics have argued that the provision of social citizenship through collectivist welfare-state provision in fact has served to undermine the individual freedoms enshrined within civil and political citizenship rights.

In chapter 1, we have discussed in brief the neo-liberal argument that attempts to achieve equality of outcome through, for example, programmes of affirmative action for disadvantaged groups might undermine legal or formal equalities (see above, p. 5–6). In a similar vein, libertarian critics of welfare-state provision have argued that the *compulsory* redistribution of income should be kept at a minimum, and that individuals should be free to determine the nature and extent of their own welfare provision. These arguments do not imply that those without resources should be left to starve, but they do indicate the targeting (that is, means-testing) of the benefits which are available in any 'minimalist' system of provision (Peacock 1991). As Plant (1991) has argued, neo-liberals have stressed the value of negative liberty – that is, the absence of intentional coercion – as against positive liberty – that is, the actual possession of powers, resources and capacities to act. A further twist to these arguments is developed by those who suggest that collective provisions have actually had the effect of undermining individual capacities. Thus state provision for the economically disadvantaged is argued, by some right-wing theorists, to be making an active contribution to the problem it is trying to solve, through the creation of 'welfare dependency' and thus the development of an underclass.

We have already encountered variants of these arguments in previous chapters. Saunders, for example, has identified the 'major fault line' in countries like Britain as being between 'a majority of people who can service their key consumption requirements through the market and a minority who remain reliant on an increasingly inadequate and alienative form of direct state provision' (1987: ch. 3). This split, he argues, is affecting 'the material life chances and cultural identities' of the people involved – that is, they are increasingly disempowered in respect of the ('normal') majority who can service their needs through the market. In a similar vein, Murray has written of the 'Great Society' welfare reforms in the United States in the 1960s that:

> The first effect of the new rules [i.e., increases in welfare] was to make it more profitable for the poor to behave in the short term in ways that were destructive in the long term. Their second effect was to . . . subsidize irretrievable mistakes. We tried to provide more for the poor and produced more poor instead. (*1984: 9*)

It should be recognized that the 'underclass' is a highly contentious concept. Some have argued that the term has been developed not in order to describe an objective phenomenon or set of social relationships but, rather, as a stigmatizing label which effectively 'blames the victims' for their misfortunes. Thus Dean has argued that: '"Underclass" is a symbolic term with no single meaning, but a great many applications . . . It represents, not a useful concept, but a potent symbol' (1991: 35). However, the implications of the arguments which have been developed using the term, which suggest the unravelling and virtual abolition of the rights of social citizenship, are simply too important to be disregarded on account of terminological niceties.

In fact, the notion of an underclass has a long history, although this is not always the label that has been used. Marx, for example, described the 'lumpenproletariat' of the nineteenth century in terms which closely resemble twentieth-century accounts of the underclass. In the most general terms, the concept describes those in persistent poverty, who are not able, for whatever reason, to gain a living within the dominant processes of production, distribution and exchange. In one sense, it might be suggested that the existence of such an underclass is in fact normal in a competitive capitalist society, which will inevitably produce losers as well as winners. As we have seen, social citizenship has been regarded as a kind of legitimate compensation for these losers, hence its role in 'class abatement'. Perhaps because the underclass is defined with respect to its *lack* of direct structural relationship to the dominant processes of production and exchange, there has been a constant tendency to conceptualize it with respect to its supposed characteristics, rather than in respect to its relationship to other classes. These characteristics have usually been negative. It is, therefore, in the explanation of poverty – or why some people are losers whilst others are not, whether the causes of poverty are primarily structural or primarily cultural – that the 'underclass' concept assumes its contentious aspect.

A frequent explanation of individual inequality is that some people are simply more talented, and ambitious, than others; they deserve, therefore, to succeed. It is perfectly possible to hold to this meritocratic view, however, without designating the less talented and less ambitious as 'worse' – as in the phrase: 'There's always got to be a bottom brick'. Bottom bricks may be bottom bricks, but they are essentially the same bricks as the top ones. It is but a short step, however, from recognizing talent and ambition in the more successful to the argument that the more fortunate are in fact better, and therefore *morally* superior to the losers. Nineteenth-century debates on poverty linked such arguments to wider economic questions; charity was seen not only as destroying incentives amongst the poor but as jeopardizing the nature of the capitalist enterprise itself: 'Hunger must be permitted to do its work so that labourers are compelled to exert themselves. Otherwise they will reduce their efforts and destroy their only safeguard against starvation' (Bendix 1964: 58) – and not only the labourers, but the enterprise as a whole, will suffer. To these arguments Malthus added his theory of population: the poor have a natural tendency to increase their numbers beyond that sustainable by the available food supply; this improvidence results from ignorance and a lack of moral restraint. Nothing less than a new set of moral values, therefore will serve to improve the lot of those in poverty.

We may see, therefore, that arguments which hold the poor to be, in varying degrees, responsible for their own plight have a long history, as have arguments to the effect that charity (or welfare) simply stops the poor from helping themselves. It is not surprising, therefore, that such arguments such have resurfaced with the increasing influence of 'New Right' perspectives on welfare – although the intention of these brief remarks has been to suggest that they are not, in fact, so 'new'. Murray (1984) has argued that the 'Great Society' welfare reforms have created an 'underclass' in the United States. Murray identifies the underclass amongst particular groups of the poor – unmarried single mothers, labour-force drop-outs, and those engaged in criminal activities – and attempts to demonstrate that all of these activities have been positively encouraged by welfare reforms.

Murray argues, for example, that changes in the benefits systems associated with Aid to Families with Dependent Children (AFDC) have made unmarried parenthood, without employment, a more attractive option for *both* parents. He also argues that the decline in rates of arrest has increased the possibility of getting away with criminal activity, and thus its economic attractions. Welfare reforms have taken away the incentive to work. Thus for those in the black ghetto (in the United States, these arguments have focused almost entirely on the problems of poverty amongst urban blacks) there has been, with these changes in incentives, a change in attitude. The black 'underclass' is demoralized, the capacity for self-help in the community has been cumulatively undermined by the policies of well-meaning white liberals. Although Murray has developed his empirical arguments largely in the US context, he also argues that such as 'underclass' is developing in Britain, and for similar reasons: 'Britain has a growing population of working-aged, healthy people who live in a different world from other Britons, who are raising their children to live in it, and whose values are now contaminating the life of entire neighbourhoods' (Murray 1990: 4).

There are two steps, therefore, to Murray's arguments: first, well-meaning reforms exacerbate the problem they are trying to solve – poverty. Then, the poor develop a moral stance which effectively removes the will to effort and further deepens the cycle of poverty. Murray's empirical evidence has been widely contested. Wilson (1987, 1991) has argued that there are compelling structural reasons for the increase in persistent poverty, and other 'social pathologies' such as single parenthood, in the black ghettos of the US Northwest. The loss of manufacturing employment during the economic restructuring which followed upon the crisis of the 1970s had a particularly significant impact upon these regions. In any case, Wilson argues, if Murray's thesis was correct, trends in black joblessness and family dissolution should have gone into reverse when the real value of welfare programmes (to the recipients) declined sharply during the 1970s; in fact, they continued to increase. Rising unemployment has also been accompanied by a fall in the real value of wages, and thus an increase in poverty. The pattern of migration flows has kept the age structure of the ghetto disproportionately young (and therefore more likely to have children), and the real decline in employment opportunities means that young black women are confronting a shrinking pool of marriageable – that is, employed – men. The very success of Equal Opportunity and Affirmative Action programmes has created an increasing black middle class who, given the long-term decline of overt discriminatory practices, have moved out of the ghetto – leaving those behind as the 'truly disadvantaged'. Thus vital elements of the black infrastructure, once provided by black professionals, have been removed, and with them the role models for the next generation.

Wilson, therefore, is not concerned to deny the increase in crime, poverty, single parenthood, and so on which has occurred in the urban ghettos of America. He is, however, concerned to emphasize the macro-structural factors which have brought about such changes, and his analysis suggests that only macro-structural changes can alter the situation. The problems of the truly disadvantaged, he argues, require *non-racial* solutions. Macrœconomic policies are needed to promote growth and tight labour markets, and there should be increased resources devoted to education and training, in combination with universalist child support programmes and access to child care. In short, Wilson advocates the establishment of a 'corporatist democracy', in which social policy is integrated with economic policy.

As far as arguments relating to the moral values of the poor are concerned, Wilson associates himself with a broadly structuralist perspective – that is, that specific social values emerge from specific social circumstances and life chances and reflect class and racial posi-tions. This position has also been forcefully argued by British critics of Murray, who have emphasized the similarities between Murray's arguments and previous theories which have stressed the significance of the 'culture of poverty' (Lewis 1959) in contributing to 'cycles of disadvantage' (Walker 1990). Empirical work in Britain on 'cycles of disadvantage' had failed to demonstrate its malign and enduring effect: 'At least half of the children born into a disadvantaged home do not repeat the pattern of disadvantage in the next generation. Over half of all forms of disadvantage arise anew each generation' (Rutter and Madge 1976).

Although Wilson is clearly a 'structuralist' rather than a 'culturalist' as far as the explanation of poverty is concerned, this does not mean that he does not recognize the contribution which the socio-cultural context might make to the exacerbation of the problems of poverty. Weak labour-force attachment will tend to lower percieved self-efficacy, for example. Such beliefs 'are part of what I have called "concentration effects", that is the effects of living in a neighborhood that is overwhelmingly impoverished' (Wilson 1991: 11). In a similar vein, Merton's analysis of the conflict between societal or cultural goals and the institutionalized means through which they could be achieved has already provided a framework through which 'deviant' responses might be understood. Thus when the goal of economic success is dominant, but the individual lacks the means through which to achieve it, 'innovation' (illegal activity) is a possible response. This argu-ment, of course, is perfectly compatible with Murray's underlying logic. However, as Merton emphasized: 'These categories (such as 'innovation') refer to role behavior in specific types of situations, not to personality. They are types of more or less enduring response, not types of personality organization' (Merton 1965: 140).

To return to the broader sociological themes discussed above in chapter 2, therefore, it would not be particularly helpful to attempt to deny the capacity for autonomous action amongst those in poverty. It is important, however, that this capacity is not linked automatically to arguments like Murray's to the effect that it is the *peculiar* nature of the poor's capacity for action – in particular, their lack of moral values stemming from a 'culture of poverty' – which explains their material circumstances. Murray would argue (as would other right-wing sociologists such as Saunders) that they wish to *restore* the capacity for action to a population which has been deprived of it by the excesses of bureaucratic state welfare. As Murray has argued:

> Government cannot identify the worthy, but it can protect a society in which the worthy can identify themselves. I am proposing triage of a sort, triage by self-selection. In triage on the battlefield, the doctor makes the decision – this one gets treatment, that one waits, the other one is made comfortable while waiting to die. In our social triage, the decision is left up to the patient. The patient always has a right to say 'I can do X' and get a chance to prove it. Society always has a right to hold him to that pledge. The patient always has the right to fail. Society always has the right to let him. (*1984: 234*)

'The right to fail', however, has a chilling echo in the nineteenth-century arguments of Thomas Malthus:

> A man who is born into a world already possessed, if he cannot get subsistence from his parents on whom he has a just demand, and if the society does not want his labour, has no claim of right to the smallest portion of food, and, in fact, has no business to be where he is. At Nature's mighty feast there is no vacant cover for him. She tells him to be gone, and will quickly execute her own orders. (*Malthus cited in Bendix 1964: 65*)

Conclusions

Despite the many inadequacies that may be discovered in Marshall's original account of the growth and development of citizenship in modern industrial societies, his threefold distinction between civil, political and social citizenship has proved invaluable in understanding developments in social stratification since the nineteenth century. The universalistic ideologies of liberal democracy made it possible (and still make it possible) for those excluded to argue that the barriers to their status as citizens should be removed. Citizenship, however, has only been achieved through struggle, rather than granted as a right. Both industrial citizenship (that is, collective bargaining rights) as well as the rights of social citizenship (particularly welfare rights) may be regarded as being in conflict with the interests associated with the dominant capitalist order.

It is legitimate, therefore, to view many of the citizenship gains of the population at large as the outcome of actual or anticipated class conflict. Despite Marx's predictions, class conflict in Western industrial societies has largely concerned itself with gaining some kind of protection from the ravages of the market for the subordinate classes, as well as (or perhaps, rather than) the revolutionary transformation of society itself. Paradoxically, therefore, class struggles have been significant in achieving significant *status* gains on behalf of subordinate classes – and amongst the most important of these has been the status of citizenship.

Initially, however, citizenship gains were largely achieved on behalf of a white, male working class. The rights of social citizenship, in particular, were modelled on patriarchal family structures. Parallel with working-class struggles, therefore, there have also been struggles on behalf of excluded groups such as women and blacks, initiated by non-class social movements. It is not being suggested that exclusion from, and gradual entry into, the status of citizenship is a sufficient explanation of the location of women and blacks within the stratification order; nevertheless, these processes are crucial to any understanding of their contemporary situation. In the modern era, new social movements are seeking to extend further the boundaries of citizenship to include animals and children, as well as more general concerns with the environment lived in by all 'citizens'.

As we have seen, much of the contemporary political debate over 'citizenship' is concerned with negative liberties rather than positive liberties, with personal freedoms rather than the redistributive issues – which Marshall (correctly) saw as the major implications of social citizenship. An emphasis on the importance of personal freedoms, however, should not be allowed to override the simple fact perceived by an earlier generation of commentators (including Marx, and Marshall himself) – that is, that personal freedoms do not count for much in a situation characterized by gross material inequalities. It is paradoxical, therefore, that the rights of social citizenship are now under sustained attack by those, such as Murray, claiming to be motivated by the need to preserve personal freedoms.[8] These arguments, it cannot be stressed too often, repeat those in widespread use before not only social, but civil and political citizenship rights had been gained: 'The slave must be compelled to work; but the freeman should be left to his own judgement and discretion' (Rev. Townsend cited in Bendix 1964: 58).

Despite the caveats which should be entered in respect of women in particular, citizenship rights are universal. The erosion of citizenship, therefore, affects more than just the working class. It is in this sense that the arguments of those who have argued that 'class' has become less significant in contemporary politics might be conceded. The roll-back of social citizenship affects all of those who have gained from its implementation, or who might hope to benefit from its extension. The defence of citizenship, therefore, cuts across the boundaries of social class.

Notes

1   Indeed, it might be argued that government actions during the miner's strike in Britain (1984) included the erosion of aspects of civil citizenship concerned with freedom of movement, the right to protest, etc.
2   The 1789 declaration in France of 'the Rights of Man and Citizen' did not include women, and the Code Napoleon served further to establish the subordinate legal status of women in France.
3   Pateman argues that, to create a properly democratic society, it is necessary to 'deconstruct and reassemble our understanding of the body politic . . . The most profound and complex problem for political theory and practice is how the two bodies of humankind and feminine and masculine individuality can be fully incorporated into political life. How can the present of patriarchal domination, opposition and duality be transformed into a future of autonomous, democratic differentiation?' (1989: 53). Pateman does not give an answer to this question, and it certainly lies outside this author's capacities.
4   It should be noted that the 'male breadwinner' model is particularly appropriate to the British case. In other European countries such as France, where women have historically been involved to a greater extent in paid employment, maternity legislation, family allowances, etc. have been developed on the assumption that women, even mothers with children, would remain in full-time employment. See Jenson (1986); Crompton et al. (1990).
5   This generalization is broadly correct for Britain and the United States; there are, however, European variations, paticularly in the timing and extent of first-wave feminism. See Evans (1987).
6   It should be noted that there are considerable differences, by ethnic group, *within* the black community in respect of these social indicators (see Brown 1984). These reflect important differences in family structures, regional variations, as well as the timing of successive waves of immigration.
7   A theoretical debate which has been of considerable relevance to the US case has concerned whether the situation of Southern blacks should be

explored using the concept of 'caste' or 'class'; see Dollard (1957) and Cox (1959).

8 A theoretical rejection of these arguments is developed in Plant (1991).

7
Lifestyle, Consumption Categories and Consciousness Communities

Introduction

To emphasize the pervasive links between stratification systems and varying patterns of consumption might appear to be nothing but a statement of the obvious. The consumption and display of scarce material and cultural goods has always, throughout the prehistory and history of human societies, been used as a marker of power and domination, whatever the sensual advantages and gratifications associated with the possession of and access to these (relatively) scarce resources might also be (Veblen 1934). However, a common theme which links a number of somewhat diverse approaches focusing on consumption is the suggestion that in the advanced industrial societies, the increase in economic productivity and the capacity for wealth-creation which has taken place since the Second World War has reduced (relatively) the significance of the production and acquisition of basic material needs in the lives of families and individuals in general. Thus with the rise in standards of living, it is argued that issues related to *consumption*, rather than production, are becoming more relevant; and that 'lifestyles', rather than 'classes' are playing an increasingly important part in shaping a whole range of attitudes and behaviours.

Thus there has been a recent and rapid increase in the level of sociological attention directed at consumption. Not surprisingly, these discussions have also been linked to the rapid flux of cultural change which has accompanied the social and economic changes associated with the development of industrialism in the late twentieth century – not only have we had a move from 'Fordism' to 'post-Fordism', apparently, but also a move from 'modernity' to 'postmodernity'. Another common feature of debates relating to consumption is the observation that whereas there exist a range of elaborated social science concepts (including, for example, class) for the analysis of economic and production relationships, the sphere of consumption is conceptually underdeveloped (Offe 1985a; Bagguley et al. 1989). Warde (1990) has identified two, 'as yet largely unconnected' fields in which the sociology of consumption has operated. The first is a predominantly British debate located within the 'new urban sociology' relating to the significance or otherwise of 'consumption-sector cleavages'. This debate has been closely associated with issues relating to occupational class, and has taken up many of the themes, as well as the methodologies, associated with this approach to 'class analysis' (for example Dunleavy 1980; Saunders 1990b).

The second field identified by Warde is the increase in the attention being paid to consumerism, taste and consumer culture. Theoretical developments in these areas have tended to make rather different assumptions, and draw on rather different approaches, to issues relating to social class than those found within the debates relating to consumption-sector cleavages. They are characterized by an emphasis on the cultural and social, rather than the economic, construction of 'classes', and therefore a feature of all such accounts is their emphasis on the *active* construction of social differences. Indeed, full-blown 'culturalism' views culture as largely autonomous; thus class cultures are seen to *shape* class processes rather than being ideological reflections of them (Hall 1981). In this chapter, therefore, we will be returning again to the theoretical issues raised in chapter 2 – that is, the nature of the links between 'structure' and 'action', 'classes-in-themselves' and 'classes-for-themselves'; as well as giving some prominence to another topic which has always been important within stratification theory – the relative significance of the economic versus the cultural in the structuring and perpetuation of systems of social inequality.

Consumption-sector cleavages

Much of the debate surrounding the issue of consumption cleavages has focused on the (often polemical) work of Saunders, which has been discussed in previous chapters. His arguments are also linked to the social consequences of the development of the entitlements of citizenship, which were examined in the last chapter. It will be remembered that Saunders has argued that, with the advent of the 'welfare-state deal', new social divisions, arising out of the process of consumption, were emerging in 'welfarist' industrial societies. The major axes of differentiation of such societies were, increasingly, not to be found in relations of production and/or the market, but between those who are able to satisfy their main consumption needs through personal owner- ship, on the one hand, and those who are forced to rely on collective provision through the state on the other. As we have seen in the last chapter, this argument has been further elaborated by those who have argued that, as a consequence of the kinds of cleavage which Saunders identifies, there has developed a dependent and disadvantaged underclass.

Reliance on the state for the provision of consumption is a matter of degree rather than absolutes; public health and education, for example, are consumed more widely within the British population than transport, housing or reliance on state benefit for cash income. Saunders argues that those reliant on state or socialized consumption suffer a disadvantage parallel to that experienced by the non-owners of productive capacity (1987: 312). Furthermore, a process of 'social restratification' is in process in that consumption cleavages are becom- ing more, not less, important. This 'breakdown of productivism' is already apparent in the phenomenon of 'class dealignment' in vot- ing behaviour in Britain. As discussed in previous chapters, 'class alignment' in voting refers to the situation, which persisted for many years after the emergence of Labour as a mass political party, in which a majority of the occupationally identified working classes voted for the Labour Party. However, between the general elections of 1945 and 1983 the Labour share of the working-class vote fell from 62 per cent to 42 per cent (Sarlvik and Crewe 1983).[1]

Saunders's major empirical arena for the exploration of his arguments, however, has been in the area of housing. He argues that those in the population who are disadvantaged in the market, and thus forced into a reliance on state-provided (local-authority) housing have emerged as a peculiarly deprived 'underclass' in Britain. Thus when the Conservative government, elected in 1979, put into practice its policy of selling off local-authority-owned housing to tenants at sub- stantial discounts, Saunders welcomed this as a move in the extension of the privatization of consumption, and thus the extension of real consumer power. His arguments are accompanied by others, drawing on biology and psychology, concerning the individualistic tendencies of the British. These, Saunders argues, are satisfied through the 'ontological security' engendered by a 'home of one's own'.

Marxist urban sociologists had argued, echoing earlier debates concerning 'false consciousness', that home ownership should not be seen as an expression of some kind of natural desire, but rather has been a means by which capitalists have manipulated and fragmented the working class, as well as fuelling a variant of 'commodity fetishism' which perpetuated their ideological domination. However, many non-

Marxist experts in the field of social policy have also been highly critical of the neo-liberal strategies of the British government of the 1980s (including the privatization of local-authority housing), which have exacerbated the range of material inequalities in British society (Walker and Walker 1987).

These changes, it is argued, have important political effects. Those who satisfy their consumption needs through private purchase, it is argued, will tend to align themselves with political parties which stress the importance of individual self-reliance, and the market, rather than the state, provision of consumption requirements in fields such as housing, health, education and transport. As we have seen, the resurgence of right politics and government has, indeed, been associated with an emphasis on the need to roll back state provision in these areas, and to reprivatize significant aspects of civil society. Whether these changes have been structurally driven by the 'fiscal crisis of the state' (that is, the fact that the costs of welfare-state expenditure simply outran the state's capacities to provide them), or whether they are, rather, a consequence of the *political* motivations of governments in power is an important question which will not be pursued here (Hamnett 1989). For the moment, however, we will focus on those arguments which have explored Saunders's assertion that consumption should be regarded as an *independent* dimension of social stratification.

The empirical procedures through which these arguments have been addressed have been straightforward. The nature (that is, whether public or private) and extent of access to the different aspects of consumption – education, health care, transport and, most importantly, housing – has been measured against occupational class, and the strengths of the different associations evaluated. In a review of this empirical evidence, Hamnett (1989) has concluded that in all of these respects, occupational class is still powerfully associated with variations in consumption, and that although occupational class cannot be held to *determine* patterns of consumption at the individual level, at the aggregate level, occupational class remains the primary determinant of consumption patterns.[2] A further stage of the argument concerns the relative strength of the association between occupational class, on the one hand, and consumption-sector measures, on the other, to attitudinal indicators such as voting behaviour and political preferences (Dunleavy 1980). This kind of evidence assumed particular relevance in the debates which surrounded the Conservative government's policy of selling (at a discount) local-authority (that is, public-sector) housing to sitting tenants. The 'right to buy', it was argued, caused a change in political allegiance, as those who had purchased their council houses switched their votes from Labour to Conservative as their housing status was transformed.

As with the association between occupational class and patterns of consumption, the empirical evidence relating to the association between housing tenure and political preference, and occupational class and political preference, suggests that the strongest association remains that with occupational class – despite the fact that the 'right to buy' does appear to have changed a number of individual instances of voting behaviour (Saunders 1990b). It is important to stress, however, that the continuing strength of the association between occupational class and a range of behavioural and attitudinal factors does not mean that nothing has changed.[3] The transformations of the occupational structure, as well as the massive changes in the distributions of housing tenure and other patterns of consumption in Britain which have taken place since the end of the Second World War, have had a considerable impact on the overall pattern of stratification. It is the *association* between the different factors which has remained relatively constant, rather than their form or composition. What the consumption-sector debate has demonstrated, however, is that, for the reasons which have been extensively rehearsed in previous chapters of this book, occupational or employment class (in all its variety) still remains as a very powerful indicator of the structure of material advantage and disadvantage, and associated attitudes, in contemporary societies.

Much of the dialogue relating to consumption-sector cleavages, therefore, has been conducted within a framework of 'class analysis' which broadly follows the parameters established within sociology after the Second World War, and which has been described in chapter 2. It brings together, through the use of employment-derived 'classes', theoretical debates relating to 'social class' with empirical analyses of material inequalities and attitudes or 'class consciousness'. Using a suitable class scheme, a 'class structure' is located within the employment structure. The relationship between this structure and various factors corresponding to attitudes, consciousness or action can then be explored. The linkages between structure and consciousness may be regarded as contingent, but to the extent that they are demonstrated, then this may be taken as evidence to support the continuing validity of this approach to 'class analysis'. 'Consumption sector' has been suggested as an alternative to 'occupational class' (that is, a 'consumption scheme' has been argued to be more closely associated with particular factors, such as voting, than a 'class scheme'), but in fact the empirical evidence suggests that the strongest associations of different aspects of behaviour and attitudes are still those with occupational class. There does not seem to be any firm evidence that 'consumption categories', as identified by the dominant source of consumption provision (state or private) are actually in the process of developing into 'consciousness communities'. Thus causality is imputed to occupational class rather than consumption sector (which, amongst other things, enables 'class analysts' of all political persuasions who have engaged in these debates to argue for the continuing relevance of class despite the changes associated with contemporary industrialism).[4]

The debates relating to consumerism and taste, however, proceed from a rather different set of assumptions relating to 'class analysis'. The investigation of 'lifestyle', it may be suggested, assumes from the beginning that social reality is actively constructed. Those concerned with the sociology of consumerism has also used investigative strategies rather different from those developed within the occupational employment class approach to class analysis, and have drawn on anthropological, as well as sociological, approaches.

Culture, class and occupation

Notwithstanding the above remarks, occupational class has been widely utilized as an element in discussions relating to the culture of consumption. The components of different lifestyles have been systematically related to employment-derived aggregates or classes; 'taste maps' have been identified which correspond to 'occupational maps' (Bourdieu 1986; Douglas and Isherwood 1980). That the consumption of goods correlates broadly with social standing, and that occupation provides a reasonable indication of this social standing, are both generalizations which would be widely accepted. The way in which consumption has been used to indicate or claim rank or special status has been a source of endless human fascination, and the inspiration for countless novels, artistic works, media representation and other forms of cultural expression. For example, at the time of writing there is appearing on television a situation comedy in which the main storyline is provided by the central character's relentless efforts to display the 'correct' consumption behaviour ('Keeping up Appearances'[5]); and classic drama has also used this theme (for example Molière's *Bourgeois Gentilhomme*). However, although the association of consumption and rank is a perpetually fascinating aspect of human behaviour, the mapping of taste by itself remains a largely descriptive exercise – although it is one which endlessly repeated.

The sociological interest in the relationship of taste to stratification systems, however, goes beyond the mere demonstration of their association to explore the ways in which taste may be seen to be a resource which is deployed by groups within the stratification system in order to establish or enhance their location within the social order. In the next section we will examine the work of Bourdieu, who has developed these insights in his analysis of the significance of 'cultural

capital'. First, however, we will briefly examine some of the methodological implications of the cultural exploration of occupational
differentiation, with particular reference to the contrasts between this
approach and aggregate-level explorations of the occupational-class
structure.

The empirical demonstration, at the aggregate level, of the association between occupational classes and patterns of advantage and disadvantage, attitudes, and so on has been firmly established – it has
been demonstrated by, amongst other things, the outcome of the
consumption-sector cleavages debate in urban sociology which has
been briefly reviewed above. However, the analysis of occupational
aggregates has not been directly concerned with the empirical examination of the actual forces which are transforming the occupational structure. Indeed, as we saw in chapter 3, in the case of social-mobility
research, the continuing transformations of the occupational structure
present serious methodological problems for this approach which have
only been partially overcome.

Occupational and employment-based class schemes, therefore, have
been mainly concerned with the examination of the *outcomes* of
occupational differentiation, rather than the processes themselves,
despite the original protestations of those who initially developed
'theoretical' class schemes (see above, chapter 3). As Savage et al.
have argued: 'It is very difficult to integrate a theory of class based
on a synchronic examination of class positions into an account of
diachronic historical change . . . it tends to lead to a mode of class
analysis in which the structure of class positions is taken as given and is
not itself subject to inquiry' (1992: 227). This does not mean, however,
that those who work with such schemes are indifferent to the processes
of occupational structuring. As we have seen, theoretical occupational
and employment-based class schemes, such as those of Goldthorpe and
Wright, are derived from theoretical accounts, particularly those of
Marx and Weber, which seek to explain the nature of occupational
differentiation. Wright has painstakingly attempted to map his Marxist
account of the development of modes of production on to the job
structure. Goldthorpe's theoretical account of the generation of his
class scheme is less specific, but nevertheless he is explicit that the
occupational aggregates he identifies 'represent the past product and
current expression of inequalities in social power and advantage'
(1983: 467). He distinguishes this account of occupational differentiation sharply from functional theories of occupational inequality, which,
as we have seen in chapter 3, was the dominant sociological tradition
against which Goldthorpe directed his initial arguments.

Empirical research at the macro-level attempts to discern, within the
occupational structure as a whole, the *outcomes* of these processes of

class structuring (or class formation). The investigation of the relation-ship between class and culture or 'lifestyle', however, has a major focus on the exploration of the *processes* themselves.[6] Thus, in this approach, occupations are not taken, albeit implicitly, as 'givens', but are regarded as the outcomes of struggle and conflict – and the direct investigation of these struggles is the major focus of empirical work. In short, the very fluidity of the occupational structure is itself an object of investigation. This has led to a significant difference in emphasis as far as the theoretical arguments concerning 'structure' and 'action' in respect of class analysis are concerned. Whereas both Goldthorpe and Wright regard 'structure' and 'action' as analytically separable, the work of authors such as Bourdieu (and Savage et al. 1992) is associated with an ontology which assumes the 'intrinsically double' nature of social reality and thus, as in Giddens's account of 'structuration', holds together 'structure' and 'action' in their empirical accounts of class processes (or formation).

Social class and the work of Pierre Bourdieu

Bourdieu's (1986, 1987) work has been the subject of increasing atten-tion in Anglo-American sociology. His conceptualization of social class is extremely general, going beyond both Marx and Weber, who both defined class in respect of the economy – notwithstanding their very real theoretical differences. However, although Bourdieu has been influenced by both Marx's and Weber's theoretical work, as Brubaker has argued:

> The conceptual space within which Bourdieu defines class is not that of production, but that of social relations in general. Class divisions are defined not by differing relations to the means of production, but by differing conditions of existence, differing systems of dispositions pro-duced by differential conditioning, and differing endowments of power or capital. (*1985: 761*)

Thus Bourdieu identifies four different 'forms of capital' – economic, cultural, social and symbolic – which together empower (or otherwise) agents in their struggle for position within 'social space'. As a con-sequence of these different empowerments, individual classes come to develop and occupy a similar habitus: 'understood as a system of dispositions shared by all individuals who are products of the same conditionings' (1987: 762). This description bears a superficial resemblance to the conventional sociological strategy of 'class analysis' described earlier – that is, 'class-producing' factors are first identified, then linked with attitudes and predispositions or 'consciousness'. However, whereas the approach of authors such as Lockwood, Dahrendorf, Goldthorpe and Wright locates the class structure, in a relatively *concrete* fashion, within the occupational (or employment) structure, Bourdieu's emphasis on the diverse and socially constructed nature of 'classes' leads him to describe class boundaries as like 'a flame whose edges are in constant movement, oscillating around a line or surface' (1987: 13).

Although, therefore, Bourdieu employs aggregate-occupational categories in his vast ethnographic study of the French class structure (1986), he does not consider these categories to constitute 'classes', even though he recognizes that occupation is generally a 'good and economical' indicator of position in social space, and provides information on occupational effects such as the nature of work, the occupational milieu, and 'its cultural and organizational specificities' (1986: 4). Nevertheless, the classes so identified are not 'real, objectively constituted groups' (p. 4). The commonalities of their location, their similar conditions of existence and conditioning, might indeed result in similarities of attitude and practices. However, Bourdieu argues, in terms similar to those argued in chapters 4 and 5 above, that:

> contrary to what Marxist theory [he is here making specific reference to Wright's attempt to construct a Marxist occupational class scheme] assumes, the movement from probability to reality, from theoretical class to practical class, is never given: even though they are supported by the 'sense of one's place' and by the affinity of habitus, the principles of vision and division of the social world at work in the construction of theoretical classes have to compete, *in reality*, with other principles, ethnic, racial or national, and more concretely still, with principles imposed by the ordinary experience of occupational, communal and local divisions and rivalries. (*1987: 7*)

In *Distinction* Bourdieu uses the class concept, therefore, as a generic name for social groups distinguished by their conditions of existence and their corresponding dispositions (Brubaker has described the aggregates identified by Bourdieu as 'status groups'). The conditions of existence identified by Bourdieu include economic capital, which describes the level of material resources – income, property, and so on – that may be possessed by an individual or a group, as well as cultural capital, which is largely acquired through education, and describes the intangible 'knowing' which, amongst other things, can both secure and perpetuate access to economic capital. Thus his approach leads to an exploration of the *processes* of social differentiation which goes beyond the mere mapping of tastes. The exploration of these processes requires the interpretation of the aggregate-level association between occupational groups and patterns of consumption, as well as the development of cultural case studies which have also focused upon the uncovering of causal links.

Bourdieu's work, therefore, is primarily concerned with the active processes of class structuring, or class formation. Thus his major focus has been on *change*, as new groups emerge out of the struggle for position within social space. In some contrast, as we have seen in chapter 4, much of the discussion relating to occupational and employment-based class schemes has been concerned with whether newly emerging occupations and jobs can be fitted into *existing* occupational classifications. This focus within Bourdieu's work on the emergence of the new is no doubt one of the factors which has resulted in the widespread application of his insights to the analysis of the 'new middle class', and it is to this that we now turn.

The 'new middle class' – the ultimate consumption category?

There is no single 'new middle class'. Although there have been considerable theoretical differences between those who have attempted to analyse this contentious category, there would nevertheless be a level of widespread agreement to the effect that the term encompasses a wide variety of occupational groupings, distinguished only by the fact that they are *not* manual workers. Thus they would include quite low-level service employees – such as, for example, workers in the hotel and restaurant trade or 'hospitality industry' – as well as the new service professionals – social workers, librarians, physiotherapists – associated with the growth and development of the welfare state.

The way in which the established frameworks of class analysis have approached the topic of the new middle class(es) has reflected this diversity. In chapter 4 we saw that Marxists (and those influenced by Marx's work such as Abercrombie and Urry 1983) have distinguished between the routine, deskilled, non-manual workers and the upper levels of management; these higher levels would be located by Wright in the bourgeosie, by Abercrombie and Urry in the 'service class'. Similarly, the categories of Weberian class analysis have distinguished between 'service', 'subaltern service' and 'intermediate' locations in the occupational structure (Goldthorpe 1987). A common feature of these established frameworks of class analysis, whether Marxist or Weberian, is that production and/or market relationships are regarded as crucial to the placement of the 'class'. Thus implicitly the class placement of these newly emerging groups is decided with reference to conventional, economically derived criteria of class location.

However, the growth of the service sector, and service work more generally, reflects not only a change in the structure of class places but also a change in the kind of work undertaken by many individuals who might be considered objectively 'working-class' in occupational terms. For increasingly, the qualities demanded of service workers rest not simply on labour or even technical skills, but *social* skills. That is, skills of welcoming, selling, soothing, and so on (as has often been noted, these have conventionally been regarded as particularly 'feminine' qualities, and women, of course, predominate in service employment). These demands for social skills, it may be suggested, have affected the *content* of the employment relationship, if not its form. Thus low-level service employees receive training in 'customer care', and there has been an increasing focus on personnel strategies such as 'human resource management'. Managers in all sectors of the economy are now encouraged, not simply to produce maximum output from their employees via rational accounting techniques, Taylorist systems of work organization, and so on, but also to build a *commitment* to the organization at all levels of employment (Peters and Waterman 1982). Such prescriptions go beyond established strategies of socially responsible control such as paternalism, or 'human relations' (Mayo 1975), and the 'needs' of the worker are seen as incorporating not just the satisfaction of material needs, and satisfying social relations, but nothing less than the realization of the full human being. Employers and their representatives, therefore, are increasingly calling upon the services of a new breed of experts concerned with the management of the body and the emotions – counsellors, assertiveness trainers, and so on.

Such experts would themselves be considered to be members of the new middle class. Within the sociology of consumption, there have developed arguments to the effect that the growth of these (and related) occupational categories is not merely a response to the changing requirements of the economy, but rather, that their rise to prominence should be seen as an outcome of the wider cultural changes which have created demands for the satisfaction of new needs. Those whose occupations are concerned with the satisfaction of these needs are also viewed as having taken an *active* role in both the identification of the needs and the manner in which they are met. In these arguments, the significance of the supposed cultural shift towards 'postmodernism' looms large.

'Postmodernism' is a term currently in widespread use within the humanities and social sciences, but it is one which is exceptionally difficult to define – not least because its ramifications can be extended to incorporate practically every aspect of the human condition. In art and culture (understood as symbolic representations) postmodernism has been contrasted with the modernist aesthetic ideal, which, although laying stress on creativity and self-invention, was seen as exhausted, and institutionalized in the museum and the academy. In contrast, postmodernism in the arts is characterized by:

> the effacement of the boundary between art and everyday life; the collapse of the hierarchical distinction between high and mass/popular culture; a stylistic promiscuity favouring eclecticism and the mixing of codes; parody, pastiche, irony, playfulness and the celebration of the surface 'depthlessness' of culture; the decline of the originality/genius of the artistic producer; and the assumption that art can only be repetition. (*Featherstone 1991: 7–8*)

Thus broken pediments on skyscrapers, the artfully mixed and pastiched covers of magazines such as *The Face*, and pop music phenomena such as punk rock – are all manifestations of these cultural trends.

The shift from 'modernism' to 'postmodernism' in artistic production is seen as being accompanied by a corresponding shift from 'modernity' to 'postmodernity' in social thought. 'Modernity' has been conceptualized in the contrast with 'traditional' societies, and it has been argued that the project of modernity began with the efforts of the Enlightenment thinkers 'to develop objective science, universal morality and law, and autonomous art according to their inner logic' (Habermas 1983). Thus modernity is concerned with the processes of rationalization, order, and the identification of the systems and structures which achieve this ordering. The development of capitalist industrialism and the modern world occurred together; indeed, the development of the social sciences – as represented by the works of Marx and Weber – might be regarded as integral to modernity as a project. As Featherstone has noted, therefore, 'to speak of postmodernity is to suggest an epochal shift or break from modernity involving the emergence of a new social totality with its own distinct organizing principles' (1991: 3).

Some have argued that a shift to a new social totality is occurring because of the inherent weaknesses of the Enlightenment project. The calculation and rationality of social thought might have created substantial material advances – but it has also contributed to the horrors of Nazi death camps, and Stalin's Soviet Union. Others have located this shift in the increasingly frantic pace brought about by modernity itself. Harvey (1990) argues that in the modern world, the dimensions of space and time have been subject to the persistent pressure of capital circulation, accumulation and crisis, and that, in periods of uncertainty, the search for a solution inevitably involves a loss of confidence in rational, 'scientific' reasoning. He suggests that:

> The crisis of overaccumulation that began in the late 1960s and which came to a head in 1973 has generated exactly such a result. The experience of time and space has changed, the confidence in the association between scientific and moral judgements has collapsed, aesthetics has triumphed over ethics as a prime focus of social and intellectual concern, images dominate narratives, ephemerality and fragmentation take precedence over eternal truths and unified politics, and explanations have shifted from the realm of material and political-economic groundings towards a consideration of autonomous cultural and political practices (*1990: 327–8*)

In short, the economic and political changes described above in chapter 4 have also been associated with profound *cultural* changes which, some have argued, are reshaping the very nature of the world. The demise of modernity, therefore, is also argued to signify the end of the era of 'totalizing discourses', or 'meta-narratives' (large-scale theoretical interpretations of purportedly universal application) which seek to explain and control the human condition.

'Postmodernism', therefore, is a huge topic, and in abstracting from it those aspects relating to the 'new middle classes' we can deal with only particular and highly selective aspects. Indeed, class analysis might be viewed as a particular example of a 'totalizing discourse' which postmodernist thinking might reject; as we have seen, such theories in any case stand accused of reductionism by critics not associated with 'postmodernist' sensibilities (Hindess 1987). However, perhaps because of the very diversity and fragmentation of the 'middle classes', 'postmodernist' ideas have been increasingly applied to the analysis of the social situation of these groupings.

Many of these commentaries have drawn upon the empirical work of Bourdieu (Featherstone 1987; Lash and Urry 1987; Wynne 1990; Savage et al. 1992). Within the dominant class, Bourdieu draws a basic distinction between the bourgeoisie – high on economic capital, relatively low on cultural capital – and the intellectuals – high on cultural capital, relatively low on economic capital. Tastes within these groupings differ; whereas the intellectuals have a preference for aesthetic modernism, bourgeois taste tends towards the baroque and flamboyant. The younger elements within the bourgeoisie, however, tend to be high on both economic and cultural capital – the bourgeoisie in France having retained their children's positions by, amongst other things, the strategic use of the *Grandes Ecoles* and the US business schools. Thus the new bourgeoisie, writes Bourdieu:

is the initiator of the ethical retooling required by the new economy from which it draws its power and profits, whose functioning depends as much on the production of needs and consumers as on the production of goods. The new logic of the economy rejects the aesthetic ethic of production and accumulation, based on abstinence, sobriety, saving and calculation, in favour of a hedonistic morality of consumption, based on credit, spending and enjoyment. (*1986: 310*)

There is in this argument of Bourdieu's a clear parallel with those developed by Bell in *The Cultural Contradictions of Capitalism* (1976). Bell argued that contemporary American society is comprised of three distinct realms – the economic, the political and the cultural – each of which is governed by a different 'axial principle'. The culture of modernism sought to substitute for religion or morality an aesthetic justification for life, but in sharp contrast to this, postmodernism has completely substituted the *instinctual*. Thus impulse and pleasure alone are considered as real and life-affirming. As a consequence, American capitalism has lost its traditional legitimacy, which was based on a system of reward rooted in the Protestant sanctification of work, and 'the hedonism as a way of life promoted by the marketing system of business, constitutes the cultural contradiction of capitalism' (Bell 1976: 84).

However, whereas the logic of Bell's arguments suggest the need for some kind of moral renewal, Bourdieu's analysis is more concerned with the way in which different groups struggle for position within the changing social space – a space which they are simultaneously creating. Bourdieu suggests that in their struggles to establish their dominance, the new bourgeoisie finds a natural ally, both economically and politically, in the 'new petite [petty] bourgeoisie'. This group 'recognizes in the new bourgeoisie the embodiment of its human ideal' – the 'dynamic' executive – and 'collaborates enthusiastically in imposing the new ethical norms (especially as regards consumption) and the corresponding needs' (1986: 366). Thus the new petty bourgeoisie is represented in occupations involving presentation and representation, and in all institutions providing symbolic goods and services, cultural production and organization. Such occupations would include sales, marketing, advertising, public relations, fashion, interior design, as well as journalists and other media employees, craftspersons etc. Occupations concerned with bodily and emotional regulation would also be included – vocational guidance, youth and play leaders, sports and exercise experts, and quasi-medical professions such as dietitians, psychotherapists, marriage guidance counsellors and physiotherapists (1986: 359). These 'indeterminate' positions, argues Bourdieu, are attractive to those individuals endowed with a strong cultural capital (that is, superior family background) imperfectly converted into educational capital, or rising individuals who have not obtained completely the educational capital needed for the top positions, and lack the cultural and social capital required to make this final leap. Thus the new petty bourgeoisie is split between the *déclassé* and the upwardly mobile.

These 'need merchants', 'new cultural intermediaries', as Bourdieu describes them, act as a transmission belt to pull into the race for consumption and competition those from whom it means to distinguish itself (1986: 365). In a similar vein, Lash and Urry (1987) draw upon the insights of Baudrillard to argue that in contemporary consumer capitalism we no longer consume products, but *signs*, thus the 'new petite bourgeoisie' (for Lash and Urry part of the lower echelons of the 'service class') have developed as 'sign-producers', to some extent displacing the 'commodity-producers' of 'organized' capitalism. Such groups and individuals are using their cultural capital to establish new systems of classification which actively *create* the jobs to suit their ambitions. Featherstone (1991) emphasizes the rapid inflation in consumer tastes, as dominant tastes (or 'positional goods') are brought within the reach of an ever-widening circle of consumers. Foreign holidays, cheap champagne, designer sportswear – all these goods lose their relative cultural value as they become more accessible, and in the 'leap-frogging social race to maintain recognizable distinctions', the cultural producers, the 'specialists in symbolic production', come into their own (1991: 89).

Bourdieu has drawn a distinction between the *déclassé* and the upwardly mobile within the new petty bourgeoisie. Featherstone emphasizes the difference – which may be a source of conflict – between the 'economic' and the 'cultural' producers, differentiated by their relative possession of economic and cultural capital. Both of these groups may be upwardly mobile, but whereas the 'culturally' upwardly mobile have achieved such mobility through formal educational routes followed by entry into professional occupations, the 'economically' mobile may lack such qualifications, having 'made the grade' through work-life mobility, usually in the private sector. Wynne (1990) has described the differentiation of the lifestyles of these two groups, which broadly reflect the kinds of differences of taste which Bourdieu identified between the bourgeoisie and the intellectuals. The 'economic' petty bourgeois are described by Wynne as the 'drinkers', characterized by a leisure style which besides regular convivial drinking includes family holidays taken in hotel packages, eating out at steakhouses, entertainment preferences for musical comedy and large spectacle, and a preference for comfort and tradition in home furnishing. In contrast, the 'cultural' 'sporters' are more preoccupied with style, rather than comfort, to holiday in a *gîte* or make other personal arrangements, to join hobby clubs and voluntary associations, and to patronize avant garde theatre and classical music concerts. Thus through their very different lifestyles, the economic and the cultural petty bourgeois are constructing and affirming their social position.

Work by Savage et al. (1992) has developed further this mapping of cultural (consumption) tastes on to different sections of the middle class. Public-sector professionals (whose tastes closely resemble those of the 'sporters' identified by Wynne) are revealed, by market research surveys, to have an 'ascetic' lifestyle which is characterized by sport and healthy living, a relatively low consumption of alcohol, combined with 'high-cultural' activities such as plays, classical music, and contemporary dance. This group is high on cultural, but low on economic, capital. A further group identified by Savage et al. correspond broadly to the 'drinkers' identified by Wynne. Managers and government bureaucrats, on the other hand, are characterized by 'undistinctive' patterns of consumption, having average or below average consumption scores on high culture and exercise alike, and showing a preference for a cleaned-up version of the 'heritage' or 'countryside' tradition in their consumption patterns. As Savage et al. note, this 'undistinctive' group are not identified within Bourdieu's framework, perhaps because of the anti-intellectualism which has characterized managerial groupings in Britain, in some contrast to France.

The third group of middle-class consumers identified by Savage et al. are the 'postmoderns'. This postmodern lifestyle is characterized by an absence of a single organizing principle in respect of consumption: 'high extravagance goes along with a culture of the body: appreciation of high cultural forms of art such as opera and classical music exists cheek by jowl with an interest in disco dancing or stock car racing' (1992: 108). These patterns may be broadly associated with the 'hedonism' identified (and lamented) by Bell, as well as with the 'new petite bourgeoisie' described by Bourdieu. However, Savage et al. emphasize that these consumption patterns are found not just amongst the newer occupations centred upon the cultivation of the body and the emotions, but amongst professionally educated private-sector workers more generally: 'barristers, accountants and surveyors partake in the post-modern lifestyle as much as sex therapists or advertising agents' (1992: 128). Cultural assets have been commodified, and practices considered to have an 'auratic' (or 'special') quality by previous generations – opera, skiing holidays, historic housing (albeit a luxury conversion or newly built in a traditional style) – are now accessible to those who have the money to pay for them. In non-sociological language, this is 'yuppie' culture.

The cultural fragmentation within the middle class, therefore, reflects the economic and spatial fragmentation within these groupings which had already been identified by those working within more orthodox frameworks of 'class analysis' (Savage et al. 1988, 1992, Crompton 1992). What those writers who have emphasized the significance of the development of 'postmodernism' and associated lifestyles argue, however, is that (a) culture should be regarded as an *independent* variable in the construction and consolidation of class position or 'habitus', and that (b) the hyper-inflation of symbols associated with the growth of consumer capitalism has, relatively, increased the significance of culture in the processes of class structuring. A major consequence of these changes is the development within the middle occupational stratum of a 'cultural mass' of symbol-producers. These changes have also had political consequences which are succinctly summarized by Harvey:

> The politics of the cultural mass are . . . important, since they are in the business of defining the symbolic order through the production of images for everyone. The more it turns in upon itself, or the more it sides with this or that dominant class in society, the more the prevailing sense of the symbolic and moral order tends to shift . . . the cultural mass drew heavily upon the working-class movement for its cultural identity in the 1960s, but the attack upon, and decline of, the latter from the early 1970s onwards cut loose the cultural mass, which then shaped its own identity around its own concerns with money power, individualism, entrepreneurialism, and the like. (*1990: 348*)

These arguments are highly suggestive, but they raise important questions relating to both causality and the permanance or otherwise of their impact. Have cultural changes actually *caused* the neo-liberal turn to 'marketization' – of which the commodification of culture may be regarded as one aspect – which has taken place over the last decade? Or might it be that a political emphasis upon the overwhelming legitimacy of 'market forces' has created a cultural anomie, a situation exceptionally favourable to the challenging and commodification of normative cultural judgements of all kinds? Savage et al.'s arguments suggest the latter interpretation. They argue that the significance of bureaucratic structures to middle-class careers is declining as firms increasingly use market mechanisms, rather than managerial hierarchies, to structure their activities, externalizing aspects of production, drawing on the labour of specialists, and so on (the so-called 'flexible firm'). They also argue that in Britain, the role of the state in both legitimating cultural assets and providing direct employment to large numbers of professional workers has changed to one of underwriting market provision. These twin factors, they suggest, have changed the basis of the legitimation of cultural assets: 'Increasingly cultural assets can be legitimised through their role in defining and perpetuating consumer cultures associated with private commodity production. Those receptive to the post-modern lifestyle increasingly look to the market to legitimate and reward their cultural assets' (1992: 215). However, what the market giveth, it also taketh away. Viewed from the standpoint of the recession of the 1990s, the 1980s yuppie culture of 'postmodernist' consumption may appear more as the transient activities of the *nouveaux riches* than as a manifestation of a deep-seated cultural change.

Summary and conclusions

This chapter has explored two specific dimensions of the sociology of consumption which have been developed with reference to the analysis of social stratification. It was shown that the debates relating to 'consumption-sector cleavages', first introduced by Saunders and Dunleavy, have operated within a terrain which was largely marked out by the orthodox sociological tradition of occupational-class analysis represented by authors such as Goldthorpe and deriving from the work of Bendix, Lipset, Dahrendorf and Lockwood, whereby theories of social class are used to locate occupational 'classes', in relational terms, within the structure of employment. As the defenders of this position have not been slow to point out, in statistical terms, occupational class remains the most important single variable associated with patterns of consumption and consumption-related attitudes (Goldthorpe and Marshall 1992).

In contrast, the debates relating to consumerism have not been cast within the framework of orthodox occupational-class analysis. This is not particularly surprising. As has been argued in chapter 5 above, one feature of the development of occupational-class analysis was that its practitioners, neo-Marxist and neo-Weberian alike, were at some pains to distinguish their development of 'theoretical' class schemes from the occupational rankings and prestige schemes which characterized earlier empirical approaches – such as Warner's – to the study of social stratification. An unanticipated consequence of this drawing of a (legitimate) analytical distinction between 'class' and 'status', however, is that the systematic investigation of culture – understood as status or prestige – has developed independently of the analysis of 'social class' as economically defined.

As we have seen in chapter 2, the classic theories of Marx and Weber identified 'classes' as groups within the social structure emerging from the dominant patterns of production, distribution and exchange. The relationship to the dominant mode of production assumed most significance for Marx; the workings of the capitalist market were more significant for Weber. Social scientists have developed these insights in order to distinguish, within the structure of employment, occupational (or employment) aggregates with particular characteristics deriving from the economic processes which Marx and Weber identified. However, the extent to which this sociological venture has proved successful has always been contested.

In the first place, the analytical split between structure and action, upon which attempts to identify a 'class structure' rest, has been contested by developments in social theory. The indivisibility of structure and action, that is, the intrinsically double nature of social reality, have been emphasized by authors such as Giddens and Bourdieu:

> Human agency and structure ... are logically implicated with one another ... Understood as rules and resources implicated in the 'form' of collectivities of social systems, reproduced across space and time, structure is the very medium of the 'human' element of agency ... agency is the medium of structure, which individuals routinely reproduce in the course of their activities. All social life has a recursive quality to it, derived from the fact that actors reproduce the conditions of their social existence by means of the very activities that ... constitute that existence. (*Giddens 1987: 220–1*)

There is in any case a persisting tradition within 'class analysis' which has forcefully denied the possibility of such a separation. A major representative of this approach within social history is E. P. Thompson, those work has had a considerable influence on other social scientists. The development of humanistic Marxism in the Gramscian tradition similarly held to the impossibility of the analytical movement, in a mechanistic fashion, from economic 'base' to ideological 'superstructure'.[7] Within sociology more generally, the empirical analysis of social class has always incorporated the systematic linking, through case-study research, of social imagery and economic class position.

Another major challenge to the possibility of the precise empirical identification of an economic 'class structure' within the structure of employment has come from those authors who have argued for the indivisibility of the 'economic' from the social or cultural within the stratification order. Arguments against the economic reductionism or determinism which has sometimes characterized 'class analysis' have emphasized the continuing significance of the *status* order in the location and structuring of occupations – where status is understood as both the persistence of 'custom and practice' (Wootton 1955) as well as the projection of group attributes on to occupational roles – as is evidenced, for example, by the historical devaluation of 'women's work'.

However, because of the sharp distinction which has been drawn between (economic) 'class' and (cultural) 'status' in stratification theory and research, the contemporary investigation of status and 'lifestyle' has proceeded along rather different channels from those dominant in 'class analysis'. Much influenced by the work of Bourdieu, these investigations have from the beginning assumed the intrinsically double nature of the social world, and have focused upon the investigation of the processes by which groups attain, establish and retain their positions within the social order. In these struggles, both economic and cultural factors (or 'economic capital' and 'cultural capital') are seen as important. In contrast to orthodox class analysis, therefore, the 'cultural' and the 'economic' have not been separated. The sociology of consumption has additionally argued that taste, culture and lifestyle are, with the development of 'postmodernity', becoming more significant in class structuring – particularly in respect of elements of the 'new middle class'.

Yet one need not necessarily adhere to the view that there has been an epochal shift in the direction of 'postmodernity' in order to recognize that the increasing attention that has been paid to the analysis of 'lifestyles' has provided us with a number of important insights into contemporary social changes.[8] The analysis of the processes of occupational structuring (or class formation) is as important to stratification theory and research as the investigation of their outcomes through the analysis of occupational or employment-based aggregates. The claim that cultural or 'lifestyle' factors have become more significant in this structuring should also be taken seriously. Empirical evidence to support this contention may be drawn from the rapid increase in the number of cultural producers – for example, Harvey cites evidence which compares the two thousand or so artists who practised in and around Paris in the mid-nineteenth century with the 150,000 professional artists registered in New York in the late twentieth (1990: 290). The expansion of the service economy is itself an indication of the increase in the resources devoted to consumption activities, and time-budget studies demonstrate the increase in leisure time (Gershuny and Jones 1987). Nevertheless, the increasing significance of consumption and lifestyle in late twentieth-century capitalism should not be allowed to obscure the fact that the economic factors identified by the nineteenth- and early twentieth-century theorists of social class still play a major part – indeed, *the* major role – in the structuring and persistence of systems of social inequality.

Notes

1   A part of the decline in the working-class element in the Labour vote is to be explained by the long-term decline in the 'working class' within the employed population. The extent to which class dealignment is also a consequence of vote-changing within the working class is a matter of some controversy. See Marshall et al. (1988, ch. 9).

2   Hamnett (1989: 227) states that: 'we can reject the view that variations in housing tenure, educational attainment and health conditions are primarily a product of culture rather than class'. His use of the concept of 'culture', however, is rather odd given that none of the statistical evidence he reviews provides a measure of 'culture'.

3   Edgell and Duke (1991: 212) have explored the relationship between sector and radical attitudes and behaviour through their Greater Manchester study, and have demonstrated that 'public-sector controllers' emerge as the most radical group within their sample.

4   As we have seen in previous chapters, those engaging in the consumption sector debates within urban sociology have not always been aware of, or sensitive to, the theoretical differences between different occupational-class schemes.

5   BBC television. These efforts are constantly frustrated by the behaviour of her decidedly working-class relatives.

6   Aggregate-level indicators, it must be stressed, also give insights into the ways in which occupational aggregates seek to maintain and reproduce their position within the system of stratification – e.g. in their consumption of different kinds of education.

7   Nevertheless, relatively sophisticated versions of the base–superstructure frame of argument can give useful insights into current developments. In the case of the 'new middle class', for example, Thrift (1989) has described how the current emphasis on country-living tradition – indeed the whole of the 'heritage industry' (museums, stately homes, etc.) contributes to the establishment of 'hegemonic' upper-class values.

8   For example, the application of these insights to the analysis of inner-city regeneration or 'gentrification' (Zukin 1988).

8
Conclusions

Introduction

Previous chapters have identified the various strands, theoretical and empirical, which have contributed to the diverse project of class and stratification analysis in sociology. Conceptualizations of social class, as well as empirical work within the area of social stratification, have been much influenced by developments in social theory, including the critique of positivism and normative functionalism, the revival of interest in theoretical Marxism, and the turn to philosophical 'realism' – as well as more recent critiques of 'totalizing discourses' from within the postmodernist perspective. These changing theoretical perspectives and emphases have been accompanied by wide-ranging economic and social developments which have included the transformation – if not collapse – of manufacturing industry in the West consequent upon recession and economic decline, the restructuring of the service economy and the technological changes which have accompanied it, the rise to prominence of new social movements and the political transformations within the Eastern bloc.

As we have seen, these developments have also been accompanied by arguments to the effect that the idea of 'class' is out of date and of declining significance. It is argued, within the sociological community, that transformations of work and the structure of employment have blurred established class boundaries. Work and employment is seen to be of less significance in shaping the attitudes and behaviours of individuals and families, and social and spatial mobility is argued to have broken up established class traditions. In politics, 'class' is seen to be in decline as a focus for collective organization and representation. On the political right, 'class' is rejected as outdated and out of place within the 'new individualism': 'Class is a communist concept. It groups people as bundles and sets them against one another' (Margaret Thatcher, *Guardian*, 22 April 1992).

The range of different reasons given for the rejection of 'class' serves to reinforce the argument, developed in chapter 1, that class is a concept with a variety of meanings. Sociologists have always been anxious to distinguish the sociological use of the term from its every-day applications (Scase 1992) but they have been slower to recognize that the variations in the meanings attached to the concept have been at least as great, if not greater, within the academic community as between 'sociological' and 'commonsense' usage.[1] It has been argued that one source of confusion within class and stratification analysis in sociology in recent years has been the developing, but largely unacknowledged, gulf which has emerged between, on the one hand, the macro-level analysis of employment aggregates ('classes') using theoretical class schemes in combination with large data sets and, on the other, contextual and historical analyses of class formation and class action, which usually employ some variant of the case-study method.

Sociological attempts to devise empirical strategies for the precise theoretical measurement of the class structure, deriving from the struc-ture of employment, rest upon arguments relating to the impact of class relations upon the structuring of jobs and occupations. Dahrendorf, Lockwood and Braverman have been identified as sociologists who, drawing upon the work of Marx and Weber, have attempted to demon-strate these connections. The assumption that the impact of 'class processes' on employment *may* be so identified, and in a fairly straight-forward fashion, is still widespread: 'Class relations, and the changes that occur within control relations, are the underlying forces that determine the nature of job tasks, the delineation of work roles and the structuring of occupations' (Scase 1992: 80). However, this par-ticular approach may been seen to have been from the start possessed of a number of flaws. These have prevented the ultimate realization of ambitious projects which incorporate the attempt to construct a universally valid theoretical class scheme based upon the structure of employment (whether these attempts have been Marxist or Weberian in their inspiration). In brief, these flaws are:

1 The empirical impossibility of identifying 'class' independently of other processes, such as work context, organizational size and sector, cultural stereotyping, and the segmentation of the labour force by gender, ethnicity and age, which also structure both the kinds of work people do and the *de facto* nature of their employment relationships.

2 A tendency to reductionism, associated with the systematic attempt to

exclude the effect of these other sources of structuring of social position – in particular, status.

3 Stereotypical assumptions relating to the division of labour, particularly in respect of gender.

4 The analytical separation of class structure from class action. Thus class consciousness and identity is either (a) treated as a manifestation of 'attitude' or (b) seen as articulated by organizations such as political parties and trade unions, the investigation of which lies outside the scope of the manipulation of occupational aggregates.

However, there has been an increasing tendency for the employment-aggregate approach to be identified with the sociological project of 'class analysis' as a whole (a tendency, it should be said, which has been encouraged by the assumptions of the leading practitioners employing these methodologies). This has led to a number of pseudo-debates deriving from the 'qualified theoretical failure' of the different approaches – both Marxist and Weberian – to structural class analysis (Waters 1991).[2] Briefly, these are:

1 A tendency to prolonged disputes as to which class scheme is 'correct'. The position taken in this book is that as no single scheme can be said to provide a definitive measure of 'class', the task of the sociologist is to establish which particular scheme is best suited to the investigation of particular problems.

2 Empirical disputes as to the continuing utility of employment class as a variable in sociological investigations are treated as (conclusive) debates relating to the utility of 'class analysis' as a whole. Concrete examples of areas of pseudo-debate would include (a) women and class analysis, (b) class and politics, and (c) class and consumption-sector cleavages.

3 The assumption that the macro-level investigation of employment aggregates *does* represent sociological 'class analysis' in its entirety has also led to the rejection as irrelevant of arguments and evidence generated by other methods.

How might pseudo-debates be avoided in the future? One strategy might be to engage in a complete shift of intellectual focus – that is, to reject altogether this approach to 'class analysis'. A recent critic of Wright's work would seem to be arguing for this outcome:

> The task is to elucidate the dialectic between class structure and class agency . . . rather than endlessly elaborate the supposedly independent variable of structure . . . the core of class theory does not lie in 'constructing the (w)right classes' . . . at a structural level but rather in exploring the movement from theoretical to practical group. (*Wacquant 1991*)

However, there is of course in this strategy the danger of simply abandoning the advances in our theoretical and empirical knowledge which have been gained through the employment-aggregate approach. The way forward, therefore, would seem to be to attempt to consolidate insights that have been gained, rather than to throw the baby out with the bathwater. Employment or occupational class will not cease to be a significant variable employed in a wide range of empirical investigations: it is simply too useful. As has been described in chapter 5, employment-derived class schemes can and should be further refined and developed. Although the (w)right class scheme for all purposes and all times may not have been – indeed, will never be – constructed, debates as to how it *might* be have led to further refinements – statistical and theoretical – of employment classifications and thus empirical investigations.[3] For example, although Goldthorpe's class scheme may be based upon a contestable set of *a priori* assumptions, and the agglomeration of some apparently disparate occupational categories, the cross-national similarities in social fluidity that have been demonstrated by those working on the CASMIN project has identified empirically measurable mobility barriers in contemporary industrial societies.

In this concluding chapter, however, we will return briefly to two important topics within the area of stratification and 'class analysis': class formation; and class consciousness and action. These will provide a framework for the discussion of a series of issues relating to the whole range of 'classes' within contemporary captalism.

Class formation

Describing inequality: contemporary 'class maps'

The persistence of the kinds of material differences revealed by macro-level employment-based class analysis demonstrates that the class processes identified by the classical theorists such as Marx and Weber are still major factors shaping the broad contours of inequality in capitalist industrial societies. That is, we may describe capitalist industrial societies as being characterized by groupings having different levels of material and symbolic advantage and disadvantage as a consequence of their differential access to, and participation in, property, production and the market, and which reflect the advantages and disadvantages brought to these situations. Class processes are not the only factors contributing to this structuring (gender, race and age, for example, are also highly significant), and there will also be important cross-national variations.[4] This 'class structure' has commonly been described within the social sciences via heuristic 'class maps', which draw upon a range of empirical evidence including macro-level data relating to the distribution of wealth, power and occupational inequalities, historical evidence, as well as contextual studies of the manner in which material and cultural advantage is gained and retained within particular 'classes', occupations and localities. Such maps, therefore, are constructed out of the theoretical and empirical tradition of class analysis as a whole.

These heuristic descriptions of the contours of stratification in advanced industrial societies are of long standing.[5] In recent years, a variety of new maps have been suggested, all of which reflect the changes associated with late twentieth-century capitalist industrialism (Waters 1991; Runciman 1990; Miliband 1989; Pahl 1988). They are not necessarily linked to employment-derived class schemes, although they clearly reflect the broad contours of the occupational order. A feature of these recent accounts is that, although the shape of the suggested structure might vary, there are important continuities in the different categories (or 'classes') identified. All view the structure as hierarchical, with proportionately more of the population in the lower reaches than the higher; but whereas some conceive the structure as a pyramid with a very small apex (Miliband 1989), others suggest the possibilities of the development of a more onion-shaped distribution (Pahl 1988).

All of these heuristic maps identify a relatively small dominant or 'upper' class, which includes the major wealth holders and controllers of capitalist industrialism. All identify a 'middle' class – or rather, middle classes, which comprise a number of different groupings, depending upon their possession of marketable skills (for example, professionals), organizational locations, etc. All identify a 'working' class (or classes) which cut across the conventional manual/non-manual boundary – that is, the working class of late twentieth-century class maps incorporates routine non-manual workers in sales and office work. The identification of an 'underclass' is also a feature of all of these accounts.

Despite their different theoretical emphases, therefore, these varying class maps all reflect the major social and economic changes which have taken place since the end of the Second World War. These include: a move away from the conventionally established 'class' boundary between manual and non-manual work following the expansion of the service sector and the routinization and feminization of much lower-level white-collar employment; an emphasis upon the diversity of middle-class locations, and the identification of the poorest and most deprived as an 'underclass' – this identification being linked, to varying degrees, with the condition of state dependency. A major element of continuity, however, lies in the persisting concentration of economic, organizational and political power within an 'upper' class which comprises only a small minority of the population.

The 'upper class'

If for no other reason, this *de facto* concentration of wealth and power in capitalist industrial societies should be sufficient to clinch the argument that these are still 'class societies'. There has been some redistribution of wealth in Britain, for example, since the early years of this century, but the data suggest that much of this redistribition has taken place within wealthy families – thus wealth is no longer concentrated amongst the top 1 per cent. but rather amongst the top 10 per cent of the population (Coates 1989). In both manufacturing industry and the financial sector, large enterprises predominate. The continuing increase in the scale of the capitalist enterprise has been argued to have been associated with a separation of ownership and control, or the advent of 'managerialism' and thus the disappearance of the capitalist 'class' (Berle and Means 1968). However, propertied families continue to monopolize positions of strategic control in modern capitalist economies through an interlocking network of ownership in combination with directorships and managerial positions (Scott 1982, 1991; Zeitlin 1982). As Scott has argued: 'The business class as a whole is characterised by a high degree of social cohesion, the main supports of this cohesion being its system of kinship and educational experience (1982: 158). Scott has therefore emphasized the significance of *status* in the consolidation and perpetuation of the upper class: 'The hierarchy of status . . . is . . . an important element in the legitimation of power structures, and the dynamics of status group relations are . . . integral elements in class reproduction and in the formation of power blocs' (1991: 5). The features which he identifies in his discussion of status processes – education, leisure patterns, and so on – closely correspond to the 'cultural capital' which Bourdieu has similarly identified as being of crucial significance to class formation.

The unity of educational experience amongst the upper class – in the British case, as exemplified by the public-school system and the universities of Oxford and Cambridge – is also reflected in the social backgrounds of those in the higher levels of administration and government, amongst the judiciary, the miliatary, the civil service, and in parliament – particularly Conservative MPs. For example, much was made of the supposed shift from old-style, patrician Conservatism, imbued with a sense of *noblesse oblige*, with the advent of the Thatcherite brand of Conservative politics. However, an analysis of the social backgrounds of Conservative MPs who first took office in 1987 revealed that over half had been educated at public school, 44 per cent at Oxbridge, and that not a single one had a working-class family background (as defined by father's occupation). As Borthwick et al. comment: 'John Major's "classless society" is thus far from realisation in the party he leads' (1991: 714).

There is ample empirical evidence, therefore, that political and economic power in the advanced industrial societies of the West remains concentrated within a relatively small upper class, and that this power is inextricably linked to the ownership and control of capitalist property.[6] Thus the constitution of the apex of all of the heuristic class maps identified above has remained remarkably constant over time, in respect of the characteristics of the component parts, as well as in its continuity across generations. Explanations of this continuity have been extensively rehearsed (Scott 1991; Bottomore and Brym 1989) – and the role of family and kinship networks are clearly very significant. This does not mean that upper-class membership is static, as, despite the social pretensions of the existing membership, large capital holdings are invariably a sufficient condition for entry (Francis 1980).

However, the effectiveness of kinship and other social networks in sustaining upper-class dominance serves to reinforce another theme of this book. This is that *non*-capitalist institutions continue to have a very significant impact upon class and stratification systems in capitalist societies. With tongue in cheek, one might suggest that, even if the argument that the public 'welfare state' has contributed to the development of an 'underclass' is highly debatable, the fact that a private 'welfare state' has sustained the upper class is not. Nevertheless, the relative openness of the upper classes to the siren calls of large wealth holdings, as theorists of social mobility have argued, has contributed to the continuing dominance of the capitalist mode of production as a whole. To the extent that changes in Eastern Europe result in a move in the direction of capitalism, we may anticipate that the power of the capitalist upper class will be further reinforced (Bottomore 1991).

Changes in the class structure, therefore, have largely taken place in the levels below its topmost reaches. However, we should be careful not to repeat a mistake often found within the social sciences. This is the assumption that purportedly universal sociological concepts developed in a particular context may be safely carried forward over time – as in, for example, the construction of ostensibly 'neutral' occupational-class schemes which in fact reflected the gendered division of labour characteristic of mid-twentieth-century Western capitalism. We should not expect, therefore, that the now-current contours of the stratification system will be straightforwardly reproduced into the twenty-first century. Nevertheless, the task for the sociologist is to suggest, however tentatively, which of the current stratification developments might prove to be more or less permanent, and which might be more sensibly viewed as contemporary artefacts.

The 'underclass'

A common theme of contemporary discussions of stratification, which is reflected in all of the heuristic maps discussed above, concerns the emergence of an 'underclass'. The identification of the phenomenon rests upon a number of linked factors:

1 an increase in long-term unemployment;
2 an increase in family households with only one parent, usually the mother;
3 spatial concentration of the poorest members of society in deprived inner-city areas, and/or undesirable local-authority housing estates;
4 the economic dependence of such groupings upon public or 'welfare state' provision.

In the United States, these features are also systematically associated with ethnicity. Two closely related arguments have been developed in consequence:

1 that it has become progressively more difficult for the poorest to escape from their multiply deprived circumstances;
2 that a 'culture of dependency' has developed amongst the resulting 'underclass', which serves to perpetuate their circumstances and those of their children.

In chapter 6, it was emphasized that it has always been the case that there will be losers in a competitive capitalist society; thus in this sense, there will always be an 'underclass' in such societies. The point at issue is whether this grouping has increased in size and, more importantly, whether this has been accompanied by ideological and attitudinal changes which have led to the emergence of a relatively permanent and stable grouping, buttressed and perpetuated by state welfare. In short, does the 'underclass' represent a qualitatively *new* stratification phenomenon? In answering this rhetorical question, it is useful to examine the discourse which accompanied the class maps developed in the 1950s and 1960s (which did not, incidentally, identify an 'underclass'). The pervasive optimism which accompanied these accounts is one of their most striking features. For example, although Mayer (1963: 466) noted the presence of 'a lower class of impoverished people' in his description of the American class (occupational) structure, his major arguments focused upon the development of a 'diamond-shaped' occupational distribution, and he argued that there was little doubt that 'differential life chances will diminish further and cultural gaps will continue to narrow down' (1959: 625). Similarly, commentaries in the United Kingdom enthused about the long-term trend which was now 'decisively in favour of greater equality. There is no going back' (Millar 1966: 44). In short, sociologists and other social commentators shared in the optimism of the postwar decades in which economic growth appeared to be continuous, and social and economic policies seemed to be capable of resolving some of the more intractable problems of capitalist industrialism. However, even in the 1960s, the poor were constantly being rediscovered by social scientists. (Coates and Silburn 1970). As we shall see, the extent of poverty has increased in recent decades, and the optimism of the 1950s and 1960s would be shared by few commentators today.

As has been argued in chapter 6, debates relating to the 'underclass' have been shaped by varying conceptions of the 'class' concept itself. Thus an 'underclass' may be identified as largely composed of ethnic minorities and immigrant workers, lacking in market capacities and full access to 'citizenship rights' (Giddens 1973). In such a model, it is the relationship of the 'underclass' to the established working class which is crucial to their identification. Other writers have stressed the significance of persisting economic disadvantage associated with unemployment and underemployment (the extent of such economic marginality is held to have increased with increasing dualism in employment practices). Here, the question of the internal homogeneity and stability of composition of this 'class' over time is regarded as crucial (Gallie 1988: 472). From the New Right, there is the 'moral turpitude' argument, in which the 'underclass' is distinguished by its relative lack of moral capacities (Murray 1990).

The position taken here is that the current emphasis upon the development of a putative underclass has two major sources, both of which should be evaluated within the context of recent economic, social and political developments. First, the lot of the very poorest in countries like Britain and the United States has worsened over the last decade, as a consequence of economic recession as well as politically inspired cuts in the nature and level of welfare provision. The political strategy of systematically attempting to increase the extent and level of market competition has also increased the numbers of potential losers. Thus the number of people in Britain living in a household with an income below half of the national average doubled between 1979 and 1987 and increased by nearly half between 1985 and 1987, and the proportion of children in *two-parent* families who were poor has increased from 5 per cent to 13 per cent (Piachaud 1991: 215). Second, ideologists of the right have always held the poor to be personally responsible for their situation; thus we might expect to see a resurgence of such arguments at a time when 'New Right' ideologies are politically dominant. Confident assertions as to the emergence of a permanent 'underclass', therefore, may prove to be a mistake of 1980s sociology. In competitive capitalism, there is always an 'underclass'; it has not 'emerged' over the last twenty years.

The decline of the traditional 'working class' and the increase in the 'middle classes'

Two other features, however, may be suggested as relatively permanent changes as far as the stratification systems of capitalist industrialism are concerned. These are, first, the proportionate decline of an internally homogeneous working class and, second, the continuing development of a heterogeneous array of middle classes. Goldthorpe's evidence relating to social mobility suggests that these middle (or, as he describes them, 'service') classes are able to maintain their positions of relative advantage over time; thus there has been an increase in the relative stability and affluence of large sections of the population.[7] The increasing employment of women has also had an impact on the contours of the stratification structure. If the units comprising the structure are taken to be individuals, then the persistence of occupational segregation means that some of its elements are dominated by feminized occupations – notably professionals in health and education, routine clerical work, and unskilled manual and service work. Women are also over-represented in the 'underclass' (Mann 1986; Waters 1991).[8] If the units comprising the structure are taken to be families, then the impact is, if anything, even greater. Pahl has identified the growing divide between 'work-rich' households, and those in which only one member may be employed, or there may be no employment at all (Pahl 1984, 1988). Piachaud has argued that women's employment is possibly the major factor keeping a household out of poverty. An even more significant effect, however, may be discernible at the upper-middle levels of the stratification hierarchy. Current trends suggest that: (a) more women are moving into higher-level jobs; (b) such women are more likely to remain in employment during the family-formation phase, and less likely to suffer occupational downgrading; and (c) more likely to be in households in which a partner is also relatively affluent (Crompton et al. 1990; McRae 1991). These trends in women's occupational achievement and work-life experiences will be likely to further extend the material gap between the relatively affluent households and those which are not. Thus the proportion of two-earner couples in the top 20 per cent of household incomes in the UK has increased from 43 per cent to 57 per cent between 1968 and 1986 (Davies and Joshi in Dale and Joshi 1992).

Class consciousness and action

If class and stratification analysis were to be effectively limited to the description and explanation of structured social inequality (that is, class formation or structuration), then debates in the area would be largely concerned with matters such as the relative significance of, say, social structural as compared to motivational factors in the explanation of inequality – as we have seen, for example, in the debate between the New Right and the liberals concerning the origins and persistence of the so-called 'underclass'; or meritocratic arguments as to the relative significance of education as compared to inherited wealth – as we have seen in contemporary debates concerning the social backgrounds of political leaders – and similar kinds of issues. However, in practice, the concept of class has been inextricably linked to the further questions of consciousness and action. To a very considerable extent, this has occurred because of the perceived political importance of the questions raised by the legacy of Marx's work, and his predictions concerning the revolutionary potential of the working class and its role in transforming capitalist society. Although they were critical of many aspects of Marx's theoretical analysis, Bendix and Lipset's (1967b) discussion was of considerable importance in placing the questions of class consciousness and action firmly on the sociological agenda, as well as in making the analytical separation between 'structure' and 'action' which, it has been suggested, has in certain respects proved counterproductive for class and stratification analysis. Indeed, the 'failure' of structurally identified classes to 'act' has been identified, by some authors, as evidence of the failure of 'class analysis' itself (Hindess 1987; Pahl 1989).

It is not being suggested here that the topic of class action is unimportant, or should be abandoned as an area of sociological investigation. It is important, however, to recognize that there is no single, overarching theory of action – 'class' or otherwise – and that class action can in no sense be simply 'read off' from class position. Two related, but rather different, emphases have been identified in discussions relating to class action. These are, first, the actions of classes in respect of class structuration or class formation: 'the whole set of creative strategies of distinction, reproduction and subversion pursued by all the agents . . . situated at the various theoretically pertinent locations in social space' (Wacquant 1991: 52). Empirical examples of this kind of approach would include 'realist' accounts of class structuring such as Lash and Urry's description of the emergence of the 'service class', or Savage et al.'s recent (1992) investigation of the middle classes. Issues relating to structuration obviously overlap to a considerable extent with explanations of inequality, as discussed in the above section of this chapter. The second emphasis, however, is upon the analysis of class action (or the potential for action) which within sociology has been identified as beginning with the work of Bendix and Lipset. That is, they identified the question of class consciousness and action as a suitable topic for sociological investigation.[9] This work is often associated with an 'action approach', and seeks to establish the circumstances in which the 'common economic conditions and common experiences of a group will lead to organised action' (Lockwood 1958; 1989: 217–18). Very simply, this may be seen as action *following* from class structuration or formation and corresponds to the Marxist notion of a class 'for itself', or what Giddens would describe as 'conflict consciousness'. Empirical examples of this kind of approach would include Lockwood's study of clerical workers, Newby's study of agricultural workers, Gallie's comparative research on refinery workers, and so on.[10]

It may be suggested that one major reason for the persistence of the interests → consciousness → action (Mann 1973), and/or structure → consciousness → action (Pahl and Wallace 1988) links in the sociological class analysis chain is that, as described in the previous section, the upper class in capitalist societies *does* manifest all the signs of being both conscious of its material interests and capable of protecting them. Offe and Weisenthal (1985) have argued that the stability of the dominant or capitalist class is not only a question of its superior resources, but also of the distinctive organizational capacities of the dominant, in contrast to the subordinate, classes. Capitalist interests are not difficult to identify, and the legitimacy of this interest (enterprise success and profitability) is widely accepted in society, and supported by the state. As a consequence, capitalist organizational forms are 'monological', that is, interest transmission is direct via the leadership. Not all capitalists need to be organized in order to represent the interests of the whole, and short-term conflicts of interest may be accommodated. In contrast, oppositional forms of organization are 'dialogical'; they do not possess the same 'taken-for-granted' legitimacy. Workers have to be persuaded that their interests have to be articulated (and are distinct from those of the capitalists), and organization is rarely successful unless all workers are involved. In short, the capitalist upper class is at an advantage not only in terms of its resources, but also in that its organizational strategies are simpler to generate and sustain than oppositional forms.[11]

The 'working class'

The sociology of class and stratification in Britain since the end of the Second World War has had something of an obsession with the 'working class', particularly concerning the prospects – or otherwise – for working-class consciousness and action.[12] Although the arguments have been couched in suitably academic language, much of this debate may be seen as a continuing dialogue with the 'ghost of Marx'. Besides the theoretical difficulties associated with the Marxist conceptualization of proletarian action (Lockwood 1981), there are a number of empirical reasons why the crude Marxist model of the mass, class-conscious proletariat should finally be abandoned. The conventional use of the manual/non-manual occupational boundary to signify a 'class' division has, as we have seen, been superseded, and the 'working class' is now seen to incorporate lower-level clerical and service occupations. Many such occupations involve the provision of personal services, and incorporate day-to-day employment relationships quite different from those associated with the 'mass proletarian' model. Many of these workers are women. Thus the existing difficulties of 'dialogical' working-class organizational forms identified by Offe and Wiesenthal can only be compounded by this further fragmentation within the 'working class'. The break-up of traditional, established, working-class communities is an additional factor making it less likely that daily life experiences will give rise to collectivist forms of social organization directed at change – Holton and Turner (1989), for example, have claimed that 'gemeinschaft is dead'. In fact, Therborn (1983) has suggested that the existence of such relatively closed-off local cultural communities are of only minor importance as far as political activity is concerned; what is of more significance is, first, the extent to which a class is constituted as a national political collectivity and, second, as a labour process collectivity (1983: 41). However, changes in the organization of production, together with the shift to the service economy, have substantially eroded the latter source of (potential) working-class collective action. Technological advance has rendered obsolete the mass (or 'Fordist') assembly line, and has facilitated the centralization of control together with the decentralization of decision-making. Thus there has been a decline in unit size in both the manufacturing and service sectors (Bannock and Daly 1990). The stress on *personal* skills within the service economy, it may be suggested, will be likely to result in an emphasis on co-operation, rather than conflict, within the workplace. Sustained high levels of unemployment have further eroded the basis of collective action, and by 1988 trade union membership in the United Kingdom had declined by fully 24 per cent from its peak level of 13.3 million members in 1979 to just over 10 million (Bird et al. 1991).

Much of the postwar debate on the working class was not primarily concerned with this class's role in the revolutionary transformation of society. It was rather with the relative success of organizations representing working-class interests in gaining benefits and protection for their members and their families – what Rex has described as the 'welfare-state deal', and Offe as the 'old politics' of economic growth, distribution and security. The working class was seen as reformist, rather than revolutionary; nevertheless, it was regarded as the major class which possessed the capacity, by virtue of its collective organization and resulting institutional pressures, to bring about major reforms.

The historical record provides ample evidence of the role of organized labour in bringing about the kinds of changes which have substantially transformed competitive capitalism – in particular, those features associated with the development of social 'citizenship'. In some countries (for example, Sweden), the trade union movement has been the major collective actor in the setting of a 'corporatist' bargain which persisted for many decades, and is still important today (Korpi 1978; Therborn 1983). However, in chapter 6 we saw that non-working-class organizations and pressure groups have also been of considerable significance in achieving citizenship gains – in Britain, for example, welfare feminism played an important role in establishing the welfare state – and the liberal ideology of universalism has from the first provided an entry into the discourse of 'citizenship' for non-class groupings such as ethnic groups.

The relative decline of the 'traditional' organized working class in the West, organized around mass industries such as mining, metal manufacture and engineering, must lead, relatively, to a decline in the significance of groups and organizations representing this 'working class' in the maintenance and extension of citizenship rights. This does not mean, however, that organized working-class pressure, and working-class action, is no longer of any importance. Macro-level surveys of attitudes have demonstrated consistent variations associated with occupational class; and although these cannot be taken as providing conclusive evidence relating to class consciousness and action, the data suggest that the factors giving rise to different expressions of social consciousness are not randomly distributed within the population at large.

It would not be sensible to deny, therefore, that the political significance of the organized working class has waned – but neither would it be sensible to argue that as a consequence 'class is dead'. That the contours of the stratification order, as well as material distribution within the different categories, *can* be changed may be illustrated by the sharp increase in inequality in Britain following the election in 1979 of a Conservative government committed to the ideology of the 'New Right'. The increase in the number of the very poorest – the so-called underclass – has been briefly described above, but Conservative policies were also directed at increasing the extent of inequality amongst the population at large. Unemployment, the government claimed, was caused by workers 'pricing themselves out of jobs'. Thus legislation was introduced which facilitated the payment of lower wages to workers who were often poorly paid in the first place. These policies included the removal of rights granted by the Employment Protection Act of the mid 1970s;[13] the privatization of public-sector services, as a consequence of which those workers who did not lose their jobs were often re-hired at lower rates of pay; subsidies to encourage low wage rates for young workers; and the removal of wages council protection in low-paid industries. As a consequence of these changes, the proportion of the British workforce falling below the Council of Europe's minimum 'decency threshold' for wages has increased from 36 per cent to 42 per cent (Byrne 1987). Over the same period, direct tax cuts disproportionately benefited the better-off. Between 1979 and 1986, it has been calculated that out of the £8.1 billion in tax cuts, nearly half went to the richest 10 per cent and almost two-thirds went to the richest 20 per cent. The share of total household income of the bottom 40 per cent of households in Britain has declined from 10.2 per cent in 1976 to 6.3 per cent in 1985; that of the top fifth has increased from 44.4 per cent to 49 per cent.

The policies which produced these outcomes were accompanied by arguments which stressed the need for national economic regeneration, but it is clear that their material impact has disproportionately affected different groups – or classes – within the population. This might be taken as an illustration of the force of Offe and Wiesenthal's argument – that policies clearly in the interests of a particular class (acpitalists) are seen as being in the 'national' interest. A straightforwardly utilitarian account of action in respect of voting would suggest that 'classes' will identify 'their' interests and act (vote) accordingly. Although this model is somewhat over-simplistic, it does serve to illuminate the broad outlines of political preferences and behaviours. For example, although capitalists are only a minority of the population in Britain, at the individual level, a majority have benefited materially (in respect of net income) from Conservative policies, even though inequalities have widened. Thus the (modest) material advantage enjoyed by the majority, even in a period of recession, may be used in an explanation of the persisting electoral success of the right.[14]

However, as sociologists never tire of reminding economists and psychologists, human action is (a) rarely determined by material factors alone, and (b) not undertaken by individuals in isolation. As Granovetter had argued: 'Actors do not behave or decide as atoms outside a social context, nor do they adhere slavishly to a script written for them by the particular intersection of social categories that they occupy. Their attempts at purposive action are instead embedded in concrete, ongoing systems of social relations' (1985: 487). The sociological fascination – indeed, obsession – with class action has not resulted in any single, coherent theory of political action, but both theoretical arguments and empirical researches in this area have supplied a number of valuable insights into the circumstances which might generate particular forms of consciousness and action which could be directed at structures of material inequality with the intention of changing, as well as maintaining, them.

'Classes' as such do not act, however the concept is defined. It is certain that the occupational or employment aggregates, as constituted by the various 'class' schemes available, do not 'act'. Even when 'classes' are viewed as being actively constructed – as in, for example, the work of E. P. Thompson or in Giddens's account of 'structuration', 'actions' are undertaken not by the classes as such, but by leaders and organizations acting on their behalf. 'Organization' is being used here to describe informal social groupings such as families and friendship networks, as well as the formally constituted bodies more usually described by the term. In the case of the upper classes, we have seen that both families and friendship networks (or 'status groups', where the term 'status group' is taken to refer to a consciousness community) are of considerable significance in the protection and furtherance of its interests, but formal organizations, such as Conservative political parties, private clubs, and others associated with elite schools, or cultural and sporting activities, are also important. In the case of the middle and lower classes, informal kinship and friendship structures are also of considerable significance in the protection of their interests, even if only in a defensive sense (Pahl 1984; Humphries 1982). Formal organizations, such as political parties, trade unions and occupational associations, have also been developed in the furtherance of particular 'class' interests. Thus late twentieth-century capitalism is characterized by a continuing conflict at the national level between 'provisions' parties and 'entitlements' parties (Dahrendorf 1988); between advocates of 'dualism' and 'corporatism' (Goldthorpe 1984a), whose arguments and policies are reflected by and in the broad contours of the 'class structure'.

The 'middle classes'

Because of the absolute decline in the 'working class' (as conventionally identified), an increasing amount of attention has been directed at the middle classes. Wright, for example, has argued that the central problem of class analysis is 'to solve . . . the location of the middle class within the class structure' (1989: 271). However, the position taken here is that it would *not* be particularly fruitful to continue to elaborate and attempt to specify the precise theoretical location of the fragmented middle classes within the structure of jobs/occupations, not least because there are compelling theoretical and empirical arguments, documented in this book, which suggest this task will never be success-fully accomplished. We can, however, use our sociological insights in order to suggest how particular kinds of consciousness and action might develop amongst these diverse groupings.[15]

Although a class's interests cannot be straightforwardly inferred from its structural location, neither are ideas, consciousness, motiva-tions to act, etc, simply plucked out of the air. In Britain, the events of the last decade have supplied numerous examples of how intended actions can have a direct impact on the distribution of wealth and income and thus the stratification system. The ideas and actions which generated these changes, however, have not gone unopposed. Without falling into the trap of either structural over-determinism or complete voluntarism, it is possible to suggest how diverse 'images of society', and thus potential motivations to act, might be generated within the middle classes.

The renewed emphasis on the significance of consumption, the current preoccupation with the supposed influence of postmodernist culture and the preoccupation with 'lifestyle', should be evaluated against the background of these political arguments. Turner, for example, suggests that we may be moving towards 'a social system based upon somewhat different principles of stratification, which will render much contemporary sociology redundant' (1988: 76). Conventional hierarchies within the cultural system are increasingly fragmented and diversified and, he argues, the cultural realm is becom-ing dissociated from the economic and political, as kitsch is celebrated and the cultural marketplace becomes increasingly important within the occupational order. In making these suggestions, it may be suggested that Turner is in danger of taking the outpourings of the 'chattering classes' too seriously. One of the arguments of this book has been that Bourdieu's (1973) argument – that 'cultural capital' (which would include 'taste' and 'lifestyle') does make an important contribution to the acquisition and maintenance of social class position – should indeed be accepted. However, cultural differentiation alone can neither sustain nor explain the stratification order. Developments and changes in cultural identity can, however, affect the stratification order in an indirect fashion if such changes are reflected in significant and persistent shifts in support for political parties. Thus Harvey, for example, has suggested that the new middle-class 'cultural mass' drew upon the working-class movement for its cultural identity in the 1960s, but that from the 1970s it has been more concerned with 'money power, individualism, entrepreneurialism' – and the suggestion is that this has been reflected in political preferences and behaviour, and thus growing support for right-wing parties, amongst the new middle classes.

There is a danger here of getting embroiled in a 'chicken-and-egg' type discussion concerning cause and effect in the determinants of political preferences and behaviour. A stated objective of the Conservative leadership in Britain, at the beginning of the 1980s, was that a change in attitudes was required; after a decade of 'greed is good', however, the leader was deposed, financial scandals proliferated, unemployment and house repossessions rose, consumers were no longer buying and 'society' looked about to be rediscovered even by the political right. A sociologist not entirely caught up in the 'postmodernist' explanatory whirlwind might also wish to develop the argument that, within the diverse and fragmented middle classes, there are coherent social-structural, as well as cultural, grounds upon which to argue that collectivist, as well as individualist, images of society, and associated political preferences and behaviours, might develop.

Arguments along these lines have been rehearsed at some length elsewhere (Crompton 1991, 1992; Savage et al. 1992), and will be only briefly summarized in the following paragraphs. The 'service class' has been described as a 'conservative force' (Goldthorpe 1987), but it has been argued that (a) the extent of fragmentation within the middle classes suggests that it is misleading to conceptualize this occupational aggregation as a single 'force', and (b) that the middle classes include more radical, as well as conservative, elements. Two major aspects of the employment situation cross-cut each other in this regard. These are, first, the employment sector, and second, the predominant mode of occupational regulation of expert labour. The growth of public-sector employment has been one of the most striking features associated with the development of welfare states since the Second World War: 'Modern welfare states . . . have . . . become virtual employment-machines . . . the Danish and Swedish welfare states employ about 30 per cent of the labour force' (Esping-Andersen 1990: 149). In contrast to private-sector managers and professionals, middle-class employees within the state sector in Britain, particularly professional employees in health, education, and so on, are more likely to favour 'collectivist' or 'corporatist' modes of macro-level economic regulation than those in similar occupations in the private sector. This is indicated both by their attitudinal responses and their political preferences (Marshall 1988; Savage 1991; Edgell and Duke 1991). These findings are perhaps not particularly surprising, as professional employees in these fields will have experienced at first hand the impact of more entrepreneurial and individualistic macroeconomic policies on both their clients and themselves.

The question of employment or occupational regulation cuts across employment sector. By 'employment regulation' is meant the means by which the use of expert labour may be brought under some kind of control. It has long been recognized within the sociology of work and organizations that it is difficult to subject 'experts' to direct controls, whether they be 'manual' or non-manual workers. Thus the employment regulation of different groups of experts may be primarily entrepreneurial (that is, regulation by market forces alone), professional self-regulation, or via some kind of organizational incorporation such as is found in, for example, IBM, or amongst the managerial staff of the major British clearing banks – a non-UK example would be 'Japanese' employment systems.[16] The contrast between professional and entrepreneurial modes of employment regulation is of long standing (Halmos 1970; Perkin 1989). The socialization of the professional includes the norm of 'institutionalized altruism' (Merton 1982) which, although it is by no means always observed, advocates a universalistic standard in the provision of expert services which might be expected to contribute to an ideology of collectivism, rather than individualism. Some empirical evidence which suggests that this might be the case is to be found in Savage et al.'s re-analysis of the 1987 British General Election Survey. Self-employed professionals, for example, (*not* state employees) were much more likely to have voted for the Alliance rather than for the Conservative Party (1992: 191). 'Professionalism' has been described as conflicting with organizational loyalties (Blau and Scott 1963). Organizational incorporation is likely to result in a measure of collectivism at the level of the organization, in combination with a highly competitive orientation towards other groups and external organizations. This outcome may also be associated with an increasing tendency towards dualism in the economy as a whole.

This brief discussion has focused upon the manner in which employment location, and the socialization of different groups within the employment relationship, may contribute to variations in social consciousness within the 'middle classes'. However, there are also a whole range of other major institutional factors which contribute to the shaping of social consciousness, and which are characterized by systematic cross-national variations. For example, education is a central element in the creation and reproduction of cultural capital amongst the new middle classes. Inglehart (1981) has argued that there has been amongst the better-educated a development of 'post-materialist' perspectives, and such views are likely to differ from the values of 'money power, individualism and entrepreneurialism' identified as significant by Harvey. National education systems, it has been demonstrated, do have a systematic impact upon organizations and hierarchical structures (Maurice et al. 1986). Esping-Andersen's work (1990) describing different welfare-state 'regimes' has demonstrated how different welfare states (liberal, corporatist, and social-democratic) are systematically related to variations in the structuring of the labour force in the countries concerned – and the nature of particular national welfare state regimes is itself likely to have an impact upon the degree of 'collectivism' – or otherwise – manifest within national populations.

The increasing number of women amongst the new middle classes further complicates the situation relating to the possibilities of consciousness and action. The persistence of occupational segregation means that a large number of women are concentrated in service-related professional work, particularly in the state sector. Historically, the presence of women has been viewed as a factor which has worked against the potential for radicalization and organization within a class fragment or occupational group; this has certainly been the case, for example, argued within the schoolteachers' unions in Britain in the past. However, women are concentrated amongst state-employed service providers, and they have shared in the rising levels of radicalism amongst these groupings. The concentration of women amongst the state-employed service providers is particularly marked in the Scandinavian welfare states, thus opening up the possibility of major cleavages by gender. As Esping-Andersen has argued: 'the Swedish employment-structured is evolving towards two economies: one, a heavily male private sector; the other, a female-dominated public sector . . . one might easily imagine a war between (largely) male workers in the private sector and (largely) female workers in the welfare state' (1990: 2151, 227). Besides this scenario, the possibilities opened up by 'equal-value' legislation have stimulated the incidence of collective action *by women* to improve the relative position of female-dominated occupations.

Concluding remarks

The brief summary above suggests that the investigation of the circumstances in which the 'common economic conditions and the common experiences of a group will lead to organised action' (Lockwood 1958; 1989) remains a fruitful area of sociological investigation. Capitalist industrial societies are still stratified, and theories of social class still provide us with essential insights into the manner in which established inequalities in wealth and power associated with production and markets, access to educational and organizational resources, and so on have systematically served to perpetuate these inequalities over time. However, class processes are not the only factors contributing to the maintenance and reproduction of inequality. Cultural practices are deeply involved in both reproduction and maintenance, and indeed, the very visibility and high profile of cultural practices means that they are often described, not as manifestations of 'class', but as 'classes' themselves. In practice, it is exceptionally difficult to separate, theoretically or empirically, the 'economic' from the social or 'cultural'. This point is particularly relevant as far as ascriptively identified groups such as women, or ethnic groups, are concerned. In these cases, a socially constructed inferior status has facilitated economic exploitation of a particularly intense kind.

The study of structured social inequality, therefore, remains a central feature of the sociological enterprise. Since the end of the Second World War, a number of different approaches to class and stratification analysis have been developed, which have been reviewed at length in this book. The aim of this exposition has not been to attempt to determine a 'best buy' amongst the different approaches that are available, but rather to illustrate their strengths and weaknesses in relation to what is perceived to be their major objective – the understanding of structured social inequality in late twentieth-century capitalist industrialism, together with its associated pattern of beliefs and actions.

Neither has this book, therefore, attempted to develop a comprehensive new approach to the topic. This is in part because no single theory or approach has the capacity to encompass the complexities of structured social inequality in their entirety, but also because, despite the criticisms which have been levelled at the different approaches to class and stratification analysis, there are nevertheless adequate theories and techniques already available to pursue this task. What is required are not so much new theories or methodologies, but rather, a flexible approach which recognizes the connectedness of the different aspects of the complex area of stratification as a whole. It might also be suggested that this objective might best be realized through the comparative analysis of stratification systems. Such a strategy would not, however, rest upon the application of a single conceptual framework across different societies, and would consciously anticipate diversity, as well as uniformity, in stratification outcomes.

These kinds of arguments, however, would require another textbook for their development. In this book, we have examined many hotly contested issues within class and stratification analysis. These have often been described as 'pseudo-debates' between practitioners following different approaches to 'class analysis', talking past, rather than to, each other. Besides providing a review of the options and strategies available within the area of 'class analysis', therefore, it is hoped that a modest contribution has been made to the avoidance of pseudo-debates in the future, and thus to the further development of our understanding of this important field.

Notes

1 A graphic illustration of the gulf which exists between different approaches may be found by examining the contents of two books on class in Britain published in consecutive years: Marshall et al.'s *Social Class in Modern Britain* (1988), and Miliband's *Divided Societies*, subtitled *Class Struggle in Contemporary Capitalism* (1989). Both books include substantial chapters on class structure, class politics, and class consciousness, but Marshall et al.'s text is largely taken up with the analysis of data using Wright's and Goldthorpe's class framework (and makes no mention of Miliband), whereas Miliband discusses similar topics without making any reference to Wright at all, and with but a single mention of Goldthorpe's work (on corporatism).

2 Waters (1991) identifies three main traditions in class analysis, Marxist, Weberian, and functionalist, each of which attempts to identify a structure of class positions. He argues that the weakness of the Marxist approach is 'A continuing insistence on the reality of class structure and the epiphenomenal status of class experience' – i.e., the failure to link structure and action. The weakness of the Weberian approach lies in the 'absence of a clear specification of the upper class'. Waters's identification of the weaknesses of the functionalist approach parallel those discussed in previous chapters of this volume.

An argument similar to that developed in this book is also made in Savage et al. (1992): 'In the past decade class analysis has become the 'jewel in the crown' of quantitative research. But it is our contention that the hegemony of quantitative class analysis has exacerbated many long-standing problems in class analysis and has hence allowed a powerful critique to expose some of these weaknessess' (p. 220).

3 For example, Edgell and Duke (1991) have carried out an empirical investigation of class changes during the era of 'Thatcherism' in Britain using a modified version of Wright's class scheme in combination with sectoral location. Their results have demonstrated e.g. the impact of 'New Right' policies on 'public-sector controllers' – key elements within the 'service class'.

4 For example, in Japan, employment conditions, wages and job security are all considerably better in the large-firm sector than in the small-firm, 'secondary' sector of industry. Thus the class situation of individuals and families is shaped most crucially by sector, rather than occupation, formal skill/qualification level, etc. See Morishima (1982).

5 See Goldthorpe et al. (1969: 7). The shape identified by different authors will, of course, reflect the criteria they employ in allocating units to

categories. The units constituting the categories also vary. Thus Runciman conceives of classes as composed of individuals; 'sets of roles whose common location in social space is a function of the nature and degree of economic power (or lack of it) attaching to them through their relation to the institutional processes of production, distribution, and exchange (1990: 377). In contrast, for Pahl, the units are households.

6 Theoretical debates exist as to the nature of the label that should be attached to this grouping – whether 'elite', 'capitalist class', 'service class', or whatever (Bottomore 1991). For the purposes of this discussion, however, we will use the simple descriptive term 'upper class'.

7 It may be noted that in respect of these 'middling' groupings the optimism of 1960s sociology may be argued to have been partially justified.

8 Care should be taken, however, not to assume that these are relatively permanent 'classes'. Patterns of occupational segregation may have been remarkably persistent, but they have also changed over time. Following the widespread introduction of equal-rights legislation, and the impact of 'second-wave' feminism, increasing numbers of women are moving into what had been previously male-dominated occupations. In Britain, the finance sector is a good example (Crompton and Sanderson 1990).

9 Note that Lockwood also identifies the work of Geiger as being of considerable importance here. See Lockwood (1958; 1989: 217).

10 It may of course be argued that this distinction cannot be maintained, given that the actions of classes in respect of structuration will often correspond to the actions of classes in pursuit of their perceived interests. This account, however, describes the characteristic assumptions made in respect of 'action' by the different empirical researchers who have addressed the topic.

11 There is an interesting parallel between Offe and Weisenthal's discussion of 'dialogical' organization forms and Lockwood's critique of the Marxist theory of action. 'Dialogical' forms of organization, it may be argued attempt to create the 'higher-order' rationality which Lockwood associates with Marx's account of proletarian action. However, Lockwood's critique of Marx does not affect the argument being advanced here – i.e. that the essentially utilitarian legitimacy accorded to capitalist ends makes organization in their pursuit easier to achieve.

12 For example, the whole of the first section of a recent collection of essays (Rose 1988) was devoted to papers on this topic.

13 The Employment Protection Act had been a major piece of legislation enacted during the period of the neo-corporatist 'social contract' of the previous Labour government. The refusal (at Maastricht in December 1991) of Conservative government representatives to accept the regulations of the EC Social Charter may be seen as a continuation of this policy.

14 It should also be remembered that living standards for the majority rose during the interwar recession, which was also a period of Conservative governments (Pollard 1983).

15   A common feature of empirical discussions relating to the 'middle class' has been to demonstrate the *lack* of homogeneity within this category, and subsequently to argue that, as a consequence, it cannot be considered to be a 'class' (Child 1986; Savage et al. 1988). These arguments, it may be suggested, are engaging with approaches to 'class analysis' in which the identification of the class *structure* is viewed as the starting-point. It is being suggested here that it is more fruitful to view the 'class structure' as being actively constructed rather than as capable of precise specification in abstract, theoretical terms. Rather than continuing to attempt to fit these diverse middle-class groupings within the procrustean bed of theoretical class schemes, therefore, it is better to begin with the assumption of heterogeneity.

16   Savage et al. (1992) have developed an argument relating to the middle classes which has many parallels to the one which is being set out here. They identify three middle-class assets – cultural, organization and property assets – which are the bases of middle-class formation. The argument here, however, relates to the development of possible 'images of society' and thus possible action, rather than class *formation*. Thus the focus of this discussion is upon modes of regulation, rather than assets.

References

Abercrombie, N. and Turner, B. S. 1978: The dominant ideology thesis. *British Journal of Sociology*, 29 (2), 149–70.

Abercrombie, N. and Urry, J. 1983: *Capital, Labour, and the Middle Classes*. Allen & Unwin: London.

Abrams, P. 1980: History, sociology, historical sociology. *Past and Present*, 87.

Althusser, L. 1969: *For Marx*. Penguin: Harmondsworth, Middlesex.

Andrews, G. (ed.) 1991: *Citzenship*. Lawrence & Wishart: London.

Archer, M. 1982: Morphogenensis versus structuration: on combining structure and action. *British Journal of Sociology*, 33 (4), 445–83.

Bagguley, P., Mark-Lawson, J., Shapiro, D., Urry, J., Walby, S. and Warde, A. 1989: *Restructuring Place, Class and Gender: Social and Spatial Change in a British Locality*. Sage: London.

Banks, O. 1981: *Faces of Feminism*. Martin Robertson: London.

Bannock, G. and Daly, M. 1990: Size distribution of UK firms. *Employment Gazette* (May), 255–8.

Banton, M. P. 1967: *Race Relations*. Tavistock: London.

Barbalet, J. M. 1988: *Citizenship: Rights, Struggle and Class Inequality*. Open University Press: Milton Keynes.

Barrett, M. 1980: *Women's Oppression Today*. Verso: London (2nd edn 1988).

Bauman, Z. 1982: *Memories of Class*. Routledge: London.

Bechhofer, F. and Elliot, B. (eds) 1981: *The Petite Buurgeoisie: Comparative Studies of the Uneasy Stratum*. Macmillan: London.

Bell, D. 1976: *The Cultural Contradictions of Capitalism*. Heinemann: London.

Bendix, R. 1964: *Nation-Building and Citzenship*. John Wiley: New York.

Bendix, R. and Lipset, S. M. (eds) 1967a: *Class, Status and Power*. (2nd edn) Routledge: London.

Bendix, R. and Lipset, S. M. 1967b: Karl Marx's theory of social classes. In Bendix and Lipset 1967a.

Benton, T. 1984: *The Rise and Fall of Structural Marxism*. Macmillan: London.

Berger, P. L. 1987: *The Capitalist Revolution: Fifty Propositions about Prosperity, Equality and Liberty*. Gower: Aldershot.

Berger, P. L. and Luckmann, T. 1966: *The Social Construction of Reality*. Penguin: Harmondsworth, Middlesex.

Berle, A. A. and Means, G. C. 1968: *The Modern Corporation and Private Property*. Harcourt, Brace: New York.

Bird, D., Stevens, M. and Yates, A. 1991: Membership of trade unions in 1989. *Employment Gazette* (June), 337–43.

Blackburn, R. H. and Mann, M. 1979: *The Working Class in the Labour Market*. Macmillan: London.

Blau, P. and Duncan, O. D. 1967: *The American Occupational Structure*. John Wiley: New York.

Blau, P. M. and Scott, W. R. 1963: *Formal Organizations*. Routledge: London.

Borthwick, G., Ellingworth, D., Bell, C. and Mackenzie D. 1991: The social background of British MPs. *Sociology*, 25 (4), 713–17.

Bottomore, T. 1991: *Classes in Modern Society* (2nd edn). HarperCollins Academic: London.

Bottmore, T. and Brym, R. J. (eds) 1989: *The Capitalist Class: An International Study*. Harvester Wheatsheaf: London.

Bourdieu, P. 1973: Cultural reproduction and social reproduction. In R. Brown (ed.), *Knowledge, Education and Cultural Change*. Tavistock: London.

Bourdieu, P. 1986: *Distinction: A Social Critique of the Judgement of Taste*. Routledge: London/New York.

Bourdieu, P. 1987: What makes a social class? *Berkeley Journal of Sociology*, 22, 1–18.

Bowles, S. and Gintis, H. 1976: *Schooling in Capitalist America*. Routledge: London.

Braverman, H. 1974: *Labor and Monopoly Capital*. Monthly Review Press: New York.

Brown, C. 1984: *Black and White Britain*. Heinemann: London.

Brown, R. and Brannen, P. 1970: Social relations and social perspectives amongst shipbuilding workers, I & II. *Sociology*, 4 (1), 71–84; 197–211.

Brubaker, R. 1985: Rethinking classical theory. *Theory and Society*, 14, 745–73.

Bulmer, M. 1975: *Working-class Images of Society*. Routledge: London.

Burawoy, M. 1979: *Manufacturing Consent: Changes in the Labor Process under Monopoly Capitalism*. University of Chicago Press: Chicago.

Burawoy, M. 1989: The limits of Wright's Marxism and an alternative. In Wright 1989.

Byrne, D. 1987: Rich and poor: the growing divide. In Walker and Walker 1987.

Calvert, P. 1982: *The Concept of Class*. Hutchinson: London.

Carchedi, G. 1975: On the economic identification of the new middle class. *Economy and Society*, 4 (1).

Castells, M. 1977: *The Urban Question*. Edward Arnold: London.

Chalmers, A. F. 1982: *What is this Thing called Science?* (2nd edn). Open University Press: Milton Keynes.

Child, J. 1986: New technology and the service class. In K. Purcell, S. Wood, A. Waton and S. Allen (eds), *The Changing Experience of Employment*. Macmillan: Basingstoke.

Clark, J., Modgil, C. and Modgil, S. (eds) 1990: *John H. Goldthorpe: Consensus and Controversy*. Falmer Press: Basingstoke.

Coates, D. 1989: Britain. In Bottomore and Brym 1989.

Coates, K. and Silburn, R. 1970: *Poverty: The Forgotten Englishmen*. Penguin: Harmondsworth, Middlesex.

Cockburn, C. 1991: *In the Way of Women*. Macmillan: Basingstoke.

Cohen, G. A. 1978: *Karl Marx's Theory of History: A Defence*. Oxford University Press: Oxford.

Collins, R. 1971: Functional and conflict theories of educational stratification. *American Sociological Review*. 36, 1002–19.

Connell, R. W. 1982: A critique of the Althusserian approach to class. In Giddens and Held 1982.

Cox, O. C. 1959: *Caste, Class and Race*. Review Press: New York.

Crompton, R. 1987: Gender, status and professionalism. *Sociology*, 21 (3), 413–28.

Crompton, R. 1989: Class theory and gender. *British Journal of Sociology*, 40 (4), 565–87.

Crompton, R. 1990a: Professions in the current context. *Work, Employment and Society* (special issue).

Crompton, R. 1990b: Goldthorpe and Marxist theories of historical development. In Clark et al. 1990.

Crompton, R. 1991: Three varieties of class analysis: comment on R. E. Pahl. *International Journal of Urban and Regional Research*, 15 (1), 108–13.

Crompton, R. 1992: Patterns of social consciousness amongst the middle classes. In R. Burrows and C. Marsh (eds), *Comsumption and Class*. Macmillan: Basingstoke.

Crompton, R. and Gubbay, J. 1977: *Economy and Class Structure*. Macmillan: London.

Crompton, R. and Jones, G. 1984: *White-Collar Proletariat: Deskilling and Gender in the Clerical Labour Process*. Macmillan: London.

Crompton, R., Hantrais, L. and Walters, P. 1990: Gender relations and employment. *British Journal of Sociology*, 41 (3), 329–49.

Crompton, R. and Sanderson, K. 1990: *Gendered Jobs and Social Change*. Unwin Hyman, London.

Crossick, G. 1978: *An Artisan Elite in Victorian Society*. Croom Helm: London.

Crowder, N. D. 1974: A critique of Duncan's stratification research. *Sociology*, 8.

Dahrendorf, R. 1959: *Class and Class Conflict in the Industrial Society*. Routledge: London.

Dahrendorf, R. 1969: On the origin of inequality among men. In A. Beteille (ed.), *Social Inequality*. Penguin: Harmondsworth, Middlesex.

Dahrendorf, R. 1988: *The Modern Social Conflict*. University of California Press: Berkeley/Los Angeles.

Dale, A., Gilbert, G. N. and Arber, S. 1985: Integrating women into class theory. *Sociology*, 19 (3), 384–409.

Dale, A. and Joshi, H. 1992: The economic and social status of British women. Social Statistics Research Unit, City University: London.

Davis, K. and Moore, W. E. 1945; 1964: Some principles of stratification. Reprinted in L. A. Coser and B. Rosenberg (eds), *Sociological Theory*. Collier-Macmillan: London.

Dawley, A. 1979: E. P. Thompson and the peculiarities of the Americans. *Radical History Review*, 19 (Winter), 33–60.

Dean, H. 1991: In search of the underclass. In P. Brown and R. Scase (eds), *Poor Work: Disadvantage and the Division of Labour*. Open University Press: Milton Keynes.

Department of Employment 1988: *Employment for the 1990s*. HMSO: London (White Paper).

DeVault, I. A. 1990: *Sons and Daughters of Labor*. Cornell University Press: Ithaca, New York.

Dollard, J. 1957: *Caste and Class in a Southern Town*. Doubleday: New York.

Douglas, J. W. B. 1964: *The Home and the School*. Panther: London.

Douglas, M. and Isherwood, B. 1980: *The World of Goods*. Penguin: Harmondsworth, Middlesex.

Dubin, R. 1956: Industrial Workers' worlds: a study of the central life interests of industrial workers. *Social Problems*, 3.

Duke, V. and Edgell, S. 1987: The operationalisation of class in British sociology: theoretical and empirical considerations. *British Journal of Sociology*, 38 (4).

Dunleavy, P. 1980: *Urban Political Analysis: The Politics of Collective Consumption*. Macmillan, London/Basingstoke.

Durkheim, E. 1957: *Professional Ethics and Civic Morals*. Routledge: London.

Durkheim, E. 1968: *The Division of Labour in Society*. Free Press: New York.

Edgell, S. and Duke, V. 1991: *A Measure of Thatcherism*. HarperCollins Academic: London.

Eisenstein, Z. 1981: *The Radical Future of Liberal Feminism*. Longman: New York.

Engels, F. 1940: *The Origin of the Family, Private Property and the State*. Lawrence & Wishart: London.

Equal Opportunities Commission 1990: *Annual Report*. HMSO: London.

Erikson, R., Goldthorpe, J. H. and Portacarero, L. 1982: Social fluidity in industrial nations. *British Journal of Sociology*, 33 (1), 1–34.

Erikson, R. and Goldthorpe, J. H. 1988: Women at class crossroads: a critical note. *Sociology*, 22, 545–53.

Esping-Andersen, G. 1990: *The Three Worlds of Welfare Capitalism*. Polity Press: Cambridge.

Evans, R. J. 1987: *Comrades and Sisters: Feminism, Socialism and Pacifism in Europe 1870–1945*. Wheatsheaf: Brighton.

Featherman, D. L., Jones, L. and Hausser, R. M. 1975: Assumptions of mobility research in the U.S.: the case of occupational status. *Social Science Research*, 4, 329–60.

Featherstone, M. 1987: Lifestyle and consumer culture. *Theory, Culture and Society*, 4 (1), 55–70.

Featherstone, M. 1991: *Consumer Culture and Postmodernism*. Sage: London.

Field, F. 1989: *Losing Out: The Emergence of Britain's Underclass*. Blackwell: Oxford.

Finch, J. and Groves, D. 1983: *A Labour of Love*. Routledge: London.

Francis, A. 1980: Families, firms and finance capital. *Sociology*, 14 (1), 1–27.

Gallie, D. 1978: *In Search of the New Working Class: Automation and Social Integration in the Capitalist Enterprise*. Cambridge University Press: Cambridge.

Gallie, D. 1988: Employment, unemployment and social stratification. In D. Gallie, (ed.), *Employment in Britain*. Blackwell: Oxford.

Geras, N. 1987: Post-Marxism? *New Left Review*, 163 (May/June).

Gershuny, J. and Jones, S. 1987: The changing work/leisure balance in Britain: 1961–1984. In J. Horne, D. Jary and A. Tomlinson (eds), *Sport, Leisure and Social Relations*. Routledge: London.

Gerth, H. and Mills, C. W. (eds) 1948: *From Max Weber*. Routledge: London.

Giddens, A. 1973: *The Class Structure of the Advanced Societies*. Hutchinson: London (2nd edn 1981).

Giddens, A. 1982a: Hermeneutics and social theory. In *Profiles and Critiques in Social Theory*. Macmillan: London/Basingstoke.

Giddens, A. 1982b: Class division, class conflict and citizenship rights. In *Profiles and Critiques in Social Theory*. Macmillan, London/Basingstoke.

Giddens, A. 1984: *The Constitution of Society*. Polity Press: Cambridge.

Giddens, A. 1987: *Social Theory and Modern Sociology*. Polity Press: Cambridge.

Giddens, A. 1990: Structuration theory and sociological analysis. In J. Clark, C. Mogdil and S. Mogdil (eds), *Anthony Giddens: Consensus and Controversy*. Falmer Press: Basingstoke.

Giddens, A. and Held, D. (eds) 1982: *Classes, Power and Conflict*. Macmillan: London/Basingstoke.

Giddens, A. and Mackenzie, G. (eds) 1982: *Social Class and the Division of Labour*. Cambridge University Press: Cambridge.

Glass, D. V. (ed.) 1954: *Social Mobility in Britain*. Routledge: London.

Goldthorpe, J. H. 1967: Social stratification in industrial society. In Bendix and Lipset 1967a.

Goldthorpe, J. H. 1973: A revolution in sociology? *Sociology*, 7.

Goldthorpe, J. H. 1978: The current inflation: towards a sociological account. In F. Hirsch and J. H. Goldthorpe (eds), *The Political Economy of Inflation*, Martin Robertson, London.

Goldthorpe, J. H. (with C. Llewellyn and C. Payne) 1980: *Social Mobility and Class Structure in Modern Britain*, 2nd edn, Clarendon Press: Oxford (2nd edn 1987).

Goldthorpe, J. H. 1982: On the service class, its formation and future. In Giddens and Mackenzie 1982.

Goldthorpe, J. H. 1983: Women and class analysis: in defence of the conventional view. *Sociology*, 17 (4).

Goldthorpe, J. H. 1984a: The end of convergence: corporatist and dualist tendencies in modern Western societies. In J. H. Goldthorpe (ed.), *Order and Conflict in Contemporary Capitalism*. Clarendon Press: Oxford.

Goldthorpe, J. H. 1984b: Women and class analysis: a reply to the replies. *Sociology*, 18 (4).

Goldthorpe, J. H. and Hope, K. 1974: *The Social Grading of Occupations: A New Approach and Scale*. Clarendon Press: Oxford.

Goldthorpe, J. H., Lockwood, D., Bechhofer, F. and Platt, J. 1969: *The Affluent Worker in the Class Structure*. Cambridge University Press: Cambridge.

Goldthorpe, J. H. and Marshall, G. 1992: The promising future of class analysis: a response to recent critiques. *Sociology*, 26 (3), 381–400.

Gorz, A. 1982: *Farewell to the Working Class*. Pluto: London.

Granovetter, M. S. 1985: Economic action and social structure: the problem of embeddedness. *American Journal of Sociology*, 91 (3), 481–510.

Gray, R. Q. 1976: *The Labour Aristocracy in Victorian Edinburgh*. Clarendon Press: Oxford.

Gregory, D. 1982: *Regional Transformation and Industrial Revolution*. Macmillan: London.

Gregory, D. and Urry, J. (eds) 1985: *Social Relations and Spatial Structures*. Macmillan: London/Basingstoke.

Habermas, J. 1983: Modernity – an incomplete project. In H. Foster (ed.) *The Anti-Aesthetic*. Bay Press, Port Townsend, Washington.

Hakim, C. 1980: Census reports as documentary evidence: the Census commentaries 1801–1951. *Sociological Review*, 28 (3).

Hall, S. 1981: Cultural studies: two paradigms. In T. Bennett, G. Martin, C. Mercer and J. Woollacott (eds), *Culture, Ideology and Social Process*. Batsford Academic and Educational: London.

Hall, S. and Jaques, M (eds) 1989: *New Times: The Changing Face of Politics in the 1990s*. Lawrence & Wishart: London.

Halmos, P. 1970: *The Personal Service Society*. Constable: London.

Halsey, A. H. et al. 1980: *Origins and Destinations*. Clarendon Press: Oxford.

Halsey, A. H. (ed.) 1988: *British Social Trends since 1900*. Macmillan: Basingstoke/London.

Hamnett, C. 1989: Consumption and class in contemporary Britain. In Hamnett et al. 1989.

Hamnett, C., McDowell, L. and Sarre, P. (eds) 1989: *Restructuring Britain: The Changing Social Structure*. Sage: London.

Harloe, M., Pickvance C. and Urry, J. 1990: *Place, Policy and Politics: Do Localities Matter?* Unwin Hyman: London.

Hartmann, H. 1981: The unhappy marriage of Marxism and feminism: towards a more progressive union. In L. Sargent (ed.), *Women and Revolution*. Boston: South End Press.

Harvey, D. 1990: *The Condition of Postmodernity*. Blackwell: Oxford.

Heath, A. 1981: *Social Mobility*. Fontana: London.

Heath, A. and Britten, N. 1984: Women's jobs do make a difference. *Sociology*, 18 (4), 475–90

Heath, A., Curtice, J., Jowell, R., Evans, G., Field, J. and Witherspoon, S. 1991: *Understanding Political Change: The British Voter 1964–1987*. Pergamon: Oxford.

Hindess, B. 1973: *the Use of Official Statistics in Sociology*. Macmillan: London.

Hindess, B. 1987: *Politics and Class Analysis*. Blackwell: Oxford.

Hirsch, F. 1977: *Social Limits to Growth*. Routledge: London.

HMSO 1966: *Census 1961*: Occupation Tables. London.

Hodge, R. W., Siegel, P. M. and Rossi, P. H. 1964: Occupational prestige in the United States: 1925–1963. *American Journal of Sociology*, 70, 286–302.

Hodge, R. W., Treiman, D. J. and Rossi, P. H. 1967: A comparative study of occupational prestige. In Bendix and Lipset 1967a.

Holmwood, J. and Stewart, A. 1983: The role of contradictions in modern theories of social stratification. *Sociology*, 17 (2).

Holton, R. J. and Turner, B. 1989: *Max Weber on Economy and Scoiety*. Routledge: London.

Humphries, J. 1982: Class struggle and the persistence of the working-class family. In Giddens and Held 1982.

Ingham, G. K. 1970: Social stratification: individual attributes and social relationships. *Sociology*, 4 (1), 105–13.

Inglehart, R. 1981: Post-materialism in an age of insecurity. *American Political Science Review*, 75 (4), 880–900.

Jenkins, R. 1988: Discrimination and equal opportunity in employment: ethnicity and 'race' in the United Kingdom. In D. Gallie (ed.), *Employment in Britain*. Blackwell: Oxford.

Jensen, J. 1986: Gender and reproduction: or babies and the state. *Studies in Political Economy*, 20.

Jensen, J., Hagen, E. and Reddy, C. (eds) 1988: *Feminization of the Labour Force: Paradoxes and Promises*. Oxford University Press: New York.

Johnson, R. 1979: Culture and the historians. In J. Clarke, C. Critcher and R. Johnson (eds), *Working-class Culture: Studies in History and Theory*. Hutchinson: London.

Johnson, T. 1990: Ideology and action in the work of John Goldthorpe. In Clark et al. 1990.

Kaye, H. J. 1984: *The British Marxist Historians*. Polity Press: Cambridge.

Keat, R. and Urry, J. 1975: *Social Theory as Science*. Routledge: London (2nd edn 1981).

Kelley, J. 1990: The failure of a paradigm: log-linear models of social mobility. In Clark et al. 1990.

Kerr, C., Dunlop, J. T., Harbison, F. and Myers, C. A. 1973: *Industrialism and Industrial Man*. Penguin: Harmondsworth, Middlesex (1st edn 1963).

Klein, J. 1965: *Samples from English Cultures*, Routledge: London.

Klingender, F. D. 1935: *The Condition of Clerical Labour in Britain*. Martin Lawrence: London.

Korpi, W. 1978: *The Working Class in Welfare Capitalism*. Routledge: London.

Kurz, K. and Müller, W. 1987: Class mobility in the industrial world. *Annual Review of Sociology*, 13, 417–42.

Laclau, E. and Mouffe, C. 1985: *Hegemony and Socialist Strategy*. Verso: London.

Laclau, E. and Mouffe, C. 1987: Post Marxism without apologies. *New Left Review*, 166, (Nov./Dec.), 79–106.

Lakatos, I. 1978: *The Methodology of Scientific Research Programmes*. Cambridge University Press: Cambridge.

Lash, S. and Urry, J. 1987: *The End of Organized Capitalism*. Polity Press: Cambridge.

Lenski, G. 1988: Rethinking macrosociological theory. *American Sociological Review*, 53, 163–71.

Leiulfsrud, H. and Woodward, A. 1987: Women at class crossroads: repudiating conventional theories of family class. *Sociology*, 21 (3), 393–412.

Lewis, O. 1959: *Five Families: Mexican Case Studies in the Culture of Poverty*. Basic Books: New York.

Lipset, S. M. and Bendix, R. (eds) 1959: *Social Mobility in Industrial Society*. Heinemann: London.

Lipset, S. M. and Zetterberg, H. L. 1959: Social mobility in industrial societies. In Lipset and Bendix 1959.

Lockwood, D. 1958: *The Blackcoated Worker*. Allen & Unwin: London (2nd edn 1989).

Lockwood, D. 1964: Social integration and system integration. In G. K. Zollschan and W. Hirsch (eds), *Explorations in Social Change*. Houghton Mifflin: Boston.

Lockwood, D. 1966: Sources of variation in working class images of society. *Sociological Review*, 14 (3), 244–67.

Lockwood, D. 1974: For T. H. Marshall. *Sociology*, 8 (3), 363–7.

Lockwood, D. 1981: The weakest link in the chain? In S. Simpson, and I. Simpson (eds), *Research in the Sociology of Work: 1*. JAI Press: Greenwich, Conn.; reprinted (1988) in D. Rose (ed.), *Social Stratification and Economic Change*. Unwin Hyman: London.

Lockwood, D. 1986: Class, status and gender. In R. Crompton and M. Mann (eds), *Gender and Stratification*. Polity Press: Cambridge.

McNall, S. G., Levine, R. F. and Fantasia, R. 1991: *Bringing Class*

Back In, Westview Press: Praeger, New York.

McPherson, K. and Coleman, D. 1988: Health. In Halsey 1988.

McRae, S. 1991: Occupational change over childbirth: evidence from a national survey. *Sociology*, 25 (4), 589–605.

Mann, M. 1973: *Consciousness and Action among the Western Working Class*. Macmillan: London.

Mann, M. 1986: A crisis in stratification theory. In R. Crompton and M. Mann (eds), *Gender and Stratification*. Polity Press: Cambridge.

Mann, M. 1987: Ruling class strategies and citizenship. *Sociology*, 21 (3), 339–54.

Marsh, C. 1986: Social class and occupation. In R. Burgess (ed.), *Key Variables in Social Investigation*. Routledge: London.

Marsh, C. and Blackburn, R. M. 1992: Class differences in access to higher education. In R. Burrows and C. Marsh (eds), *Consumption and Class: Divisions and Change*. Macmillan: Basingstoke.

Marshall, G. 1982: *In Search of the Spirit of Capitalism*. Hutchinson: London.

Marshall, G. 1983: Some remarks on the study of working class consciousness. *Politics and Society*, 12 (3), 263–302.

Marshall, G. 1988: The politics of the new middle class: history and predictions. Paper presented at the annual conference of the British Sociological Association.

Marshall, G. 1991: In defence of class analysis: a comment on R. E. Pahl. *International Journal of Urban and Regional Research*, 15 (1), 114–18.

Marshall, G., Newby, H., Rose, D. and Vogler, C. 1988: *Social Class in Modern Britain*. Hutchinson: London.

Marshall, G. and Rose, D. 1990: Out-classed by our critics. *Sociology*, 24 (2), 255–67.

Marshall, T. H. 1963: Citizenship and social class. In *Sociology at the Crossroads*. Heinemann: London.

Martin, J. and Roberts, C. 1984: *Women and Employment: a Lifetime Perspective*. HMSO: London.

Marx, K. 1843: On the Jewish Question. In L. Colletti (ed.) 1975: *K. Marx: Early Writings*. Penguin: Harmondsworth, Middlesex.

Marx, K. 1955: *The Poverty of Philosophy*. Progress Publishing: Moscow.

Marx, K. 1962a: The Eighteenth Brumaire of Louis Bonaparte. In K. Marx and F. Engels, *Selected Works*, vol. 1. Foreign Languages Publishing House: Moscow.

Marx, K. 1962b: Preface to *A Contribution to the Critique of Political Economy*. In K. Marx and F. Engels, *Selected Works*, vol. 1. Foreign Languages Publishing House: Moscow.

Marx, K. and Engels, F. 1962: *Manifesto of the Communist Party*. In

K. Marx and F. Engels, *Selected Works*, vol. 1. Foreign Languages Publishing House: Moscow.

Marx, K. 1974: *Capital*, vol. 3. Lawrence & Wishart: London.

Marx, K. and Engels, F. 1970: *The German Ideology*. Lawrence & Wishart: London.

Massey, D. 1984: *Spatial Divisions of Labour*. Macmillan: London/Basingstoke.

Maurice, M., Sellier, F. and Silvestre, J. J. 1986: *The Social Foundations of Industrial Power*, trans. A. Goldhammer. MIT Press: Cambridge, Mass.

Mayer, K. 1959: Diminishing class differentials in the United States. *Kyklos*, 12, 605–28.

Mayer, K. 1963: The changing shape of the American class structure. *Social Research*, 30, 458–68.

Mayo, E. 1975: *The Social Problems of an Industrial Civilization*. Routledge: London.

Meillassoux, C. 1973: Are there castes in India? *Economy and Society*, 2 (1).

Merton, R. K. 1959: Notes on problem-finding in sociology. In R. K. Merton, L. Broom and L. S. Cottrell (eds), *Sociology Today*. Harper & Row: New York.

Merton, R. K. 1965: Social structure and anomie. In R. K. Merton, *Social Theory and Social Structure*. Free Press: New York.

Merton, R. K. 1982: Institutionalized altruism: the case of the professions. In R. K. Merton, *Social Research and the Practicing Professions*. Abt Books: Cambridge, Mass.

Miliband, R. 1989: *Divided Societies*. Oxford University Press: Oxford.

Millar, R. 1966: *The New Classes*. Longmans Green: London.

Mitchell, J. 1975: *Psychoanalysis and Feminism*. Penguin: Harmondsworth, Middlesex.

Mitchell, J. C. 1983: Case and situation analysis. *Sociological Review*, 31.

Molyneux, M. 1979: Beyond the domestic labour debate. *New Left Review*, 116.

Morishima, M. 1982: *Why Has Japan Succeeded?* Cambridge University Press: Cambridge.

Mouffe, C. 1981: Hegemony and ideology in Gramsci. In T. Bennett, G. Martin, C. Mercer and J. Woollacott (eds) *Culture, Ideology and Social Process*. Batsford Academic and Educational: London.

Müller, W. 1990: Social mobility in industrial nations. In Clark et al. 1990.

Mullins, P. 1991: The identification of social forces in development as a general problem in sociology: a comment on Pahl's remarks on class and consumption relations as forces in urban and regional development. *International Journal of Urban and Regional Research*, 15 (1), 119–26.

Murphy, R. 1984: The structure of closure: a critique and development of the theories of Weber, Collins and Parkin. *British Journal of Sociology*, 35, 547–67.

Murphy, R. 1986: The concept of class in closure theory. *Sociology*, 20, 2.

Murray, C. A. 1984: *Losing Ground*. Basic Books: New York.

Murray, C. A. 1990: *The Emerging British Underclass*. IEA Health and Welfare Unit: London.

Murray, R. 1989: Fordism and post-Fordism. In Hall and Jaques 1989.

Myrdal, G. 1962: *An American Dilemma*. Harper & Row: New York.

Neale, R. S. (ed). 1983: *History and Class*. Blackwell: Oxford.

Newby, H. 1977: *The Deferential worker*. Allen Lane: London.

Nichols. T 1979: Social class: official, sociological and Marxist. In J. Irvine, I. Miles and J. Evans (eds), *Demystifying Social Statistics*. Pluto: London.

O'Connor, J. 1973: *The Fiscal Crisis of the State*. St James Press: London.

Offe, C. 1985a: 'Work' – a central sociological category? In *Disorganized Capitalism*. Polity Press: Cambridge.

Offe, C. 1985b: New social movements: challenging the boundaries of institutional politics. *Social Research*, 52 (4).

Offe, C. and Weisenthal, M. 1985: Two logics of collective action. In C. Offe, *Disorganized Capitalism*, Polity Press: Cambridge.

Pahl, R. E. 1984: *Divisions of Labour*. Blackwell: Oxford.

Pahl, R. E. 1988: Some remarks on informal work, social polarization and social structure. *International Journal of Urban and Regional Research*, 12, 247–67.

Pahl, R. E. 1989: Is the emperor naked? Some questions on the adequacy of sociological theory in urban and regional research. *International Journal of Urban and Regional Research*, 13 (4), 711–20.

Pahl, R. E. and Wallace, C. D. 1988: Neither angels in marble nor rebels in red: privatization and working-class consciousness. In D. Rose (ed.), *Social Stratification and Economic Change*. Hutchinson: London.

Parkin, F. 1972: *Class Inequality and Political Order*. Paladin: London.

Parkin, F. (ed.) 1974: *The Social Analysis of Class Structure*. Tavistock: London.

Parsons, T. 1965: Full citizenship for the Negro American? A sociological problem. *Daedalus*, 94, 1009–54.

Parsons, T. and Clark, K. B. 1967: *The Negro American*. Beacon Press: Boston.

Pateman, C. 1988: *The Sexual Contract*. Polity Press: Cambridge.

Pateman, C. 1989: *The Disorder of Women*. Polity Press: Cambridge.

Paukert, L. 1984: *The Employment and Unemployment of Women in OECD Countries*. OECD: Paris.

Pawson, R. 1989: *A Measure for Measures*. Routledge: London.

Pawson, R. 1990: Half-truths about bias. *Sociology*, 24 (2), 229–40.

Payne, G. 1987: *Mobility and Change in Modern Society*. Macmillan: Basingstoke/London.

Peacock, A. 1991: Welfare philosophies and welfare finance. In T. Wilson and D. Wilson (eds), *The State and Social Welfare*. Longman: London/New York.

Perkin, H. J. 1989: *The Rise of Professional Society*, Routledge: London.

Peters, T. J. and Waterman, R. H. 1982: *In Search of Excellence*. Harper & Row: New York.

Phillips, A. 1990: Citizenship and feminist theory. In G. Andrews (ed.), *Citizenship*, Lawrence & Wishart: London.

Piachaud, D. 1991: Revitalising social policy. *Political Quarterly*, 62 (2), 204–25.

Pickvance, C. G. 1977: From 'social base' to 'social force': some analytical issues in the study of urban protest. In M. Harloe (ed.), *Captive Cities: Studies in the Political Economy of Cities and Regions*. Wiley: London/New York.

Pickvance, C. G. 1992: Comparative analysis, causality and case studies. In A. Rogers and S. Vertovec (eds), *The Urban Context: Ethnicity, Social Networks and Situational analysis*. Berg: London.

Pirenne, H. 1936: *Economic and Social History of Medieval Europe*, trans. I. E. Clegg. Routledge: London.

Plant, R. 1991: Welfare and the enterprise society. In T. Wilson and D. Wilson (eds), *The State and Social Welfare*. Longman: London/New York.

Plant, R. and Barry, N. 1990: *Citizenship and Rights in Thatcher's Britain: Two Views*. IEA Health and Welfare Unit: London.

Polanyi, K. 1957: *The Great Transformation*. Beacon Press, Boston.

Pollard, S. 1983: *The Development of the British Economy: 1914–1980*. Edward Arnold: London.

Pollert, A. 1988: The flexible firm: fixation or fact? *Work, Employment and Society*, 2 (3), 281–316.

Posner, C. (ed.) 1970: *Reflections on the Revolution in France: 1968*. Penguin: Harmondsworth, Middlesex.

Poulantzas, N. 1975: *Classes in Contemporary Capitalism*. New Left Books: London.

Prandy, K. 1991: The revised Cambridge scale of occupations. *Sociology*, 24 (4), 629–56.

Price, R. and Bain, G. S. 1988: The labour force. In Halsey 1988.

Przeworski, A. 1985: *Capitalism and Social Democracy*. Cambridge University Press: Cambridge.

Rattansi, A. 1985: End of an orthodoxy? The critique of sociology's view of Marx on class. *Sociological Review*, 641–69

Reid, I. 1981: *Social Class Differences in Britain*. Grant McIntyre: London.

Reiss, A. J. 1961: *Occupations and Social Status*. Free Press: New York.

Rex, J. 1961: *Key Problems of Sociological Theory*. Routledge: London.

Rex, J. 1986: *Race and Ethnicity*. Open University Press: Milton Keynes.

Rex, J. 1987: Ethnicity and race. In P. Worsley (ed.), *The New Introducing Sociology*, Penguin: Harmondsworth, Middlesex.

Rex, J. and Tomlinson, S. 1979: *Colonial Immigrants in a British City*. Routledge: London.

Rose, D. 1988: Introduction. In D. Rose (ed.), *Social Stratification and Economic Change*. Hutchinson: London.

Rose, D. and Marshall, G. 1986: Constructing the (W)right classes. *Sociology*, 20 (3), 440–55.

Rose, D., Marshall, G., Newby, H. and Vogler, C. 1987: Goodbye to supervisors? *Work, Employment and Society*, 1 (1), 7–24.

Runciman, W. G. 1990: How many classes are there in contemporary British society? *Sociology*, 24 (3), 377–96.

Rutter, M. and Madge, N. 1976: *Cycles of Disadvantage*. Heinemann: London.

Sabel, C. F. 1982: *Work and Politics*. Cambridge University Press: Cambridge.

Sarlvik, B. and Crewe. J. 1983: *Decade of Dealignment: The Conservative Victory of 1979 and Electoral Trends in the 1970s*. Cambridge University Press: Cambridge.

Sarre, P. 1989: Recomposition of the class structure. In Hamnett et al. 1989.

Saunders, P. 1987: *Social Theory and the Urban Question*. Unwin Hyman: London.

Saunders, P. 1990a: *Social Class and Stratification*, Routledge: London.

Saunders, P. 1990b: *A Nation of Home Owners*. Unwin Hyman: London.

Savage, M. 1991: Making sense of middle-class politics: a secondary analysis of the 1987 British general election survey. *Sociological Review*, 39 (1), 26–54.

Savage, M., Dickens, P. and Fielding, T. 1988: Some social and political implications of the contemporary fragmentation of 'service class' in Britain. *International Journal of Urban and Regional Research*, 12 (3).

Savage, M., Barlow, J., Dickens, A. and Fielding, T. 1992: *Property, Bureaucracy and Culture: Middle Class Formation in Contemporary Britain*. Routledge: London.

Sayer, A. 1984: *Method in Social Science: A Realist Approach*. Hutchinson: London.

Sayer, A. 1989: Post-Fordism in question. *International Journal of Urban and Regional Research*, 13 (4), 666–95.

Scase, R. 1992: *Class*. Open University Press: Buckingham.

Scott, J. 1982: *The Upper Classes*. Macmillan: London.

Scott, J. 1991: *Who Rules Britain?* Polity Press: Cambridge.

Seccombe, W. 1974: The housewife and her labour under capitalism. *New Left Review*. 83. 3–24.

Smelser, N. J. 1959: *Social Change in the Industrial Revolution: An Application of Theory to the Lancashire Cotton Industry 1770–1840*. Routledge: London.

Smelser, N. J. (ed.) 1988: *Handbook of Sociology*. Sage: Beverly Hills, Calif.

Smiles, S. 1859: *Self-Help: With Illustrations of Conduct and Perseverance* (4th edn). Murray: London.

Smith, C. 1987: *Technical Workers, Class, Labour and Trade Unionism*. Macmillan: London.

Sombart, W. 1906: *Why Is There no Socialism in the United States?* Repr. 1976: International Arts and Sciences Press: White Plains, NY.

Stacey, M. 1960: *Tradition and Change: A Study of Banbury*. Oxford University Press: London.

Stacey, M. 1981: The division of labour revisted or overcoming the two Adams. In P. Abrams, R. Deem, J. Finch, and P. Rock (eds), *Practice and Progress: British Sociology 1950–1980*, Allen & Unwin: London.

Stanworth, M. 1984: Women and class analysis: a reply to Goldthorpe. *Sociology*, 18 (2), 159–70.

Stark, David 1980: Class struggle and the labour process. *Theory and Society*, 9 (1).

Stedman Jones, G. 1976: From historical sociology to theoretical history. *British Journal of Sociology*, 27 (3), 295–305.

Stedman Jones, G. 1983: *Languages of Class: Studies in English Working-class History*. Cambridge University Press: Cambridge.

Stewart, A., Prandy, K. and Blackburn, R. M. 1980: *Social Stratification and Occupations*. Macmillan: London/Basingstoke.

Stoecker, R. 1991: Evaluating and rethinking the case study. *Sociological Review*, 39 (1), 88–112.

Szreter, S. R. S. 1984: The genesis of the Registrar-General's social classification of occupations. *British Journal of Sociology*, 35, 522–46.

Therborn, G. 1983: Why some classes are more successful than others. *New Left Review*, 138 (March–April).

Thomas, R. and Elias, P. 1989: Development of the standard occupational classification. *Population Trends*, 55, 16–21.

Thompson, E. P. 1968: *The Making of the English Working Class*. Penguin: Harmondsworth, Middlesex.

Thrift, N. 1989: Images of social change. In C. Hamnett et al. 1989.

Thrift, N. and Williams, P. (eds) 1987: *Class and Space*. Routledge: London.

Touraine, A. 1977: *The Self-Production of Society*. University of Chicago Press: Chicago.

Tumin, M. 1964: Some principles of stratification: a critical analysis. In L. A. Coser and B. Rosenberg (eds), *Sociological Theory*, Collier-Macmillan: London.

Turner, B. S. 1986: *Citizenship and Capitalism: The Debate over Reformism*. Allen & Unwin: London.

Turner, B. S. 1988: *Status*. Open University Press: Milton Keynes.

Turner, B. S. 1990: Outline of a theory of citizenship. *Sociology*, 24 (2), 189–217.

Urry, J. 1981: *The Anatomy of Capitalist Societies*. Macmillan: London/Basingstoke.

Veblen, T. 1934: *The Theory of the Leisure Class*. Modern Library: London.

Wacquant, L. J. D. 1989: Social ontology, epistemology, and Class. *Berkeley Journal of Sociology*, 34, 165–86.

Wacquant, L. J. D. 1991: Making class: the middle class(es) in social theory and social structure. In McNall et al. 1991.

Walby, S. 1986: *Patriarchy at Work*. Polity Press: Cambridge.

Walby, S. 1988: Gender politics and social theory. *Sociology*, 22 (2), 215–32.

Walby, S. 1990: *Theorizing Patriarchy*, Blackwell: Oxford.

Walker, A. 1990: Blaming the victims. In Murray 1990.

Walker, A. and Walker, C. (eds) 1987: *The Growing Divide: A Social Audit 1979–1987*. Child Poverty Action Group: London.

Warde, A. 1990: Introduction to the sociology of consumption. *Sociology*, 24 (1), 1–4.

Warner, L. 1963: *Yankee City*. Yale University Press, New Haven, Conn.

Waters, M. 1991: Collapse and convergence in class theory: the return of the social and the analysis of stratification arrangements. *Theory and Society*, 20 (2), 141–72.

Weber, M. 1948: Class, status, party. In H. Gerth and C. W. Mills (eds), *From Max Weber*. Routledge: London.
Weber M. 1976: *The Protestant Ethic and the Spirit of Capitalism*, trans. Talcott Parsons, Allen & Unwin: London.
Westergaard, J. and Resler, H. 1975: *Class in a Capitalist Society*. Heinemann: London.
Willener, A. 1970: *The Action-image of Society*. Tavistock: London.
Willis, P. 1977: *Learning to Labour: How Working Class Kids Get Working Class Jobs*. Saxon House: London.
Wilson, E. 1977: *Women and the Welfare State*. Tavistock: London.
Wilson, W. J. 1987: *The Truly Disadvantaged: Inner City Woes and Public Policy*. University of Chicago Press: Chicago.
Wilson, W. J. 1991: Studying inner-city social dislocation: the challenge of public agenda research. *American Sociological Review*, 56, 1–14.
Wood, E. M. 1986: *The Retreat from Class*. Verso: London.
Wootton, B. 1955: *The Social Foundations of Wage Policy*. Allen & Unwin: London.
Wright, E. O. 1976: Class boundaries in advanced capitalist societies. *New Left Review*, 98.
Wright, E. O. 1979: *Class Structure and Income Determination*. Academic Press: New York.
Wright, E. O. 1980: Class and occupation. *Theory and Society*, 9.
Wright, E. O. 1985: *Classes*. Verso: London.
Wright, E. O. (ed.) 1989: *The Debate on Classes*. Verso: London.
Wright, E. O. and Martin, B. 1987: The transformation of the American class structure, 1960–1980. *American Journal of Sociology*, 93 (1).
Wright, E. O. and Singlemann, J. 1982: Proletarianisation in the changing American class structure. *American Journal of Sociology*, 88 (Supplement), 176–209.
Wrong, D. 1966: The oversocialized conception of man in modern sociology. Reprinted in L. A. Coser and B. Rosenberg (eds), *Sociological Theory*, Collier-Macmillan: London.
Wynne, D. 1990: Leisure, lifestyle and the construction of social position. *Leisure Studies*, 9, 21–34.
Zeitlin, M. 1982: Corporate ownership and control: the large corporation and the capitalist class. In Giddens and Held 1982.
Zukin, S. 1988: *Loft Living: Culture and Capital in Urban Change*. Radines/Century Hutchinson: London.
Zweig, F. 1961: *The Worker in an Affluent Society*. Heinemann: London.

Index